D1738940

Dilemmas of
Social
Democracy

Recent Titles in
Contributions in Political Science
Series Editor: Bernard K. Johnpoll

DILEMMAS OF SOCIAL DEMOCRACY

The Spanish Socialist Workers Party in the 1980s

JN
8395
.P15
S52
1989
West

Donald Share

Contributions in Political Science, Number 230

GREENWOOD PRESS
New York • Westport, Connecticut • London

Library of Congress Cataloging-in-Publication Data

Share, Donald.
    Dilemmas of social democracy : the Spanish Socialist Workers Party
in the 1980s / Donald Share.
        p.   cm. — (Contributions in political science, ISSN 0147–1066
; no. 230)
    Bibliography: p.
    Includes index.
    ISBN 0–313–26074–5 (lib. bdg. : alk. paper)
    1. P.S.O.E. (Political party) 2. Socialism—Spain. 3. Spain—
Politics and government—1975– I. Title. II. Series.
JN8395.P15S52   1989
324.246'074—dc19   88–25102

British Library Cataloguing in Publication Data is available.

Library of Congress Catalog Card Number: 88–25102
ISBN: 0–313–26074–5
ISSN: 0147–1066

First published in 1989

Greenwood Press, Inc.
88 Post Road West, Westport, Connecticut   06881

Printed in the United States of America

The paper used in this book complies with the
Permanent Paper Standard issued by the National
Information Standards Organization (Z39.48–1984).

10   9   8   7   6   5   4   3   2   1

Contents

Tables

Abbreviations

AES	Social and Economic Accord
AI	Inter-confederation Accord
ASU	Socialist University Group
CCOO	Workers Commissions
CDS	Democratic and Social Center
CEOA	Spanish Confederation of the Autonomous Right
CEOE	Spanish Confederation of Entreprenurial Organizations
CiU	Convergence and Union
CNT	National Confederation of Workers
EC	European Community
EEC	European Economic Community
FLP	Popular Liberation Front
FPS	Federation of Socialist Parties
FSM	Socialist Federation of Madrid
NATO	North Atlantic Treaty Organization
PAD	Democratic Action Party
PASOK	Panhellenic Socialist Movement
PCE	Spanish Communist Party
PCPE	Communist Party of the Spanish Peoples

PDL   Liberal Democratic Party
PRD   Democratic Reform Party
PSA   Andalusian Socialist Party
PSC   Catalan Socialist Party
PSI   Socialist Party of the Interior
PSOE   Spanish Socialist Workers Party
PSOE-H   Spanish Socialist Workers Party-Historic sector
PSP   Popular Socialist Party
UCD   Union of the Democratic Center
UGT   General Confederation of Workers
UMD   Democratic Military Union

Preface

I have been intrigued by the Spanish Socialist Workers Party (PSOE) for the past ten years. In many ways I feel as though I have personally experienced the evolution of the PSOE because I had friends and colleagues in the party before the death of Franco, during the precarious transition to democracy, and after the Socialists' stunning electoral victory of 1982. The goal of the book is not to pass judgment on the PSOE's development as a party; rather, it attempts to contribute to a better understanding of this important, complex, contradictory, and fascinating process.

Along the way I benefited enormously from the support, insight, criticism, and encouragement of far too many individuals to list here. In Spain, I would like to express my gratitude to the Centro de Investigaciones Sociológicas and the Fundación Pablo Iglesias (for their assistance in providing data), Pablo Castellano, Antonio García Santesmases, José Girón Garrote (and his graduate students at the University of Oviedo), Ludolfo Paramio, José Félix Tezanos, and Monica Threlfall.

In the United States, I would like to thank Tim Amen, David Balaam, Robert Fishman, Richard Gunther, Joel Krieger, David Lieberman, Scott Mainwaring, Felipe Pimentel, and William Haltom. The Department of Politics and Government at the University of Puget Sound provided an excellent atmosphere and considerable support for the project.

I had the good fortune to obtain generous funding for various parts of the research from the Enrichment Committee of the University of Puget Sound, the American Political Science Association, and the National Endowment for the Humanities.

I dedicate this book with love to my wife, Marjorie Newman. Her support for my work and travel was greatly appreciated, and I look forward to collaborating with her on more important and challenging projects in the future.

1

Introduction

Thanks to the crisis of Keynesian social democracies, neoliberalism has been able to launch an all-out ideological offensive under the themes of "the bankruptcy of socialism" and "market capitalism—the response to the crisis."

—André Gorz[1]

THE CRISIS OF ADVANCED CAPITALISM AND THE CRISIS OF SOCIAL DEMOCRACY

The 1980s have been hard times for West European socialist and social democratic parties.[2] In many countries the electoral performance of these parties has been disappointing, and in others sudden surges of electoral support have been short-lived.[3] Only two West European social democratic forces, the Spanish and Greek parties, were able to win consecutive absolute majorities during the 1980s. Most West European social democratic parties are currently in opposition or in minority or coalition governments. Two of the most prestigious parties, the British and the West German, have suffered severe electoral setbacks and have spent long periods in opposition.[4]

On the ideological front, the social democratic left is confronted with a crisis of perhaps greater proportions. A variety of factors have combined to undermine the traditional growth-cum-redistribution model that sustained social democratic policies in the post–World War II period.[5] Since the oil crisis of the 1970s, sustained economic growth has proved elusive in many advanced societies. Joel Krieger notes that "the global capitalist recession of the 1970s eroded the terms of the postwar [welfare state] settlements and reduced the prospects for a victimless mixed-economy capitalism."[6] Increased automation of the productive process and heightened international competition, among other factors, have created high levels of unemployment that are not easily reduced by economic growth. Social democrats' traditional faith in the redistributive role of the modern welfare state has been challenged by a new distrust of bureaucracy and taxes. The rise of "postmaterialism" has not worked to the benefit of social democrats.[7] Consequently, social democratic parties are now confronted with the emergence of a neoliberal right, which has seriously questioned the welfare state and Keynesian economic assumptions, and the "green" left, which has attacked the bureaucratization, centralization, and growth orientation of the traditional social democratic model.

Indeed, in light of the current economic crisis, much recent scholarly writing has rekindled an old debate about whether social democracy's goal of transforming capitalism from within the confines of democratic capitalism is attainable. Some have pointed to the undeniable progress made by social democratic welfare states in the delivery of basic democratic freedoms and the redistribution of income. John D. Stephens, writing about the Swedish case, notes that "a strong labor movement and a long period of socialist incumbency has led to the extension of democratic control and a very significant redistribution. There the welfare state is part of a transitional political economy between capitalism and socialism."[8] For Stephens the major reason for the failure of most European social democratic parties to move past the welfare state is their organizational weakness (compared with the high levels found in Sweden) and is not mainly the result of contradictions inherent in capitalist democracy.[9]

Others contend that democratic capitalism and socialism are incompatible. Jonas Pontusson argues that even in Sweden the crisis of the 1970s and 1980s has seriously eroded the position of the social democrats, thus disputing the optimism of Stephens and others.[10] Peter Aimer and others have pointed to contradictions and weaknesses in the Swedish Meidner Plan, designed to offset sacrifices asked of the working class with increased ownership of the means of production.[11] Przeworski goes further to conclude that "[s]ocial democrats will not lead European societies into socialism. Even if workers would prefer to live under socialism, the process of transition must lead to a crisis before socialism could be organized. To reach higher peaks one must traverse a valley, and this descent will not be completed under democratic conditions."[12] He argues that social democratic governments inevitably become dependent on big capital in order to generate the kind of growth necesary for Keynesian political economic policies and other redistributive measures. By reducing levels of class conflict and by gaining control over trade unions, social democrats are in a position to make the capitalist system work smoothly during times of rapid growth, but they are impotent to do so in times of low growth without sacrificing social democratic goals. During the periodic economic crises produced by advanced capitalism, socialist parties are faced with a serious electoral dilemma. The electoral coalition forged during times of growth and the political economic compromises that allow for redistribution of income and large profits for private enterprise come unraveled. Socialists must either advocate policies that can restore high growth rates to the economy but that are highly unpopular with traditionally socialist voters, or seek to defend the short-term interests of those voters at the risk of alienating big capital and ultimately exacerbating the economic crisis. Social democrats inevitably chose the latter strategy because, as Przeworski argues,

Once private property of the means of production was left intact, it became in the interest of wage-earners that capitalists appropriate profits. Under capitalism the profits of today are the condition of investment and hence production, employment and consumption in the future.... Social democrats protect profits from demands of the masses because radical redistributive policies are not in the interest of wage-earners. No one drew the blueprint and yet the capitalist system is designed in such a way that if profits are not sufficient, then eventually wage rates or employment must fail. Crises of capitalism are in no one's mutual interest; they are a threat to wage-earners since capitalism is a system in which economic crises must inevitably fall on their shoulders.[13]

On the internal organizational front, social democratic parties are battling to sustain membership in parties and affiliated unions and to insulate younger generations from the lure of the new right and the green left. For parties that have in many cases become identified with the establishment, the organizational challenge is particularly serious. The need to appeal to youth and new social groups (white-collar workers, women, environmentalists, immigrants, etc.) inherently brings into question the centralization and hierarchy of the traditional social democratic party model. The need to diversify the bases of electoral support has long threatened the social democrats' traditional appeals to the working class. By deemphasizing the class-oriented appeal, social democrats help to weaken class consciousness and render workers more vulnerable to the appeals of other parties. By seeking to attract a more diverse electoral clientele, social democratic parties dilute their own ideology. As Przeworski notes, "To be effective in elections they have to seek allies who would join workers under the socialist banner, yet at the same time they erode exactly that ideology which is the source of their strength among workers. They cannot remain a party of workers alone and yet they can never cease to be a workers' party."[14]

As social democratic party membership began to reflect more accurately the composition of society as a whole, problems of internal governance increased. As David Hine has noted, more middle-class members entered social democratic parties seeking greater levels of participation and different types of rewards for activity than traditional members. They tended to be more value-oriented and were far more willing to contest party leaders. The increase of white-collar members, especially civil servants, made it more difficult and contradictory for social democratic parties to trim public sector expenditures at a time when public demands for reduction in taxes and budget deficits were growing.[15]

It is therefore hardly surprising that in the 1980s many of West Europe's social democratic parties have experienced serious intramural turmoil. The internal explosion within the British Labour Party after the 1979 elections illustrates how economic and ideological crises contributed to a bitter internal party struggle.[16] A less dramatic but similar power struggle within the German Democratic Party took place after the party lost consecutive elections.[17] Relations with affiliated trade unions have almost everywhere been strained. Somewhat ironically, and despite rising unemployment, the social democratic left appears to have been the principal political victim of the crisis of the welfare state.[18]

The economic crisis and the electoral, ideological, and internal organizational crises have compounded one another. Economic crisis, by creating unemployment, weakens the working-class organizations so crucial to most social democratic parties. The unraveling of the Keynesian growth-cum-redistribution model has intensified the debate within social democratic parties between proponents of alternative models (on the left and the right) and those clinging to more traditional policies. Consecutive electoral defeats weaken party organization, which in turn hampers future campaign efforts and provides new recruits for parties to the left and right.

How have West European social democratic parties responded to the multifaceted crisis outlined above? Almost without exception, and whether in government or in opposition, the European social democrats have come to adopt neoliberal, market-oriented economic policies and centrist or even conservative domestic social policies while reaffirming a cautious foreign policy orientation. Relatively few attempts have been made to find progressive solutions to the crisis, and little headway has been made in the search for an alternative social democratic vision to replace the discarded Keynesian model. Theorist André Gorz has noted that "no traditional [social democratic] party has yet evaluated the challenges and opportunities implicit in the crisis. All of them have yet to define a long term political plan... and the long term perspectives are fundamentally distinct from the short term concerns."[19] Przeworski pessimistically concludes that because of the social democrats' adherence to Keynesian economics and their faith in the welfare state, they "find themselves without a distinct alternative of their own as they face a crisis of the international system. When in office they are forced to behave like any other party, relying on deflationary cost-cutting measures to ensure private profitability and the capacity to invest."[20]

The parties of northern Europe, in power during the 1960s and 1970s, have responded to the crisis of advanced capitalism gradually. Most of these parties had long since abandoned democratic socialist ideals for a social democratic vision that firmly embraced the capitalist system, while calling for substantial redistribution of income and political power. These societies achieved in the 1950s and 1960s a broad and solid consensus or "class compromise." The resulting "social democratic states" shared a common parliamentary government, extensive welfare systems, a large public sector, a mixed economy, and strong and politically important trade unions.[21] In response to the oil crisis of the 1970s, the governing British, West German, and Swedish social democrats implemented austerity policies that contradicted social democratic goals.[22] Despite the relative prosperity of the northern countries and the relatively weaker impact there of the economic crisis of the late 1970s and early 1980s, the adoption of such policies ultimately proved politically expensive, especially in terms of internal party coherence.

In the south, the economic crisis and the social democratic response to it transpired more rapidly and coincided initially with a sudden rise to power. Unlike northern Europe, where the social democrats shared, and often dominated, power during the postwar period, the southern European social democrats were virtually excluded from power until the late 1970s and early 1980s. Whereas in 1975 no southern European social democratic party had governed for over twenty years, by 1982 there were socialist parties in government in France, Spain, Portugal, and Greece, followed by the Italian Socialists' capturing of the prime ministership in 1983. Indeed, just as the economic crisis began to erode the social democratic hegemony in northern Europe, the southern social democrats experienced a historic sweep into power.

Although until quite recently the parties of the south formally espoused democratic socialist ideology, all of them came to power on social democratic platforms that included significant redistribution of income (including nationalization of industry in some cases), an improvement of social services, major social reforms, and a more independent foreign policy vis-à-vis the major power blocs. With the exception of Italy, the social democratization of the southern parties, a process that spanned decades in northern Europe, took place within a matter of years and partly while these parties were in power.

However, southern European social democrats soon confronted similar obstacles to those that drove their northern counterparts from power. Upon taking power, or shortly thereafter, the southern social democratic governments embraced economic austerity policies and toned down their foreign policy proposals. James Petras has noted that "the rise of southern European socialist parties was as sudden and dramatic as their subsequent shift away from social welfare policies and their declining influence."[23] However, the electoral picture was not quite as bleak as in the north: By 1987, socialist parties still governed with absolute majorities in Spain and Greece but had lost power in Portugal and France and appeared stalemated in Italy. However, the ideological bankruptcy of the social democrats was, if anything, even more apparent in southern Europe, where poorer economies, more severe inequality, weaker trade unions, and higher levels of unemployment made the neoliberal economic policies more costly and contradictory.

The rapid drift to the right of the southern European social democratic left has many interrelated causes. These will be discussed with reference to the Spanish case in the following chapters, but a number of factors common to southern Europe can be noted at the outset. Much of the ideological baggage of the southern European socialist parties had accumulated during the long years of opposition, especially where the socialist opposition struggled against authoritarian regimes (Greece, Spain, and Portugal). The environment of clandestine struggle in which the Greek, Spanish, and Portuguese parties existed contributed a great deal to these parties' revolutionary and maximalist image.

The longevity of authoritarian regimes (two of them in NATO, and all closely allied with the United States) formed the basis for a strong anti-imperialist and *tercermundista* emphasis in the foreign policy of the Greek, Spanish, and Portuguese parties. The persistence of pockets of extreme inequality in all of the southern countries also gave a more traditionally socialist hue to programs and platforms of southern parties. The presence of strong communist parties also pulled these parties toward the left. The sudden democratic transitions of Greece, Portugal, and Spain and the equally historic end of conservative domination of the French Fifth Republic caught the socialist parties unprepared for their rise to power. Thus it is hardly surprising that these parties have jettisoned much of the rhetoric of the "permanent opposition."

Spain, Portugal, and Greece shared a number of additional characteristics that contributed to the rapid moderation of their socialist parties. The end of authoritarian rule in Portugal (1974), Greece (1974), and Spain (1975) produced precarious democracies that were initially threatened with the possibility of military coups. Outdated, weak, and peripheral economies only exacerbated the impact of the economic crisis of the late 1970s, creating far higher levels of unemployment. Years of protectionist industrial and trade policy, along with paternalistic labor relations, had produced rigid and uncompetitive economies. The need to liberalize the economy and to implement austerity policies was viewed as far greater in the south, but its social costs were also far higher than in the north.

Although the timing, strategies attempted, and individual circumstances have differed in the southern European cases, the results have been strikingly similar. Petras notes with irony that "in actual experience the southern European social democrats did move 'beyond' the welfare state—back toward a version of orthodox liberal market economics that would surprise even the most right-wing of northern European social democrats.... The Socialists' international positions have, with few exceptions, fused with those of the Reagan administration."[24] Petras argues that the southern European socialist parties actively sought to "restructure capitalism" in order to better integrate their economies with European and world capitalism, even at the cost of abandoning the construction of a modern welfare state.

The Portuguese Socialists, faced with the need to consolidate a fragile democracy against the attacks from the left and right, and handed a peripheral economy in ruin, quickly sought to repair the capitalist system and almost immediately abandoned their democratic socialist rhetoric for a moderate social democratic platform and a neoliberal set of policies while in government. Papandreaou's Panhellenic Socialist Movement (PASOK) has retreated from its anti-U.S. foreign policy and has implemented a harsh economic austerity policy. As will be discussed in following chapters, the Spanish Socialists had jettisoned most democratic socialist rhetoric before coming to power, but once elected in 1982 they failed to implement a social democratic platform far more moderate than that of their French colleagues.

The French Socialists, unencumbered by the problem of regime consolidation, and given a relatively more healthy economy, embarked on an ambitious social democratic strategy in their first year of government. The French Socialists sought "not to manage the capitalist system, but to replace it," but they were ultimately forced to adopt neoliberal austerity policies because of a variety of domestic and international constraints.[25] In short, there were high hopes that in the 1980s the southern European democrats would "show the way" for their frustrated northern counterparts, but these hopes have been dashed.

Thus despite the divergent political trajectories of the northern and southern social parties, social democrats throughout West Europe are faced with an essentially similar strategic and ideological quandary. Graeme Duncan summarizes this quandary when he observes:

National parties are caught in a constricting web of international control and influence, which limits significantly their freedom of action, and economic autarchy or partial forms of it ... do not seem on the agenda. Certainly any serious attempt to break free would be extremely demanding in economic, political and cultural terms. Thus options, legroom, are sharply, even cripplingly limited. Domestic macro-economic policy sometimes seems less an instrument of national policy than the plaything of outside forces.[26]

The most urgent question facing them may be whether and how these parties can find their way back into government. New electoral alliances, whether with forces to their left or right, may need to be explored. Attempts to appeal to new social groups including women, youth, unemployed workers, environmentalists, and peace movements will have to be considered.

The very nature and worth of the traditional social democratic party organization (including its ties with the labor movement) will likely be placed on the drawing board. In an era when the role of the middle classes within the social democratic parties is on the rise, social democrats will have to experiment with changes that facilitate more grass-roots participation in decision-making processes. But as Hine notes, the increasing personalization of politics in postindustrial politics, a trend that has certainly characterized southern European socialist parties, may contradict such a participatory orientation.[27] At the very least, demands for increased participation and the trend toward personalization of party power promise to produce increased intramural conflict.

A strongly related set of ideological concerns, postponed or largely ignored until recently, must also be examined. Foremost among these is the need to articulate a new social democratic vision that can distinguish the goals of the social democratic left from those of the right and that can provide a long-term political objective from which short-term sacrifice might be justified. Ultimately, West European social democrats will have to determine the new meaning of social democracy in an age of contracting employment, slower growth, increased international competition, and greater social class complexity.

SOCIALISM IN SPAIN: POLITICAL SUCCESS AND IDEOLOGICAL CRISIS

In the context of the crisis of West European social democracy, the Spanish Socialist Workers Party (PSOE) enjoyed remarkable political success in the 1980s. The PSOE won consecutive absolute majorities in the 1982 and 1986 general elections and dominated local and regional politics during that period (discussed in more detail in Chapter 5). Though the 1987 municipal, regional, and European Parliament elections were a partial setback for the governing Socialists, the PSOE remained the most powerful political party in Spain. Unlike most of their European counterparts, the PSOE avoided serious internal party conflict during its tenure in government, despite the implementation of a number of highly controversial policies. As discussed in Chapters 4 and 5, notwithstanding the presence of some intramural dissent, the party leadership, under Felipe González, was not really challenged.

Despite this political success, the Spanish Socialists have not emerged unscathed from the crisis of advanced capitalism. As detailed in Chapter 4, the PSOE government's economic and foreign policies were highly contradictory for a party of the left. The Socialists came to power pledging to create 800,000 new jobs and to use state investment to promote economic growth. Not unlike their French neighbors, the Spanish Socialists soon implemented a set of neoliberal economic policies, including economic austerity and an industrial streamlining plan. As a result, unemployment jumped over four percentage points to an alarming 20 percent. The PSOE took power with the professed goal of removing Spain from the North Atlantic Treaty Organization (NATO) and supported a nonaligned foreign policy. Nevertheless, the Socialists eventually came to promote NATO membership and pursued a foreign policy strongly identified with the Atlantic Alliance.

By mid–1987, the PSOE was not in danger of losing power, but the Socialists were faced with rising social unrest and widespread disenchantment with the governing party. Five years of PSOE government had indicated the severity of the ideological crisis of Spanish socialism. By 1987 the *Cambio* (change) advocated by the PSOE 1982 had been all but forgotten and had been replaced with the term "modernization." The Socialists seemed unable to articulate a progressive political program that could rekindle electoral support and win the support of a variety of social sectors that had become disillusioned with PSOE rule.

FOCUS OF THE BOOK

This book seeks to explain both the rapid political success of the Spanish Socialist Workers Party in the 1980s and the PSOE's equally rapid abandonment of social democratic policies once in government. It will be argued that these two phenomena were closely, but not completely, related to each other. The PSOE's ability to bury its democratic socialist agenda was a crucial precondition for its rise to power in 1982, but the rejection of much of its social democratic program once in power was not required by political and economic constraints. Instead, a variety of considerations discussed in the following chapters must be considered in order to understand the Socialists' behavior in government after 1982.

Chapter 2 presents an overview of the PSOE's history, highlighting the themes that would later be viewed as lessons by contemporary Socialist leaders. The PSOE's bitter experience during the Spanish Second Republic, its difficult existence throughout the franquist regime, and the party's renaissance in the 1970s all provide pieces to the puzzle of the PSOE's ideological evolution after Franco's death.

Chapter 3 examines how the Socialists performed the difficult task of rebuilding a devastated party while at the same time contributing to an uncertain and risky transition to democracy. The success of both projects delivered many benefits to the PSOE but also constrained their future behavior. Once in the context of a new electoral system, the Socialists had to reconsider their party organization and ideology and adjust both to the realities of democratic society and public opinion. The ideological and organizational struggle within the PSOE came to a head in 1978, and González imposed a new party line thereafter. The organizational and ideological changes, together with changes in the Spanish party system, prepared the PSOE for its victory in 1982.

Chapter 4 turns to the record of the Socialists once in power, focusing on economic and foreign policy. In both areas the Socialists abandoned much of their 1982 commitments, creating considerable controversy both within Spanish society and within the Socialist Party.

Chapter 5 attempts to explain the Socialists' behavior, taking into account the material presented in Chapters 2 through 4 but adding a consideration of how the PSOE party organization and structure, the nature of the Spanish party system, public opinion, and internal party politics came into play.

Chapter 6 will reconsider the Spanish experience in light of the Europe-wide crisis of social democracy. To what extent can the Spanish Socialists expect to continue their political success in the 1990s? Regardless of their political prospects, the concluding chapter will discuss the prospects for an ideological renaissance within the Spanish Socialist Workers Party.

NOTES

1. André Gorz, *Paths to Paradise* (Boston: South End Press, 1985), p. 7.

2. In this book the terms "socialist" and "social democratic" and "labor" parties will be used interchangeably because contemporary social democratic parties usually adopt one of these labels. Following Kesselman and others, this book employs the following analytical distinction between social democracy and democratic socialism. Social democracy accepts control of the economy by a minority but insists on several modifications of the capitalist system: Keynesian intervention in the economy to foster growth and reduce unemployment, and strongly organized working classes with the legally sanctioned ability to protect workers' interests. Democratic socialism envisions control of the economy in the hands of the majority of citizens and thus seeks to move away from capitalism. See Mark Kesselman, "Prospects for Democratic Socialism in Advanced Capitalism: Class Struggle and Compromise in Sweden and France," *Politics and Society* 4 (1982): 397–400.

3. Among the recent comparative works on European social democracy are by Anton Pelinka, *Social Democratic Parties in Western Europe* (New York: Praeger, 1983); William Paterson and Alastair H. Thomas, eds., *The Future of Social Democratic Parties in Western Europe* (Oxford: Clarendon Press, 1986); Bogdan Denitch, ed., *Democratic Socialism: The Mass Left in Advanced Industrial Democracies* (Montclair, N.J.: Allanheld and Osmun, 1981); Stephen Philip Kramer, *Socialism in Western Europe: The Experience of a Generation* (Boulder, Colo.: Westview, 1984); Adam Przeworski and John Sprague, *Paper Stones: A History of Electoral Socialism* (Chicago: University of Chicago Press, 1986); Leo Panitch, *Working Class Politics in Crisis: Essays on Labour and the State* (London: Verso, 1986).

4. On the British Labour Party see Peter Byrd, "The Labour Party in Britain," in Paterson and Thomas, *Future*, pp. 59–107. On the German Social Democratic Party see William E. Paterson, "The German Social Democratic Party," in Paterson and Thomas, *Future*, pp. 127–152; and Stephen Padgett, "The West German Social Democrats in Opposition 1982–86," *West European Politics* 3 (1987): 334–356.

5. An excellent discussion of the crisis of the Keynesian model for industrial societies is in Joel Krieger, *Reagan, Thatcher and the Politics of Decline* (New York: Oxford University Press, 1986), pp. 22–26.

6. Krieger, *Reagan, Thatcher*, p. 24.

7. See Ronald Inglehart and Jacques-René Rabier, "Political Realignment in Advanced Industrial Society: From Class-Based Politics to Quality-of-Life Politics," *Government and Opposition* 4 (Autumn 1986).

8. John D. Stephens, *The Transition from Capitalism to Socialism* (Urbana and Chicago: University of Illinois Press, 1986), p. 174.

9. Stephens, *Transition*, p. 197. A concurring view is in Walter Korpi, *The Working Class in Welfare Capitalism* (London: Routledge, 1978).

10. Jonas Pontusson, "Behind and Beyond Social Democracy in Sweden," *New Left Review* 143 (January-February 1984): 69–96. A good overview of the tensions underlying the Swedish welfare state is in Peter Walters, "Distributing Decline: Swedish Social Democrats and the Crisis of the Welfare State," *Government and Opposition* 3 (Summer 1985): 356–369.

11. Peter Aimer, "The Strategy of Gradualism and the Swedish Wage-Earner Funds," *West European Politics* 3 (July 1985): 43–53.

12. Adam Przeworski, *Capitalism and Social Democracy* (Cambridge: Cambridge University Press, 1986), pp. 43–44.

13. Ibid., p. 43.

14. Ibid., p. 29.

15. An excellent treatment of internal fragmentation of social democratic parties is in David Hine, "Leaders and Followers: Democracy and Manageability of Social Democratic Parties of Western Europe," in Paterson and Thomas, *Future*, p. 270. See also N. Johnson, "Parties and Conditions of Political Leadership," in H. Doring and G. Smith, eds., *Party Government and Political Culture in West Germany* (London: Macmillan, 1982), pp. 160–164. This view is corroborated by Douglas Webber, "Social Democracy and the Re-emergence of Mass Unemployment in Western Europe," in Paterson and Thomas, *Future*, pp. 19–58.

16. Krieger, *Reagan, Thatcher*, pp. 36–58.

17. See Werner Hulberg, "After the West German Elections," *New Left Review* 162 (March-April 1987): 85–99; Hine, "Leaders and Followers," pp. 261–290; and Padgett, "The West German Social Democrats."

18. Mark Kesselman notes that "in most capitalist nations, the right has been the beneficiary of discontent generated by the economic crisis. Most Social democratic and welfare state coalitions have been defeated by conservative political parties or have remained in office by adopting austerity policies." See Kesselman, "Prospects for Democratic Socialism," p. 397. This view is corroborated by Webber, "Social Democracy," in Paterson and Thomas, *Future*, pp. 19–58.

19. André Gorz, "El Socialismo de Mañana," *Leviatán* 26 (1986): 113. All translations of foreign-language sources in this book are made by the author.

20. Przeworski, *Capitalism*, p. 41.

21. See Graeme Duncan, "A Crisis of Social Democracy," *Parliamentary Affairs* 3 (Summer 1985): 267.

22. The German Social Democratic government's last budget (1982) was severely criticized by the party left because of its austerity measures, which, according to William Paterson, would be implemented on the backs of workers, pensioners, and the jobless. See Paterson, "The German Social Democratic Party," p. 131. Economic austerity policies were partly responsible for the doubling of unemployment between 1980 and 1982 and were a key element in the breakup of the center-left coalition government. See Webber, "Social Democracy," p. 21.

23. James Petras, "The Rise and Decline of Southern European Socialism," *New Left Review* 146 (July-August 1984): 37.

24. Petras, "The Rise and Decline," pp. 37, 44.

25. See Brian Criddle, "The French Socialist Party," in Paterson and Thomas, *Future*, pp. 223–241.

26. Duncan, "A Crisis of Social Democracy," p. 269.

27. Hine, "Leaders and Followers," p. 283.

2

The Historical Legacy: A Century of Socialism in Spain

> I think it is fair to say, without exaggeration, that of all parties in contemporary Spanish history, the PSOE has had the most internal quarrels and divisions.
>
> —Manuel Contreras[1]

Despite being the oldest of Spain's national political parties (over a century in existence), the Spanish Socialist Workers Party entered the new democracy in 1977 with little governmental experience and a complex and ambiguous historical legacy.[2] For three quarters of its first one hundred years the PSOE was marginalized from political power. The party participated in power only during the Primo de Rivera dictatorship (1923–1930) and the Spanish Second Republic (1931–1936), and in neither case did it control the government.

The brevity and intensity of the PSOE's governmental experience, especially during the ill-fated Second Republic, and the subsequent long period of exile and clandestine existence during the franquist regime (1939–1975) has recently caused PSOE historians and intellectuals to reevaluate and reassess the party's historical legacy. In helping to consolidate the parliamentary monarchy after Franco's death, PSOE leaders could not help looking back at the brief periods of Socialist participation in government in order to exact lessons that might be applied to the new democracy. The passage of time and the emergence of a new generation of PSOE scholars created a new willingness to look back at party history with a more open mind.

To a considerable extent, contemporary Spanish Socialists have inter-

nalized a set of important historical lessons that have guided their behavior in the democratic regime. At the very least Spanish Socialists use
their own history as a yardstick with which to measure their current
performance. This chapter will highlight some of the most important
themes that emerged from the first century of Spanish socialism. Sections
of the chapter will touch on the origins and development of the PSOE,
the PSOE during the Spanish Second Republic, the Socialists under the
franquist regime, and the renaissance and reemergence of the PSOE in
the early 1970s.

While these four epochs in the history of the PSOE are briefly considered, a number of common and interconnected themes will emerge.
First, with few exceptions the PSOE has suffered from organizational
weakness. Second, the PSOE has been plagued by debilitating internal
conflict. A third and related characteristic has been the personalized
nature of leadership (and factions) within the PSOE. Finally, there has
generally been an intellectual and ideological shallowness within the
Spanish Socialist left.

By considering these themes, we can begin to understand both the
historical lessons that were later internalized by PSOE leaders, as well
as the elements of continuity present in the Socialist Party during and
after the transition to democracy.

ORIGINS AND EARLY DEVELOPMENT OF SOCIALISM IN SPAIN

Socialist ideas entered Spain in the middle nineteenth century but did
not really take root until the early twentieth century.[3] Socialism as a
political movement developed relatively late in Spain. From its inception
in 1868 until its repression in the early 1870s, the Spanish Federation
of the First International displayed serious internal divisions between
the dominant anarchist (Bakuninist) and Marxist factions.[4] This early
schism had a geographical base that would later become important: The
anarchist wing of the First International was centered in Barcelona, while
the Marxist faction was strongest in Madrid. The anarchist remnants of
the First International would later cohere around the anarchist National
Confederation of Workers (CNT). Founded in 1910, the CNT became
a powerful and revolutionary anarcho-syndicalist movement with special
strength in Catalonia (where the PSOE remained weak throughout the
Second Republic).

Pablo Iglesias, a poor typesetter who had arrived in Madrid in 1871
from his native Galicia, was expelled from the Spanish branch of the
First International a year later for his adherence to the ideas of Karl
Marx.[5] Two years later Iglesias became president of the Typesetter's
Guild, a position he used to organize a small group of about forty fellow

Marxists (mostly typesetters, but also a half dozen intellectuals). The typesetters formed an "elite" among the nascent working class of Madrid and were especially literate and involved in politics. From this nucleus the PSOE was founded in Madrid in May 1879.

Iglesias used the French SFIO as the model for a Spanish Socialist organization.[6] The initial manifesto of the PSOE revealed a clear Marxist orientation. It defined the PSOE's goals as the taking of power by the working class, the transformation of all private property into collective property, the organization of society into an economic federation based on workers' collectives, and the "end of class society and creation of one single working class."[7] But Iglesias was less concerned with ideology than with the building of a solid working-class organization, and on ideological matters he tended to defer to his French counterparts.[8] On the one hand, the early PSOE was "devoted to practical reforms rather than premature revolutionary efforts."[9] On the other hand, the PSOE adhered rigidly to a narrow working-class orientation, rejecting any alliances with or membership by the Republican middle classes.

One result of this exclusivist *obrerismo* was to alienate many Spanish intellectuals, partly explaining the poor intellectual heritage of the PSOE. Miguel de Unamuno, one of Spain's great men of letters, joined the PSOE in 1895 and was courted by party leaders to be its preeminent intellectual. Unamuno soon became disillusioned with the PSOE's fierce anticlericalism and with its rigid Marxism. Despite his personal commitment to socialist ideas, Unamuno criticized his fellow Socialists as "intolerable, foolish Marxist fanatics, ignorant, and blind to the virtues and contributions of the middle class, and unaware of the evolutionary process."[10] Unamuno, along with other intellectuals, left the party during the period 1898–1910, reflecting an early cleavage within the party between more intellectually oriented PSOE members and the majority faction led by Pablo Iglesias.

For the first thirty years of the party, Iglesias kept the PSOE small, tightly organized, and firmly under his personal control.[11] In 1882, the PSOE organized its first general strike. It was easily repressed, and Iglesias was jailed, but the strategy paid off in increased membership and publicity for the young party. In 1886, the official party newspaper, *El Socialista*, appeared. In 1891, the PSOE elected two city council members in the Basque Country. Still, in its early history the PSOE had a minuscule presence in Spain. The General Confederation of Workers (UGT), the PSOE's trade union affiliate, was not founded until 1888; and unlike other European cases, it was largely the creation of the Socialist Party. In 1899, the PSOE won only 23,000 votes (0.8 percent of the total) and had very few members. The low level of industrialization, the paucity of the urban working class, and police repression all hampered the development of a mass left. By 1900, the UGT had made important progress in the north of Spain but still had only sixty locals and 15,000 members. Spurred by the success of the German Social Democratic Party, the PSOE was able to attract 70,000 members by 1904, but by 1906, the party rolls had decreased to 34,000.

After the turn of the century the PSOE faced stiff competition from radical republicanism and anarcho-syndicalism. A serious internal polemic developed between those seeking to end the PSOE's political isolation through alliances with republican forces and followers of Pablo Iglesias, who remained stubborn in his opposition to any such collaboration. The PSOE began to enjoy its first electoral success in municipal elections, especially in Madrid. Iglesias and two other PSOE members were elected to the Madrid city council in 1905, along with seventy-one other Socialists throughout Spain. At a PSOE Party Congress in 1908 the Socialists adopted a cautious policy of alliance with bourgeois parties, and a formal electoral alliance with the Republicans was agreed upon in 1909. Iglesias was the PSOE's first deputy elected to parliament in 1910, but the Socialists did not increase their parliamentary presence until 1918, when they won six seats. The party's increased pragmatism strongly reflected the growing influence of a younger generation of PSOE leaders that included Francisco Largo Caballero, Julián Besteiro, Luís Arquistaín, Fernando de los Ríos and Indalecio Prieto. These younger members were more willing to interpret Marxism flexibly and saw real possibilities for political progress within the Spanish political system, especially after the decline of the conservative Maura. The PSOE experienced a dramatic influx of new members between 1910 and 1912, during which time the CNT was illegal.

Together with a pragmatic, moderate, and collaborationist electoral stance, the PSOE pursued a policy of mass mobilization. Its participation in the 1917 general strike, together with the anarchist CNT and other republican forces, provoked a vicious response from the government, which declared a state of war, closed down the PSOE press and local party centers, and sentenced many top PSOE organizers (including Largo Caballero and Besteiro) to life prison terms.[12] The mass uprising was efficiently crushed but weakened the parliamentary monarchy and hastened its demise.

Like all West European socialist parties, the PSOE was deeply affected by the Russian Revolution. Its principal leaders were strongly attracted to the Bolshevik model, and they contemplated seriously its application to the Spanish case. In response to the revolution, the PSOE broke its electoral alliance with Radicals and Republicans, although the party suffered as a result. The Socialists voted in 1919 to support "conditional membership" in Lenin's Third International. However, PSOE emissary Fernando de los Ríos returned from a meeting with Lenin deeply opposed to the latter's "twenty-one Conditions." Party leaders subsequently followed his advice and rejected membership in the Third International, and in 1921, PSOE congressional delegates narrowly supported this decision.[13] The resulting split of the PSOE and the creation of the Spanish Communist Party (PCE) weakened the party and contributed to a decline of over 75 percent of its membership between 1920 and 1922.[14]

The Restoration regime, begun in 1876, ended in 1923 with Spain's last military *pronunciamiento*, led by General Primo de Rivera and engineered and supported by King Alfonso XIII.[15] The Restoration regime had been moribund ever since the mass uprising of 1917. The parliamentary monarchy became an increasingly repressive and unpopular regime and in its last years ruled almost exclusively under states of siege. After the breakup of the Republican-Socialist alliance in 1919 and the formation of the PCE, the PSOE radicalized its view of the decaying constitutional monarchy. Thus while the PSOE initially opposed Primo's rise to power, the Socialists strongly favored the end of the Restoration regime and saw opportunities for reform and organizational freedom within the dictatorship.

The PSOE officially branded the Primo regime reactionary and called on its members to oppose it. But the party stopped short of taking an active stance against the dictatorship. As the contours of Primo's corporatist system began to take shape, the PSOE became more supportive of the regime. Primo's corporatist labor relations system, based on mixed employer-worker councils and state arbitration, approximated a long-standing proposal of the Socialist Party. Eager to stem the precipitous decline of PSOE and UGT membership, the Socialists implemented a policy of seeking influence in these corporatist councils.

Primo's regime brutally repressed the CNT, the PSOE's chief rival on the left, but the dictator adopted a conciliatory attitude toward the UGT and PSOE, regarding both as nonrevolutionary organizations that could enhance the legitimacy of his regime. Taking advantage of the relative freedom of action, the PSOE and UGT were able to halt the decline in membership and began to extend their organizational network among the peasantry.

In 1924, with the support of the UGT and PSOE, Francisco Largo Caballero accepted an appointment as a councillor of state, a job reserved by Primo for a representative of organized labor. Largo Caballero, a poor construction worker who was illiterate until his twenties, had become a rising star within the UGT.[16] A pure political opportunist, Largo Caballero believed that Socialists could secure important gains for the working class from positions of influence offered by the dictatorship. Largo's participation in the Primo regime provoked a storm of criticism from a wide range of political forces and from some sectors within the PSOE. Indalecio Prieto, a top member of the PSOE Executive Committee, quit the leadership in protest. Official PSOE and UGT policy allowed participation in all *elected* positions based on the view that *both* the Restoration monarchy and the dictatorship were undemocratic bourgeois regimes and that representation of the working class within either system could contribute to the goal of building socialism. The Socialists thus participated in municipal elections and the labor relations committee, as well as in governmental organizations where their presence could be justified as representing workers. This posture reflected a growing pragmatism within the PSOE, a tendency that was enhanced by the protracted illness of Pablo Iglesias and his death in 1925.

By 1926, attempts by Primo to institutionalize his regime through the election of a National Consultative Assembly deeply polarized the Socialist Party and the UGT. Although both organizations had supported temporary collaboration with the regime, attempts by Primo to extend his dictatorship were fiercely opposed. Despite the fact that Largo Caballero reacted enthusiastically to the proposal, Indalecio Prieto and Julián Besteiro, Iglesias' successor as PSOE leader, called for the establishment of a genuine democratic republic. Extraordinary congresses of the PSOE and UGT (October 1927) rejected all participation in the Assembly. This political setback, together with a deteriorating economic situation, initiated the demise of Primo de Rivera and for the Socialists began a period of distancing from and frontal opposition to the dictatorship. However, Socialists continued to support collaboration in all other representative posts and ratified this policy in a Party Congress held in 1928. Julián Besteiro, elected president, and Francisco Largo Caballero, elected vice-president, easily defeated a slate of candidates (led by Fernando de los Ríos) opposed to any further collaboration with the Primo dictatorship.

Nevertheless, in a joint PSOE-UGT document published in 1929, rejecting the past pragmatism and adopting a new principled opposition to the dictatorship, the Socialists affirmed, "[we] can best carry out our goals in a republican state, where we can obtain the full political power that corresponds to our increasing social power."[17]

The Socialists clearly benefited from the Primo de Rivera dictatorship. By 1931, the PSOE recovered somewhat from the PCE split and had built its membership up to almost 20,000 (from a low of about 8,000 from 1923 to 1927); UGT membership reached almost 100,000. The PSOE gained a new organizational presence among the peasantry when it absorbed the Spanish Federation of Agricultural Workers (FETT) and gained a crucial foothold in Andalusia. In addition to taking advantage of the illegality of competing organizations, PSOE and UGT leaders gained invaluable experience in public administration. Within the Socialist camp collaboration with the dictatorship enhanced the prestige and power of Francisco Largo Caballero and the trade union movement within the PSOE, thus setting the stage for further internal conflict during the Second Republic.

SPANISH SOCIALISM IN THE SECOND REPUBLIC

> Because of the internal divisions in the Spanish Socialist party, its support of the October 1934 revolution, its unwillingness to share the responsibilities of governing after the Popular Front electoral victory in 1936, and its extremist rhetoric and actions from 1933 to 1936, the PSOE...a factor of stability in the first period of the Republic, became a major, if not the decisive factor leading to the breakdown [of democracy].
>
> —Juan J. Linz[18]

The PSOE emerged from the Primo dictatorship as the strongest and best-organized Spanish political party. Despite differences within the PSOE over the question of collaboration with the dictatorship, the fall of Primo created a temporary consensus around the formation of a republican regime. Thus virtually the entire PSOE leadership supported the Pact of San Sebastián (August 1930), which founded the Second Republic, although it did not officially participate in the pact.

Below the surface, serious tensions persisted. Even among the most avid PSOE supporters of the Second Republic there were different priorities. Francisco Largo Caballero's main goal was the steady consolidation of the trade union movement, whereas Indalecio Prieto and Fernando de los Ríos sought to consolidate the political alliance with other republican forces.[19] In 1931, a more serious schism developed between the majority of the leadership supporting the PSOE's acceptance of cabinet posts in the Second Republic (Largo Caballero, Prieto, Fernando de los Ríos) and those opposing any participation in government (led by PSOE and UGT president Julián Besteiro). Besteiro resigned as Party leader over this issue, and six members of the PSOE Executive Committee followed him.

At the heart of the internal division was the relationship between the goals of building socialism and building parliamentary democracy. Stanley Payne notes:

[The Socialists'] initial relationship to the Republic had been ambiguous. Only reluctantly had the Socialist leadership allowed the party to be taken into the Republican coalition, and the Socialists themselves, after cooperating with Primo de Rivera's labor tribunals, had done very little to assist the coming of the new regime. Since 1918 Spanish Socialist ideology had become increasingly vague. Many Socialist spokesmen still considered themselves orthodox revolutionary Marxists, though non-Leninist and non-communist, while others ignored the issue altogether. In 1931 the Socialists made it clear that their goal was a socialist republic, not a liberal middle class parliamentary republic, but what this actually meant was far from clear.[20]

It does seem clear that what divided PSOE leaders during the first years of the Second Republic was not a conflict over the desirability of building a socialist state (although the exact nature of such a state was never clearly elucidated) but, rather, a dispute over short-term strategies for achieving such an outcome.[21] Largo Caballero's view was that collaboration with the dictatorship, and then the Republicans, was ultimately in the best interests of the working class and could facilitate the building of socialism. By 1933, faced with the reality that the PSOE agenda could not be achieved in alliance with Republicans or within the context of the Second Republic, he turned against both. Julián Besteiro opposed any participation in Republican governments from a strict Marxist perspective because he did not believe that Socialists could implement their agenda in a bourgeois republic. He advocated a position of loyal but forceful opposition to bourgeois governments, but he also opposed the October 1934 revolutionary uprising.

Indalecio Prieto came closest to supporting the Republic unconditionally and went the furthest among the top PSOE leaders to protect the regime against its enemies. Linz argues that the PSOE leadership assumed an "accidentalist" view toward democracy: "Democracy and a bourgeois parliamentary republic are of only instrumental value for a labor movement whose ultimate goal is a better society for the working class and can be abandoned for the dictatorship of the proletariat if perceived as necessary to achieve the goal."[22] Only Fernando de los Ríos, justice minister during the first Republican government, appeared to believe firmly in the value of parliamentary democracy per se, but he was always in a distinct minority.

Largo Caballero and Prieto were able to rally the PSOE behind the new Republic during its first *bienio*, with Besteiro in the minority, although the policy of collaboration was not officially approved until the PSOE Thirteenth Congress in 1932. In the first government led by the Republican Azaña, the Socialists obtained three cabinet posts, filled by Largo Caballero (Labor), Prieto (Finance), and de los Ríos (Justice). Important social gains were made by the Republican-Socialist government, especially in the area of labor relations, where Largo Caballero distinguished himself as an able administrator.

Nevertheless, by 1933 the party consensus over the strategy of allying with the Republicans and supporting the Second Republic had broken down. As Juan Linz has noted, the agenda of the first Republican government was overambitious and poorly prioritized and certainly did not satisfy the expectations of the Socialist leadership or membership.[23] Welfare and land reform issues that were priorities for the PSOE met with less enthusiasm from the bourgeois Republicans and took a back seat to items high on the Republican agenda (anticlericalism, educational reform, antimilitarism, regionalism). The policies of the Republican government, especially in the area of agrarian reform, raised expectations that could not be met. The energy expended on largely symbolic agenda items (especially anticlericalism) created hostility against the Republic that was not offset by new sources of support.

Within the PSOE there was growing hostility toward the alliance with the Republicans. In part the impatience of the Socialists reflected the dramatic swelling of party ranks after the inauguration of the Republic. Membership in 1931 was up 272 percent over the 1930 figures, growing from 18,200 to 67,000.[24] The increase in part resulted from the general politicization of society in 1931 and also from the fact that the PSOE was the strongest and best-organized party at the start of the Republic. Membership increases were especially high in agricultural areas, notably Andalusia, where peasant frustration over stagnated agrarian reform policies was especially high.

Pressure from the party base took place within a context of a serious leadership vacuum. Iglesias had dominated the PSOE until his death in 1925, and his successor, Julián Besteiro, resigned and was a constant internal critic of PSOE policy throughout the Second Republic. After 1933, the Socialist Party polarized around the tactical differences of Largo Caballero (advocating revolutionary actions) and Prieto (supporting a broad coalition to defend the Republic), and this internal schism paralyzed the party for the remainder of the Republic. Moreover, the internal fragmentation took on an institutional dimension as Prieto maintained his support within the PSOE Executive Committee and Largo Caballero increasingly depended on his support within the UGT and the Socialist Youth organization.

By the fall of 1933 the Republican-Socialist government was in total crisis. Economic decline, rapid mass mobilization, police repression, a growing revolutionary anarchist movement, the political recovery of a "semiloyal" right, overall political polarization, and a worsening international environment (Nazism in Germany and Dolfuss in Austria) formed the context for the radicalization of an important sector within the PSOE (led by Labor Minister Largo Caballero and supported by Luis Arquistaín, editor of the journal *Leviatán*) and the downfall of the coalition and government in September 1933.[25]

The PSOE's decision to run in elections separately from the plethora of republican forces that had composed the previous coalition had disastrous consequences. The PSOE dropped from 114 to 55 seats and fell from the largest to the third-largest party. The republican parties were virtually wiped out, and the rightist Spanish Confederation of the Autonomous Right (CEDA) and the center-right Radicals made spectacular gains. The PSOE viewed the electoral victory of the right as a direct threat to the survival of the republic, a reaction influenced heavily by events in Germany and Austria. After the Radical Lerroux formed his first government, Largo Caballero announced that "we have cancelled our commitments to the Republicans. True to our doctrine, the working class must have power completely in its own hands. We must fight to convert the present regime into a socialist regime."[26] Socialist leaders threatened to stage an uprising should the suspect CEDA be allowed in government. Center-right governments under the Radicals were attempted until October 1934, when it was no longer possible to marginalize the largest single party from government. The inclusion of three CEDA ministers in the government was the spark that began the ill-fated revolution of 1934.

Although the revolution was not entirely the making of the PSOE (uprisings took place among Catalan nationalists, and the CNT and PCE participated in some regions), the Socialist Party spearheaded the uprising in Asturias, where it had its greatest and most prolonged success but also the most tragic demise. Socialist leaders who masterminded the uprising prepared a program to be implemented after taking power that included abolition of the army, the nationalization of all land (but not industry, interestingly enough), and a socialist dictatorship. But the program was for naught as army troops sent to Asturias, led by General Francisco Franco, were used to crush the two-week-long rebellion, but not until over 1000 people (mostly workers) died. Widespread jailings (over 15,000) of suspected revolutionaries followed.

The PSOE electoral strategy in 1933, and the subsequent revolution in October 1934, not only contributed to the PSOE's loss in the elections and the advent of a reactionary and repressive government but also benefited the PSOE's competitors on the left, especially the PCE. The PCE won its first parliamentary seat in the 1933 elections and, through shrewd propaganda work, effectively stole the banner of the 1934 uprising away from the Socialists.

After the revolution, and as the conservative government in 1935 began to undo much of the legislation passed under the Republican-Socialist coalition, internal divisions within the PSOE reached a boiling point. The most serious division among socialists was between the more radicalized UGT and those within the PSOE who still sought collaboration with the Republic. According to Santos Juliá:

Union and Party, that had been unified behind the project of consolidating and upholding the Republican regime, had become divided, unable to formulate a policy, and torn between supporting the Republic and undertaking a definitive assault against it.[27]

Within the PSOE leadership three main camps were grouped around strategic more than ideological differences. Besteiro, increasingly isolated within the PSOE, supported the Republic but opposed collaboration with centrist or center-left governments. He was supported by a dwindling number of party activists who remained loyal to him. Prieto supported the Republic and sought alliances with progressive parties in order to fend off the threat of fascism. His approach had wide support within the Executive Committee of the PSOE. Largo Caballero, increasingly influential within the PSOE leadership, the Young Socialists, and among the party and UGT rank and file, worked actively to promote a Bolshevization of the Socialist left in collaboration with the Communist Party and the anarchist CNT.

In late 1935 Prieto attempted to form the Popular Front with the Socialists and center-left forces loyal to the republic. Largo Caballero insisted on the inclusion of the PCE, quit the leadership of the PSOE in protest over the issue, and brought the PSOE perilously close to splintering. In January 1936, Largo Caballero prevailed over the skeptical Prieto and the Popular Front was formed.

Largo Caballero's role in the radicalization is particularly peculiar given that in fewer than three years he had moved from the party right to the extreme left. Though a chief architect of the PSOE's collaboration with the Primo dictatorship and a proponent of collaboration with Republican forces after the fall of that regime, by the summer of 1933, Largo Caballero was advocating a dictatorship of the proletariat. De la Cierva explains Largo Caballero's behavior as an attempt to atone for years of collaborationist activity that by 1933 had delivered disappointing results.[28] Bizcarrondo notes the influence on Largo Caballero of Luis Arquistaín, the former Spanish ambassador in Germany whose firsthand observation of the demise of the German Social Democrats led to an abandonment of reformism, and whose journal *Leviatán* incited radicalization of the PSOE.[29] Juliá explains the radicalization as being rather consistent with Largo Caballero's narrow and "corporatist" trade union mentality. At different historical junctures, Caballero saw collaboration with the dictatorship, support for the Republic, and advocacy of a dictatorship of the proletariat as being in the best interest of the working class.

Despite the electoral victory of the Popular Front in February 1936, in which the PSOE won 99 of 267 seats and became once again the single largest parliamentary group, the internal political crisis intensified. Relations between Largo Caballero and Prieto developed into a personal feud, and those between the factions of the PSOE turned violent. The Largo Caballero wing of the PSOE that now dominated the Socialist group in parliament staunchly opposed participation in the Republican government, opting instead to support a government solely of Left Republicans. This group judged the Popular Front government as temporary and felt it provided an opportunity to move the political struggle into the streets and to unify mass organizations for a more successful 1934-style revolution sometime in the future. Immediately after the elections the peasant federations of the UGT began to occupy landed estates, a wave of strikes crippled industry, and an upsurge in political violence all combined to create a prerevolutionary atmosphere. Largo Caballero's rhetoric had become unquestionably disloyal to the Republic: he stated, "I want a Republic without a class war: but for this to happen it is necessary that one class disappears."[30]

Ironically perhaps, the extensive social revolution that took place in the Republican zone during the Civil War was not the making of revolutionary leaders as much as the spontaneous mass opposition to the rightist military uprising. Prieto and his supporters in the PSOE Executive Committee remained eager to enter into government in alliance with Left Republicans; and given the parliamentary strength of the PSOE, they felt that Prieto should be allowed to head such a government. They were, however, increasingly isolated by the radicalization of the party base, encouraged by Largo Caballero's leadership of the UGT, his influence over the Socialist Youth movement, and the growing strength of the PCE. Prieto's appointment as prime minister was ultimately blocked by the PSOE left—Largo Caballero threatened to pull the UGT out of the Popular Front, and a weak, isolated, and ineffective Left Republican was appointed prime minister.[31]

The tragic struggle between Prieto and Largo Caballero was interrupted, though by no means ended, by the outbreak of the Civil War in July 1936. If Prieto's attempts to form a progressive but prorepublican alliance were obstructed by the PSOE left, Largo Caballero's goal of unifying the mass organizations of the left (UGT, CNT, PCE, etc.) was equally unsuccessful.[32] Largo Caballero became prime minister of a broad coalition government (September 1936–May 1937), but Prieto, as defense minister, helped to bring his government down. In the end both Socialist leaders were ousted from government, victims of inter- and intraparty intrigues that debilitated the PSOE and the republic and that benefited the PCE and, ultimately, the Nationalist forces.

THE DECLINE AND RENAISSANCE OF THE PSOE DURING FRANQUISM

Relatively little has been written on the PSOE during franquism, especially during the period 1939–1955. In part this paucity of scholarship reflects the virtual obliteration of the PSOE within Spain during that period. In fact, Socialist Party activity was centered in exile (Mexico and

France) until the early 1970s. It is also true that during this period the major opposition force within Spain was the Communist Party (PCE).

Nevertheless, as Preston contends, the PCE barb that the PSOE spent forty years on vacation is grossly unfair.[33] Socialists within Spain continually attempted to regroup the PSOE but met with severe repression. From 1939 to 1953, six consecutive PSOE Executive Committees inside Spain were arrested by the franquist police. The PSOE was unable to make the transition from an open mass party to a smaller clandestine organization. Unlike the PCE, the Socialists attempted to rebuild the UGT rather than infiltrate the franquist syndical structure.[34] Socialists in the interior lacked the leadership and organizational skills and resources needed to maintain the PSOE's presence within the harsh conditions of franquist opposition. Despite the fact that the PSOE had been a far superior numerical force during the Republic, Franco's obsession with rooting out Communist opposition enhanced the prestige of the PCE and overshadowed the role of the PSOE.

Most analyses agree that the main factor weakening the PSOE during franquism was the persistence of internal divisions. Conflicts between personalities (Negrín, the last PSOE prime minister, and Prieto), geographical centers of exiled Socialists (Mexico and France), PSOE members based inside Spain and in exile, and different strategies designed to topple Franco plagued the party. These schisms became increasingly irrelevant as the franquist regime gained internal consolidation and external support and as the principal PSOE leaders from the republican period died (Besteiro, 1940; Largo Caballero, 1946; Arquistaín, 1955; Negrín, 1956; Prieto, 1962). By 1951, when Rodolfo Llopis replaced Prieto as party leader, the PSOE was little more than a "nostalgia club" in exile and was described by one writer as miserable and bitter.[35] The trauma of the Second Republic and the Civil War, along with the difficulties of adapting to new countries and languages, sapped the energy of the aging Socialist exiles.

What most united the leadership in exile was its fierce anticommunism. PSOE leaders never forgave the PCE for its infiltrations and intrigues during the Second Republic. Prieto and Llopis based their political strategies on foreign intervention against Franco, and they hoped to use their anticommunist credentials to gain support of the Western democracies in the post–World War II environment.[36] Consequently, the PSOE refused to consider any joint activity with the Communists, even when it became clear that the PCE had important organizational attributes within franquist Spain. The PSOE's stubbornness on this issue created a permanent split in the antifranquist opposition that persisted until after Franco's death. The Socialists participated in three different antifranquist coalitions (The Spanish Junta of Liberation, 1941; The Union of

Democratic Forces, 1961; and The Platform of Democratic Convergence, 1974) but boycotted organizations in which the PCE was a member.

The atrophy of the PSOE in exile contrasted with the renaissance of the Socialist movement within Spain in the mid–1950s. The official PSOE had at most 3,000 members, but Socialist opposition was growing inside Spain. More often than not, the activities were developed on the margins of the party, although many future PSOE leaders gained their start in such university, labor, and even Church organizations.[37] The mild and short-lived liberalization of the political system begun in 1956 and associated with Education Minister Ruíz Giménez provided an opportunity for these opposition groups to gain organizational ground. The Socialist University Group (ASU) was formed in 1956 in Madrid and included many students who would later join the PSOE. A group of socialist students congregated around a well-respected socialist intellectual, Professor Enrique Tierno Galván. Socialist groups emerged in Sevilla and the Basque Country. A group of Socialists organized around the progressive Catholic publication *Cuadernos Para el Diálogo*. Perhaps the most important opposition organization to emerge was the Popular Liberation Front (FLP), and its Catalan branch (FOC), an underground organization that blended Marxism, Catholicism, and anti-imperialist ideologies.[38] A number of prominent PSOE leaders emerged from the FLP/FOC, including Narcís Serra and José María Maravall, both future PSOE cabinet ministers.

At the 1958 Seventh Congress in exile (Toulouse, France) the leadership resisted growing pressure to give these organizations support and resisted making them autonomous organizations within the PSOE. PSOE members in the interior complained bitterly about lack of funds and autonomy. Only two positions on the party Executive Committee were reserved for members in the interior. Llopis opposed attempts by Tierno Galván and others to enter into contact with franquist social democrats, Christian democrats, and liberal monarchists, eventually leading many socialists to bolt the party.

In the 1960s, the influence of the Socialists inside Spain continued to grow vis-à-vis the leadership in exile. At the 1962 Munich meeting of opposition forces, PSOE delegates from the interior outnumbered exiles two to one.[39] Despite resistance from Llopis, a consensus was emerging between a wide range of antifranquist forces in the interior (including socialists) that would later facilitate the transition to democracy. Important progress was made on the Socialist trade union front in the rebirth of a Catalan socialist movement (the Catalan Socialist Movement [MSC] held its first congress in 1967), and the strengthening of the PSOE organization inside Spain. In 1968, Tierno Galván, frustrated by the intrasigence of the PSOE leadership, formed the Socialist Party of the Interior (PSI, later the Popular Socialist Party, PSP).

The growth of the socialist opposition within Spain, the rigid control of the PSOE leadership in exile, and the resulting fragmentation of socialist groups in the interior, led to a full-scale assault on the Llopis leadership between 1968 and 1974. At the 1970 Seventh Congress in exile, the delegates from the interior won important victories that reflected their growing strength. In addition to winning a large number of seats on the Executive Committee, the internal Socialist groups were able to gain some measure of autonomy from the leadership. Llopis remained in charge of the party, but the momentum for change could not be stopped. Between 1970 and 1972, Socialists in the interior formed a de facto parallel Executive Committee and began openly attacking Llopis and the leadership in exile through the PSOE press. Sensing the impending mutiny, Llopis refused to convoke the scheduled party congress in August 1972. The interior delegates held a congress in open rebellion against the PSOE leadership, and they gained the support of some members of the "official" Socialist Executive. At this conference, during which Felipe González made his presence visible for the first time, a new Executive Committee was constituted and the party leadership was officially moved to Spain.

Llopis resisted to the bitter end, convening his own congress later that year. Tierno Galván and the PSI foolishly backed Llopis, but the PSOE-*Histórico* (PSOE-H) never obtained recognition from international socialist parties. In early 1974, the Socialist International officially recognized the "new" PSOE, although the PSOE-H continued to exist and enjoyed one last moment of glory when in 1977 it was legalized before the larger Socialist Party.

The 1974 Eighth Congress in exile, held in the Parisian suburb of Suresnes, marked the definitive consolidation of a new generation of Socialist militants from the interior. Felipe González was elected Secretary General, and Enrique Múgica, Pablo Castellano, José María Benegas, and other younger militants were elected to the Executive Committee.

CONCLUSION: THE HISTORICAL LEGACY

Looking back at the history of the PSOE since its founding in 1879, several general themes are apparent, and each of them has had a visible impact on the present-day Socialists. First, although the PSOE may be viewed as one of the most stable political organizations in Spanish history, it is also true that it has been an organizationally debile party during its entire history.[40] The PSOE has only recently attracted over 200,000 members or 4,000 *agrupaciones* (party locals) (see Table 2.1). The PSOE emerged from the franquist period especially weakened but made a spectacular recovery after 1974 and has made slow but steady progress since then. The paucity of membership and organizational capacity has meant that at key historical junctures the party has been overwhelmed

Table 2.1
Membership and Number of *Agrupaciones* in PSOE, 1902–1986

YEAR	MEMBERS*	AGRUPACIONES
1902(a)	4,200	78
1905(a)	6,100	144
1908(a)	6,000	115
1912(a)	13,000	198
1915(a)	14,300	238
1918(a)	30,600	223
1920(a)	52,800	536
1924(b)	8,500	209
1926(b)	8,500	230
1928(b)	9,000	219
1930(b)	18,500	317
1932(b)	75,100	1,119
1936(b)	59,800	n.a.
1974(c)	3,500	n.a.
1977(d)	51,500	1,423
1979(d)	101,000	2,230
1981(d)	99,300	2,756
1982(d)	112,500	2,862
1984(d)	154,900	3,538
1985(d)	162,600	n.a.
1986(d)	185,000	3,897
1988(e)	215,000	n.a.

*Figures rounded down to nearest hundred.

Source: (a) José Félix Tezanos, "Continuidad y cambio en el socialismo español. El PSOE durante la transición" in Julián Santamaría, ed., *Los partidos políticos en España.* (Madrid: Centro de Investigaciones Sociológicas, forthcoming), p. 24; (b) Manuel Contreras, *El PSOE en la Segunda República: Organización e ideología* (Madrid: CIS, 1981), p. 85; (c) Paul Preston, "Decadencia y resurgimiento del PSOE durante el régimen franquista" in Santos Juliá, ed., *El Socialismo en España* (Madrid: Editorial Pablo Iglesias, 1986), p. 366; (d) *Anuario 1986, El Socialista* (Madrid: PSOE, 1986), p. 144. (e) quoted by PSOE Secretary of Organization Txiki Benegas, in *Cambio 16* (January 18, 1988), p. 23.

by relatively large infusions of new members. This occurred during three periods of rapid political change (1915–1920, 1930–1932, and 1974–1977), usually in response to mass mobilization, and each of these dramatic increases exacerbated serious ideological problems for the PSOE. During all three periods the massive influx of members was associated with an ideological radicalization of the party.

For most of its history, the PSOE was an insignificant electoral force. As seen in Table 2.2, the PSOE has gained parliamentary strength only twice in its history, during the Second Republic, and from 1977 to the present. Its most impressive electoral success was in 1931, when it won over 33 percent of the vote, and in 1982 and 1986, when it won 48.7 and 44.1 percent, respectively.

Table 2.2
PSOE **Performance in General Elections, 1891–1987**

YEAR	% OF VOTE	# OF SEATS
1891	0.1	–
1893	0.2	–
1896	0.4	–
1898	0.6	–
1899	0.8	–
1901	0.9	–
1903	1.0	–
1905	0.8	–
1907	0.8	–
1910	1.1	1
1914	1.2	1
1916	0.5	1
1918	5.0	6
1919	3.4	6
1920	1.0	4
1923	1.2	7
1931	33.8	115
1933	19.2	55
1936	16.4	92
1977	29.2	118
1979	30.5	121
1982	48.7	202
1986	44.1	184

Source: Tezanos, "Continuidad y cambio en el socialismo español," pp. 7–8.

As discussed earlier, this weakness has historically posed a severe dilemma for the Socialists. Reformists within the party pointed to steady political progress despite some temporary setbacks, but many within the PSOE doubted whether the PSOE could ever win a majority of the vote and thus opposed collaboration with the three democratic regimes. This fundamental doubt about the PSOE's ability to garner a majority mandate in part explains the Socialist collaboration with the Primo dictatorship, as well as its semiloyal behavior during the Second Republic. As will be pointed out in chapter 3, during the transition to democracy many sectors of the PSOE harbored similar doubts about the electoral possibilities of the Socialists in a democratic regime, partly explaining their initially harsh rhetoric vis-à-vis the democratization process.

Most pronounced among the historical legacies of the PSOE has been the internal division within the party. A related characteristic has been the extreme personalization of party power within the PSOE. During the early period of the PSOE's history, when founder Pablo Iglesias was firmly in control of the Socialist Party, the personalization of power prevented the ideological fragmentation of the party, although it could not prevent the breakaway of the PCE after the Russian Revolution.

When Iglesias became ill (1922), the PSOE began a long period of personal, tactical, and ideological conflict. The PSOE was on the verge of a formal division during the Civil War, remained badly divided during the franquist regime, and actually split (over totally different issues) in 1972. For much of this time the warring internal factions rallied around PSOE leaders (Prieto, Caballero, Negrín, Llopis, Tierno, etc.). After 1974, Felipe González performed a role roughly similar to that of Iglesias, acting as the founder of the "new" PSOE. As will be discussed in following chapters, González and his top aides have very successfully limited internal conflict in the organization, determined to reverse an inauspicious legacy of the PSOE past.

Finally, it is important to emphasize the intellectual shallowness of the PSOE during most of its history. One is struck by the lack of sophisticated and detached Socialist analysis, by the reactive nature of most of the PSOE's tactical decisions, and by the party's imitation of its European neighbors on major ideological questions. Often over the course of the PSOE's history, most recently during the transition to democracy, the official PSOE ideology and program appeared completely out of touch with the realities of Spanish society. As the foregoing historical survey suggests, the early anarchist influence on the socialist movement in Spain; the anti-intellectual atmosphere of the early PSOE; the rigid control of the PSOE by its founder, Pablo Iglesias; the explosive growth of the PSOE during the Second Republic; the harsh conditions during franquism; and the closed-mindedness of the PSOE leadership in exile contributed to a rather weak ideological tradition.

Although the "new" PSOE under Felipe González emerged from a break with the official party, González and his supporters identified wholeheartedly with the party past. But logically the new leaders were anxious to avoid a repetition of the problems discussed earlier. The historical lessons they internalized can be summarized as follows. First, from the disaster of the 1934 revolution, Socialists were cautioned about the dangers of mass mobilization, especially when the objective conditions (including the strength of the Socialist party organization itself) were not appropriate. In retrospect it seems that PSOE leaders were not sufficiently insulated from their party base at key junctures during the Republic.

A second historical lesson learned by PSOE leaders regarded the devastating consequences of internal party divisions and the need for strong and unified leadership. Endless arguments over ideology and tactics, the formation of personal fiefdoms within the party, and the use of affiliated organizations (the UGT, the Socialist Youth, the party newspaper, or local party branches) to bolster different factions undoubtedly weakened the PSOE. During the Second Republic these divisions had facilitated the considerable poaching of party support by the PCE, and the Communists shrewdly played PSOE factions off against each other. The "new" PSOE was created by an act of indiscipline on the part of militants in the interior (and was thus not supported by Tierno Galván). But as will become clear in Chapters 4 and 5, González implemented strong measures to prevent the recurrence of such division in the new democratic regime. In addition, the PSOE moved quickly to absorb the different socialist parties that existed during the transition to democracy in order to create a single, unified Socialist party.

Finally, most PSOE leaders emerged from the franquist regime with a greater appreciation of the value of parliamentary democracy. Forty years of authoritarian rule had been the worst possible situation for the Socialists (much less so for the PCE, which flourished in clandestine conditions); and despite occasional rhetoric to the contrary, PSOE leaders entered the transition willing to compromise and negotiate the conditions for any political outcome that led to a democratic regime. This sentiment was nicely summarized in early 1982 by Javier Solana, currently minister of culture and the chief party spokesperson:

Democracy and its consolidation come first, before our political programs.... Because the Spanish right has shown that it can live very well under both authoritarian and democratic regimes, while the left can only survive within a democratic framework. We have a lot of pain and suffering, and many years behind bars, to prove that.[41]

NOTES

1. Manuel Contreras, *El PSOE en la II República: Organización e ideología* (Madrid: Centro de Investigaciones Sociológicas, 1981), p. 39.

2. Among the general treatments of the PSOE's history are Antonio Padilla Bolívar, *El movimiento Socialista Español* (Barcelona: Planeta, 1977); Manuel Tuñón de Lara, *El movimiento obrero en la historia de España*; Santos Juliá, ed., *El socialismo en España* (Madrid: Editorial Pablo Iglesias, 1986); Ricardo de la Cierva, *Historia del socialismo en España, 1879–1983* (Barcelona: Planeta, 1983); Eñrique Moral Sandoval, ed., *Cién años para el socialismo. Historia del PSOE (1879–1979)* (Madrid: Editorial Pablo Iglesias, 1979).

3. On the early development of socialism in Spain, see Jordi Maluquer de Motes, *El socialismo en España, 1833–1868* (Barcelona: Grijalbo, 1977).

4. Stanley G. Payne, *A History of Spain and Portugal*, vol. 2 (Madison: University of Wisconsin Press, 1973), p. 601.

5. On Pablo Iglesias see María Teresa Martínez de Sas, *El socialismo y la España oficial. Pablo Iglesias, diputado a Cortes* (Madrid: Tucar, 1975); J. Losada Martin, *Ideario político de Pablo Iglesias* (Barcelona: Nova Tera, 1976).

6. De la Cierva, *Historia del socialismo*, pp. 38–39.

7. Quoted in ibid., p. 39.

8. Marta Bizcarrondo, "La Segunda República: Ideologías Socialistas," in Juliá, ed., *El socialismo en Español*, p. 257.

9. Payne, *A History*, p. 602. On the early programs of the PSOE, see A. Elorza, "Los primeros programas del PSOE (1879–1888)," *Estudios de Historia Social* 8–9 (1979): 143–180.

10. Quoted in de la Cierva, *Historia del socialismo*, p. 44. On Unamuno and the PSOE, see C. Blanco Aguinaga, "El socialismo de Unamuno, 1894–1897," *Revista de Occidente* 41 (1966): 166–184.

11. A good overview of this period is found in Luis Gómez Llorente, *Aproximación a la historia del socialismo Español (hasta 1921)* (Madrid: Cuadernos Para el Diálogo, 1976).

12. PSOE, *Reseña histórica y estructura del PSOE* (Madrid: PSOE, 1984), p. 1.

13. De la Cierva, *Historia del socialismo*, pp. 79–80. The vote among delegates was 8,808 opposed to Lenin's Twenty-One Conditions and 6,025 favoring them.

14. Enrique Moral Sandoval, "El socialismo y la dictadura de Primo de Rivera," in Juliá, ed., *El socialismo en España*, p. 194.

15. An excellent overview of the role of the PSOE in the Primo de Rivera dictatorship is found in ibid., pp. 192–211. The following discussion draws heavily on his analysis.

16. For a treatment of Largo Caballero, see Pablo Castellano, "Francisco Largo Caballero (1869–1946)," *Tiempo de Historia* 9 (1975): 15–28.

17. Quoted in Moral Sandoval, "El socialismo y la dictadura," p. 211. Other portions of the document appear in Contreras, *El PSOE en la II República*, pp. 27–28.

18. Juan J. Linz, "From Great Hopes to Civil War: The Breakdown of Democracy in Spain," in Juan J. Linz and Alfred Stepan, eds., *The Breakdown of Democratic Regimes: Europe* (Baltimore, Md.: Johns Hopkins University Press, 1978), p. 145.

19. On the first two years of the Second Republic, see J. L. García Delgado, ed., *La II República. El primer bienio* (Madrid: Siglo XXI, 1987).

20. Payne, *A History of Spain and Portugal*, p. 634.

21. Contreras's book is the most comprehensive study of the Socialist Party during the Second Republic. Two excellent works by Santos Juliá are *La izquierda del PSOE, 1935–1936* (Madrid: Siglo XXI, 1977), and "Los socialistas en la crísis de los años trienta," *Zona Abierta* 27 (1983): 63–77. Also, see Marta Bizcarrondo, *Arquistaín y la crísis Socialista en la II República (1934–1936)* (Madrid: Siglo XXI, 1975); and "La Segunda República: Ideologías socialistas," in Juliá, ed., *El Socialismo en España*, pp. 255–294.

22. Linz, "From Great Hopes," p. 166.

23. Ibid., pp. 151–153.

24. Contreras, *El PSOE en la II República*, p. 85.

25. A detailed study of this period is Bizcarrondo, *Arquistaín y la crísis*. The term "semiloyal," which can be applied to both the major party of the right, the CEDA, and the PSOE, is explained in Linz, "From Great Hopes," pp. 160–171.

26. Quoted in de la Cierva, *Historia del socialismo*, p. 132.

27. Santos Juliá, "República, revolución y luchas internas," in Juliá, ed., *El socialismo en España*, p. 231.

28. De la Cierva, *Historia del socialismo*, p. 143.

29. Bizcarrondo, "La Segunda República," p. 263.

30. Quoted in Raymond Carr, *Spain, 1805–1975*, 2d ed. (Oxford: Clarendon Press, 1982), p. 642.

31. Payne, *A History*, p. 602; and Carr, *Spain*, pp. 656–672.

32. Except for the strategy's partial success in Catalonia and of the merger of the Socialist and Communist youth movements. The PCE soon dominated both unified organizations.

33. Paul Preston, "Decadencia y resurgimiento del PSOE durante el régimen franquista," in Juliá, ed., *El socialismo en España*, p. 349.

34. Richard Gunther, Giacomo Sani, and Goldie Shabad, *Spain after Franco: The Making of a Competitive Party System* (Berkeley: University of California Press, 1986), p. 71.

35. See de la Cierva, *Historia del socialismo*, p. 216, and Mario Caciagli, *Elecciones y partidos en la transición Española* (Madrid: Centro de Investigaciones Sociológicas, 1986), p. 194.

36. Preston, "Decadencia y resurgimiento," p. 351.

37. Ibid.

38. Ibid., p. 361.

39. Ibid.

40. José Félix Tezanos, "Continuidad y cambio en el socialismo Español. El PSOE durante la transición," in Julián Santamaría, ed., *Los partidos políticos en España* (Madrid: Centro de Investigaciones Sociológicas, forthcoming), p. 2.

41. Interview with the author, January 1982.

3

Transition to Democracy, the Reemergence of the PSOE, and Ideological Crisis

The Party must represent the desire for social change of many sectors that are not identified with one class, contrary to the analysis at the start of the century. Secondly, in this historic moment the Party has an obligation to be a source of tranquility for society, transcending the boundaries of the Party itself. And it has this obligation because only the Socialist Party can play this role. That is contradictory for a party based on change. That is the whole drama of the PSOE.
—Felipe González[1]

A PECULIAR TRANSITION

The Socialist Party that emerged from the October 1974 Party Congress had to deal almost immediately with a treacherous and complex political environment. Inside Spain there was a steady resurgence of political mobilization. Although it was faced with periodic repression, the general atmosphere of liberalization (especially press freedom) allowed the democratic opposition an increasingly higher profile. By 1974, the franquist regime had evolved from a *dictadura* (a harsh dictatorship) to a *dictablanda* (a softer dictatorship). Edward Malefakis notes that

despite memories of past brutality, the subliminal recognition that *in extremis* the regime might resort to its original techniques, and the lapses—the 1970 Burgos trials, the harsh prison sentences meted out to *Comisiones* leaders in 1974—that occasionally occurred, opposition to Franco had become something of a parlor sport for upper middle class youth whose risks were minimal.[2]

At the same time, two contradictory processes were manifest within the democratic opposition. On the one hand was the emergence of a plethora of competing groups and parties after years of harsh repression. The PSOE was thus faced with a number of socialist competitors, including Enrique Tierno Galván's Popular Socialist Party (PSP), and Llopis's "historical" sector of the PSOE (PSOE-H). Parties themselves were numerous and were generally weak and without significant organizational structures or mass support. On the other hand, the opposition to authoritarian rule was gradually beginning to cohere, although its definitive unity would continue to prove elusive. In July 1974, the Democratic Junta had been formed by a wide spectrum of opposition parties and politicians, including the Communists and the PSP. Although the PSOE and a variety of centrist parties and groups refused to join the Junta (the PSOE opposed the inclusion of the PSP and the presence of monarchists, while other groups refused to collaborate with the Communist Party), most of these groups formed their own coalition, the Platform of Democratic Convergence, eleven months later.[3]

Simultaneously, the franquist regime was in the midst of a protracted internal political crisis. The assassination of Franco's confidant and hand-picked successor as head of government, Admiral Luís Carrero Blanco, in December 1973, threw the regime into disarray and triggered an intense power struggle within the franquist coalition. The internal power struggle was not resolved until after the death of Franco, but the very presence of a factional dispute among the authoritarian political families was enough to create an air of anxiety and tension in Spanish society.

Notwithstanding the increasing politicization of society, the gradual coherence of the democratic opposition, and the growing intramural crisis of the authoritarian regime, franquism remained essentially intact. Although increasingly ill, Franco continued to wield a remarkable degree of influence over the squabbling authoritarian families, preventing in the short term any fatal rift in the franquist coalition. The regime easily contained and repressed all opposition that it considered harmful to its survival.

In short, increasing societal pressures for democratization were evident, but the opposition realized that at least until the death of Franco, the conditions would not be ripe for a democratic break. The period immediately preceding Franco's death (1974–1975) was therefore a period of opposition renaissance and rebuilding; but given the weakness of the opposition and the strength of the regime, it could not be a time of frontal assault on authoritarian rule. To a considerable extent, this period of waiting suited the PSOE leadership well. The young and relatively inexperienced Socialist leaders used the period to consolidate the internal organization of the party, to make contacts with other opposition forces, and to forge strong ties with important northern European benefactors.

Although Franco's imminent death offered some hope for a democratic transition, it certainly offered no guarantee. Franco had promised to leave things *atado y bién atado* (very well secured) for his successors, and he had attempted to carry out his promise. As head of state he had groomed and trained a young monarch, Juan Carlos de Borbón, son of the legitimate heir to the Spanish throne. Franco had required that Juan Carlos swear loyalty to the overtly authoritarian principles of the National Movement. In fact, the prince's political apprenticeship had been characterized by an unyielding conformity to franquist ritual, and the future monarch never expressed democratic intentions. From the official PSOE perspective, the restoration of the monarchy in Spain was to be opposed both because the Socialists favored a republic and because the monarchy had resulted directly from an authoritarian regime.

Franco had entrusted the head of government to Carrero Blanco, his most faithful collaborator, a political veteran of authoritarian temperament and a man with an unshakable loyalty to franquism. Carrero came the closest to Franco in his ability to command respect from the disparate political families within the franquist coalition. Carrero's assassination clearly was a severe blow to the dictator's plan to control politics after his own death. Franco selected Carlos Arias Navarro, an equally loyal but far less respected leader, to succeed Carrero. Though Arias spoke initially of the need for reform, his first term as head of government was characterized by a total incapacity to convince franquist hardliners of this need.

Thus from the democratic opposition's perspective, there was little certainty about whether a transition (let alone what type of transition) might take place after Franco disappeared from the political scene. Events immediately following Franco's death (November 1975) exacerbated this sense of apprehension. As planned, Juan Carlos was crowned king, and his initial actions shocked the opposition.[4] He reappointed Arias to the presidency, a move that was taken as a sign that Juan Carlos envisioned no rapid transition to democracy. Arias's failure to promote democratic reform and the king's inability or unwillingness to do so frustrated the opposition as well as reformers within the franquist regime. Most of the opposition parties, including the PSOE, had openly opposed Arias's reform plan even before it was defeated by franquist hardliners. Arias's failure may also have encouraged the unification of the two major opposition coalitions into the Democratic Coordinator in March 1976. The organization now included parties from across the political spectrum, including Communists, Socialists, and Christian Democrats. Its perceived importance can be measured by the fact that the leadership of the new organization was almost immediately arrested and jailed, an act that only served to polarize the political environment. From January to March 1976, Spain experienced its highest level of worker and student unrest since the Civil War, and terrorist activity again began to rise.

Domestic political events encouraged much of the opposition to advocate a democratic *ruptura*, and events in southern Europe only added to this sentiment. The collapse of authoritarian rule in Greece and Portugal in 1974 simultaneously radicalized sectors of the democratic opposition *and* the hardliners of the franquist regime, apparently weakening the prospects for a gradual and peaceful democratization of authoritarian rule.

The opposition became even more pessimistic when, in July 1976, King Juan Carlos replaced Arias with Adolfo Suárez. Suárez was a young and charismatic politician, but his roots in the franquist National Movement (an organization over which he presided) and his lack of democratic credentials were cause for skepticism. Opposition leaders called openly for a *ruptura negociada*, a clean break from authoritarian rule via a coalition composed of the left, democratic conservatives, and the most reformist sector of the franquist regime. However, these calls were somewhat hollow given the overall weakness and fragmentation of the opposition, the strength of the franquist regime's coercive ability, and the generally depoliticized state of Spanish society after forty years of authoritarian rule. Noting the rise of working-class mobilization, José María Maravall noted:

The [working-class] pressure was always intense, but ... it was largely divorced from organizational strategies and was not directed by any political or trade unionist goals. In addition, this pressure never surpassed the ability of the transitional government to react because, among other things, mobilization was supported by only a limited sector of the population.[5]

As Carr and Fusi concluded, "No one had the power to restore democracy from below."[6]

If the opposition's frustration with attempts by Arias to reform the franquist regime explains the skepticism with which Suárez's appointment was greeted, the opposition's gradual acceptance of Suárez's more ambitious reform plan is explained largely by the opposition's lack of viable alternatives. However, Suárez's fast-paced reform measures, the apparent open-endedness of his proposed changes, and his willingness to conduct a dialogue with key opposition leaders made it easier for opposition leaders to justify such acceptance. The guarded optimism of opposition leaders in response to Suárez's formal announcement of a reform plan in late July 1976 was a clear contrast to the pessimism expressed during the Arias presidencies.

From July 1976, when Suárez was appointed president,* to June 1977,

---

*This book uses the term "president"—from the Spanish *presidenté del gabierno* (president of the government)—to refer to the Spanish prime minister.

when the first democratic elections were held in over forty years, Suárez initiated and implemented a democratic reform program through the franquist legal framework.[7] This program, which took the form of a constitutional amendment, included the Cortes approval of the amendment in November 1976, a popular referendum on the program in December, the legalization of most political parties in February 1977, the abolition of the franquist Syndical Organization, a decree offering amnesty to political prisoners in March, the legalization of the PCE in April, the dismantling of the National Movement in May, and the calling of general elections for June.

A key element of this progress, referred to elsewhere as "transition through transaction," was that it was initiated and implemented *from above*, although it steadily gained support from popular sectors: first the guarded adherence from opposition leaders, then the massive popular approval in the December 1976 referendum, and finally the full-scale support and collaboration of opposition parties in the spring of 1977. Franco died peacefully in his bed, and his regime did not instantly perish with him, as had often been predicted with varying degrees of optimism, gloom, and fear. From the perspective of this study, the important point is that opposition leaders were unable to force political change even with the absence of the dictator: there was no mass uprising or popular action in the period following Franco's death. The PSOE's call for abstention in the December 1976 referendum was from the start contradictory, half-hearted, and doomed to failure. The party could not advocate a "no" vote because it would ally itself with the franquist right and might contribute to a defeat of the Suárez reform, an outcome hardly desired by most PSOE leaders. Its official advocacy of abstention was rendered equally impractical given the democratic opposition's division over the matter. Two other socialist parties and much of the centrist opposition advocated a "yes" vote. The Political Reform Law was approved by 94 percent of the voters, and from that point on the PSOE never seriously challenged the Suárez reform.[8]

For an opposition that had been advocating *ruptura* and that certainly had entertained hopes of participation in some type of provisional government, the idea of accepting a democratic reform imposed from above and without any clear guarantees concerning the rules of the transition process, the protection of basic democratic freedoms, the nature of the new regime, or the amount of participation of opposition groups was stubbornly resisted. In part, such resistance was the result of an unwillingness to accept the rather obvious limits to opposition power that adherence to the Suárez reform made apparent. Acceptance of Suárez's transition through transaction was proof that the opposition could not force a more democratic alternative.

AN AMBIGUOUS RESPONSE

For the PSOE, acceptance of Suárez's reform was especially difficult. The PSOE was undergoing rapid expansion and radicalization. Between 1974 and 1977, PSOE membership rose from 3,500 to 51,500, a growth of over fourteen-fold in three years.[9] The radicalization resulted in part from this rapid growth (the entry into the party of ideologically inexperienced and hardly pragmatic cadres), in part from the rise to power of a younger leadership cohort (less experienced, less ideologically mature, and accustomed to clandestine conditions), and in part from the presence of potentially strong competitors (especially the PCE, but also other socialist parties) to the PSOE's left.[10]

The radicalization of the PSOE culminated in the December 1976 Twenty-seventh PSOE Congress, the first congress held inside Spain since before the Spanish Civil War. The PSOE was still officially illegal, but the Suárez government decided to tolerate it, perhaps as an incentive for the Socialists to embrace the president's reform program. The attendance of Europe's most prominent social democratic leaders (Willy Brandt, Olof Palme, François Mitterrand, Pietro Nenni, and Michael Foot, among others) added respectability and legitimacy to the event and created an obstacle to government harrassment.[11] However, if Suárez was banking on a show of moderation, he was sorely disappointed: the PSOE presented itself as one of the most radical socialist parties in western Europe. The party officially defined itself as "mass, Marxist, and democratic" and officially eschewed "any attempt to accomodate capitalism, or any simple reform of the system."[12] The program, which constituted a significant departure from earlier versions, advocated the socialization of the means of production "through the conquest of political and economic power" and specifically called for the nationalization of the largest banks and fifty of the biggest private enterprises. The PSOE continued to call for a democratic *ruptura*, an apparent rejection of the Suárez reform plan.

Given the weakness of the opposition (including the PSOE), such a radical stance may appear counterintuitive. But as Richard Gunther has argued, it was precisely the weakness of the Socialists that pushed PSOE delegates (though by no means all party leaders) to adopt a program more suited to a "party of mass mobilization" (with an emphasis on radical change, mass mobilization, and extraparliamentary tactics) than to a "catch-all party" similar to social democratic parties throughout Europe (parties aimed almost exclusively at winning votes, most often by appealing to the broadest possible sector of the population).[13] Although the popularly approved Law for Political Reform had provided for general elections to take place in June 1977, it was still unclear how and when the PSOE would be legalized, and the Socialists were understandably suspicious about the conditions for such a legalization. More important, however, was the party's insecurity vis-à-vis its future electoral prospects, a sentiment that made a more radicalized and mass-mobilizational approach appealing. It was unclear whether the PSOE could regain the dominant position within the left that it had enjoyed during the Second Republic. There was a widespread view at the Twenty-seventh Party Congress that the PSOE was dwarfed in size, organization, and electoral potential by the Communist Party, and that it faced a stiff battle with the PSP of Tierno Galván. Given the uncertainty of the scenario and the apparently minoritarian position of the PSOE within the opposition, the Socialists' radicalism is more understandable.

The role of Felipe González in both the radicalization and later moderation of the PSOE platform remains a matter of some debate. De la Cierva and Gunther seem to favor the view that González was swept along in the tides of radicalization, even though he always supported a "catch-all" orientation for the PSOE. From this perspective, only the success of the Suárez reform and the huge and unexpected electoral support for the PSOE allowed González to begin to deradicalize the PSOE. Others have contended that González himself pushed the PSOE to the left, either as a result of some combination of youth, inexperience, and demagoguery or as a consequence of Machiavellian calculations that enhanced his own power within the party.

To some extent it appears that both interpretations are partially valid. After 1974, González clearly used a 1960s-style radicalism to distinguish himself from the staid old guard of the PSOE, and he employed an anti-imperialist and anticapitalist rhetoric to consolidate his leadership within the PSOE and to help swell the ranks of a hitherto minuscule party. He felt most comfortable with the rhetoric and terminology of the revolutionary left, and his charismatic image was enhanced by this radicalism. At the same time, González likely considered the radical platform adopted by the PSOE in 1976 as too extreme. He had met personally with Suárez in August 1976 and was deeply impressed with the young president.[14] Shortly after, González admitted publicly that Suárez's Political Reform Law "could be a way to liquidate franquism." But despite González's growing confidence in the Suárez reform, his control over the party was too tenuous (and his own views too much in transition) to have limited the radicalism at this point. González was able to prevent the inclusion of the term "dictatorship of the proletariat" in the party program, and the leadership did succeed in preventing the chanting of republican slogans during the Twenty-seventh Congress.[15] He warned delegates not to "fall into the trap of undervaluing formal civil liberties, or of considering them preconditions that can be eliminated after some higher form of democracy is conquered."[16] It is probable that the success of the Suárez reform, his favorable interactions with both Suárez and the king, the success of the PSOE in the 1977 general elections, and the consolidation of González's leadership within the party prompted the general secretary to initiate an ideological and organizational moderation (discussed later).

The contradictions entailed by the radical PSOE program were quickly forgotten in early 1977 as Socialist elites turned to the most crucial matters at hand: (1) the need to open up the political space for parties through negotiations with the Suárez government, and (2) the urgency of building an electoral organization that could establish the PSOE as the major socialist party and the hegemonic political force on the left. Negotiations with Suárez began in early 1977 between the president and a group of nine representatives from the Democratic Coordinator, and they were generally successful in securing an orderly legalization of parties and a steady (if imperfect) protection of civil liberties.

After forty years without electoral politics, all parties were deeply insecure about their electoral prospects. With the exception of the PCE, no Spanish parties had deep organizational roots among the population. The belated legalization of parties and slow and uneven democratization of the Spanish media limited the impact of party leaders' charisma (except that of President Suárez, who had not yet declared his candidacy). Opinion polls showed that the electorate was by and large confused and undecided and offered no clear picture of the political future. In this context, the PSOE was particularly worried about competition from other socialist parties, primarily the PSP of Tierno Galván, the Federation of Socialist Parties (FPS), and the PSOE-Histórico (PSOE-H).[17] To the chagrin of González, PSP leader Tierno Galván was named one of two socialist representatives of the Democratic Coordinator's Group of Nine, thus giving the PSP equal status with the PSOE. The PSOE leadership was again miffed when Tierno was invited to meet with the king before González. When the government legalized the *históricos* before the PSOE, González pulled his party out of the Group of Nine in protest.[18] The surprise legalization of the PCE in April met a crucial demand of the Group of Nine, but it also added a serious and well-organized electoral contender to the scenario. Moreover, since the beginning of Suárez's presidency the PCE had embarked on a bold attempt to occupy the center-left, and the Communists were somewhat successful in presenting themselves as a more moderate and flexible party than the PSOE.

By May 1977, some fundamental changes had taken place in the political climate in Spain, and these changes were clearly reflected in the PSOE electoral campaign. First, the Suárez reform had borne fruit and had not only dismantled much of the franquist institutional edifice but had actually legalized all major political parties (including the PCE). With all attention focused on elections, the Socialists (together with almost all other parties) no longer spoke of *ruptura democrática*, but rather referred to the process as a *ruptura negociada* (a negotiated break). The subtle change in language reflected the Socialists' overwhelming acceptance of the transition through transaction. This view was now less the result of the lack of viable alternatives and the party now accepted the Suárez plan as the most *desirable* form of democratization.

Second, the PSOE leadership designed an electoral campaign that downplayed virtually all radical aspects of the 1976 platform. The PSOE employed the slogan "Socialism Is Liberty" and ran a slick campaign geared to project a popular, familial, and humanistic party image. It emphasized the theme "Socialism Is in Your Hand" and consistently displayed the fist and rose, the symbol of the Socialist International (a crucial provider of foreign financial aid and the main source of international legitimacy). Using a series of graphic vignettes, the PSOE emphasized concrete social problems (unemployment, educational reform, emigrants, and health care) and avoided discussion of general solutions such as the party's stand on nationalization. Most important, the PSOE campaign centered on the charismatic image of its leader, Felipe González, a tactic that was aimed at personalizing the appeal of the PSOE and downplaying ideological and programmatic issues.

Party leaders skillfully juggled this moderate national electoral campaign with the image projected to party militants. After all, the electoral campaign, in addition to being an attempt to win popular support, was also a crucial first legal opportunity to mobilize party membership and solidify the party organization. At numerous electoral *mitines* (rallies), attended mainly by party members and supporters, PSOE leaders projected an image far more consonant with the radical party platform. At these events (attended by González with incredible frequency during the three-week campaign), Socialist leaders more openly harangued the government and the right and engaged in more classic socialist ritual and rhetoric.

Perhaps the most successful aspect of the PSOE campaign was the ability to appeal to *both* the long political history and tradition of the PSOE (including its ties to social democratic parties in Europe) as well as the modern image, exemplified by its high-tech mass media campaign and its young, energetic leader.

Finally, the changed political conditions inside Spain meant that the Socialist Party (again, like most opposition parties) exercised utmost restraint when discussing the transition process itself and the franquist regime more generally. Socialist leaders very carefully avoided attacks on Suárez's past, on abuses during the franquist regime, or on leaders of the extreme right. This restraint was particularly admirable given the controversial last-minute candidacy of Suárez, Spain's most popular and visible politician. The president's entry into the race dashed the hopes of all other parties and raised questions about Suárez's use of his still considerable power to manipulate the electoral process.

THE ELECTORAL WATERSHED

Since the popular approval of the Law for Political Reform in December 1976, the PSOE leadership had effectively abandoned all talk of alternatives to Suárez's transition through transaction strategy. The electoral results of June 15, 1977, the first free elections in forty-one years, now gave the PSOE an indisputable stake in the emerging democracy.

Suárez's Union of the Democratic Center (UCD) won a plurality of the vote (34.3 percent) and lower house seats (46.8 percent), as expected, but the surprise victor of the elections was the PSOE. Carr and Fusi call the Socialists' second-place finish (with 28.5 percent of the vote and 33.7 percent of the lower house seats) "almost a miracle," given the virtual absence of the PSOE within Spain only three years before the elections.[19] Moreover, the electoral system employed strongly favored the conservative rural areas of Spain and underrepresented the cities.[20] Nevertheless, the PSOE won seats in all but three Spanish provinces, received the most votes in nine provinces, and scored impressive victories in Madrid, Barcelona, Valencia, and Seville.[21] Its percentage of the vote tripled that of the nearest competitor.[22] The electoral results made the PSOE Spain's largest political party (the UCD was a loose coalition of parties).

The PSOE electoral performance was a resounding success in a number of respects. First, it unquestionably affirmed the PSOE's hegemonic role on the left and, perhaps more important, within the Socialist left. The PCE won just over 9 percent of the vote and only 6 percent of the seats, a disappointing result given the superior organizational capabilities of the Communists. Moreover, the PCE failed to establish itself as a national party, and its votes and seats were largely concentrated in Catalonia. Within the Socialist camp, Tierno Galván's Popular Socialist Party (PSP), running in coalition with the Federation of Socialist Parties (FPS), proved totally unable to challenge the PSOE, winning a mere 4.2 percent of the vote and 1.7 percent of the seats.[23] Tierno's party faced huge electoral debts that would eventually compel it to integrate into the PSOE (April 1978). In short, the elections confirmed the PSOE's strategy of rejecting all electoral alliances with parties of the left, and the results forced most smaller parties to deal with the Socialists on the PSOE's terms.[24]

The elections were also a victory for Felipe González's leadership within the PSOE. González's increasingly moderate public image, his charisma, and his popularity played a major role in the Socialist electoral success, and party members became aware that his leadership was an indispensable part of the PSOE's future electoral fortunes.

However, the euphoria within the Socialist Party after the 1977 elections temporarily concealed an underlying ideological crisis. Many within the party saw the elections as a watershed that could (and should) separate the PSOE's radical opposition past from its more moderate future as a loyal and democratic opposition. A future electoral victory and the formation of a Socialist government no longer appeared to require a frontal assault on the franquist regime, the Suárez leadership, or the parties of the right. For others within the PSOE, the electoral success meant that the PSOE could now act with greater confidence and could feasibly attempt to implement the ambitious and radical PSOE platform in the not-too-distant future. Moreover, the electoral victory of Suárez's UCD meant that franquist politicians remained in power, convincing some Socialists that a democratic "break" was still necessary. However, these tensions remained under the surface for many months. In the meantime, the PSOE prepared to operate as a loyal opposition and to participate in the writing of a new, democratic constitution.

THE FRAGILE CONSENSUS

After the 1977 elections, the PSOE immediately moved to strengthen its organizational structure. The most important task was the consolidation of the still fragmented socialist left. Two national socialist parties (the Federation of Socialist Parties and Tierno Galván's Popular Socialist Party) had performed poorly in the elections, and a steady stream of defections by members of these parties toward the PSOE augured well for their full integration into the PSOE. In addition, there were a number of regional parties that had remained totally separate from the PSOE or that had been only loosely linked with it. The system of state financing of political parties (calculated on a per-vote basis) and the PSOE's strong ties with other European parties gave the PSOE leverage in negotiations with the different socialist groups. One by one, these parties were brought into or more fully integrated within the PSOE, and by 1979 only the Andalusian Socialist Party (PSA) remained separate. The PSP's integration was particularly difficult because of Tierno Galván's prestige. By April 1978, the two parties had agreed to a plan regulating the fusion of the PSP and PSOE leadership. As a result, Tierno was given the title of honorary PSOE president (the position was quietly eliminated in September 1978) and was promised to be designated as the PSOE candidate for mayor of Madrid.

The addition of these parties promised to deliver to the PSOE about another 5 percent of the electorate that had voted for the PSP-FPS coalition in 1977, in addition to six additional seats in the lower house. Partly as a result of these additions, PSOE membership continued to grow rapidly, almost doubling between June 1977 and May 1979. The number of party locals rose from 1,423 to 2,230 during the same period.

Although the Socialists made important gains in the consolidation and strengthening of their organization and membership, the principal focus of party leaders was on the elite-level negotiations that took place from July 1977 to late 1978. Two crucial issues facing political leaders—the writing of a new constitution, and basic accords to regulate political economic matters—were resolved by party leaders almost entirely behind closed doors. Despite the unexpected electoral windfall, and notwithstanding the growing organizational capability of the PSOE, the Socialist leadership clearly preferred this form of conflict resolution over a strategy of frontal confrontation with the right. After all, the PSOE was still a weak party in many respects. At the time of the 1977 elections the Socialists had only about 50,000 members. In the legislature the PSOE, even with the support of other leftist parties, lacked the seats to prevent the UCD from governing (with support of the right). Elite-level negotiation could potentially avoid open conflict in the legislative and mass arenas, and the PSOE leadership realized fully that the left was not ready to benefit from such confrontations.

The logic of elite-level compromise over crucial political economic issues went beyond purely utilitarian calculations. Socialist leaders were aware that the Suárez reform had created the conditions for a peaceful establishment of a genuinely democratic political system. If the 1977 electoral results were any indication, the PSOE was to be a principal actor in the future democracy. Given the persistent political and economic obstacles that threatened the consolidation of a democratic regime, the Socialists were entirely disposed to limiting mass mobilization, containing rhetoric, and restricting partisan conflict to private discussions among political elites.

Negotiating the Rules of the Game

Nowhere did elite-level negotiations take on more importance than in the writing of the Spanish Constitution of 1978, and the PSOE played a central role in the entire process. De la Cuadra and Gallego-Díaz conclude that "the history of the consensus—of which the Constitution of 1978 was the most characteristic aspect—is fundamentally . . . the history of the quarrels and reconciliations between the Union of the Democratic Center (UCD) and the Spanish Socialist Workers Party (PSOE)."[25] Although the PSOE, even in alliance with parties of the left, did not have a majority of the votes and could therefore not *impose* its constitutional agenda on the center and right, its status as the second-largest party made its approval of any constitution indispensable.

Suárez's UCD government also lacked a majority in the legislature, and the governing coalition was so ideologically diverse and fractionalized that it would hardly have been feasible to force a new constitution on a recalcitrant PSOE. It *was* numerically possible that the UCD, together with the rightist Popular Alliance (AP), could muster a majority to defeat the left, but such a strategy, while often attractive, angered the important social democratic sector of Suárez's own coalition.

The June elections produced a distribution of seats that facilitated a UCD-PSOE compromise over the constitution, but historical "lessons" in the minds of elites and widespread fears about threats to the consolidation of democracy were equally important in promoting such an outcome. PSOE leaders were well aware that during the Second Republic the right had always rejected the "Republic for Republicans," and the Socialists were eager to craft a constitution that could garner widespread legitimacy.[26] Moreover, much of the right was increasingly bitter over the unexpected course that the transition had taken under Suárez. Military leaders had become more vocal in their opposition to Suárez, especially after he unilaterally legalized the Communist Party shortly before the elections. Suárez's quick move to begin writing a constitution, while not unexpected, and the strong showing of the PSOE in the elections increased the potential for hostility from the right. The fear of a military coup was thus an important factor encouraging the PSOE to seek a broad constitutional compromise.

The task of writing a new constitution began in July 1977 and was entrusted to a subcommittee of the lower house of the legislature (the Committee of Constitutional Affairs and Public Liberties).[27] In negotiations over the distribution of the seven committee members among parties, the PSOE immediately gave way on an important issue. It was widely accepted that the PCE and AP should get one representative each and that the UCD should get the most representatives. As it became clear that either the UCD or the PSOE would have to forfeit one representative in order to allow for a Basque-Catalan representative, the PSOE agreed to cede one of its two representatives. The Socialists feared that excluding a regional representative could seriously hamper the future legitimacy of the democratic regime.[28] The decision proved costly; the UCD was left with three representatives, while the PSOE, AP, PCE, and Catalan-Basque minority had one each. Moreover, the Catalan representative, Miguel Roca Junyent, voted most often with UCD. Despite its status as the loyal opposition, when it came to writing a new constitution, the PSOE was placed on an equal footing with several far smaller parties.

The PSOE selected as its representative Gregorio Peces-Barba, a young legal scholar at the University of Madrid. Peces-Barba had a reputation within the Socialist camp as a moderate, and, importantly, he was one of the few PSOE leaders to openly declare his strong Catholic sentiments. In selecting Peces-Barba the PSOE leadership bypassed Pablo Castellano, the party's leading constitutional expert yet one who was considered too radical and confrontational.

From the start it was clear that the PSOE leadership was prepared to abandon much of the party program adopted at the 1976 Congress. For example, the PSOE's commitment to a republican form of government was absent from a secret constitutional draft written by the party leadership, even though the party clung to its support of a republic in official negotiations.[29] The Socialists' willingness to compromise was almost nullified by the strategy of the three UCD representatives on the subcommittee. Miguel Herrero de Miñón, the chief negotiator for UCD, sought to isolate the PSOE through a coalition of the UCD, the Basque-Catalan representative, and occasional support of either the AP or the PCE. The strategy became apparent in January 1978, when a draft of the constitution was published and when amendments were solicited from the full thirty-six-member committee. UCD members' amendments attempted to roll back many of the compromises agreed to behind closed doors. The subcommittee that had hammered out a draft of the constitution with broad support now began to accept the more conservative amendments by outvoting the Socialist and Communist representatives.

Through the spring of 1978, relations between the PSOE and UCD deteriorated, threatening to destroy prospects for a "constitution of consensus." In the full Constitutional Committee, more conservative proposals prospered and the left was isolated and increasingly frustrated. On May 15, the PSOE withdrew from the Constitutional Committee. Peces-Barba explained that the isolation pursued by the right put the Socialists "in a very difficult position vis-à-vis a favorable assessment of the Constitution."[30] González complained that the consensus was broken and threatened that the PSOE might be forced to include constitutional reform in its electoral platform. Alfonso Guerra, the number-two Socialist leader, warned that the constitution-writing process was on the verge of producing "the most reactionary constitution in Europe. It is the work, exclusively, of the UCD and AP. There is no longer any consensus."[31]

As was customary during the entire transition, the impasse was broken through face-to-face negotiations among political elites. Suárez, deeply worried about the increasing polarization and angered at his own negotiators for what he considered an excessive cornering of the Socialists, marginalized the most conservative sectors of his party and shifted negotiating power to more conciliatory UCD members.[32] He instructed his aides to abandon the policy of isolating the left and urged them to work out a comprehensive constitutional pact with the Socialists. On May 22, 1978, a marathon bargaining session was held among three PSOE officials (Alfonso Guerra, Enrique Múgica, and Gregorio Peces-Barba) and three top UCD officials (led by Fernando Abril, Suárez's vice-president). The meeting, convened in a Madrid restaurant and totally at the margins of the official constituent process, lasted all evening. By the time it was over, the PSOE and the UCD had renegotiated twenty-five articles of the constitution.

Fernando Abril, remembers one of those present, resembled Guerra, especially in the theatrics with which both carried on the negotiations. One then the other threatened to leave the table. They both flatly rejected proposals only to become flexible on identical proposals minutes later, and each threw papers to the floor dramatically.[33]

No longer feeling outmaneuvered, the PSOE agreed to a number of compromises that it had previously resisted. For example, it dropped demands that there be no mention of a free market economy in exchange for the UCD's agreement to water down a provision regarding employers' rights to worker lockouts. The results of the PSOE-UCD summit were spectacular. The PSOE returned to the Constitutional Committee, and on the first afternoon of business twenty-five articles were approved (it had taken ten full days to approve the first twenty-four).

When, in May 1978, it became apparent that the UCD and PSOE had basically agreed on a constitutional text (and had actually scripted out public positions and voting behavior in the committee) without consultation of other parties, the rightist AP and the Basque Nationalist Party (PNV) withdrew in protest from the Constitutional Committee. Although the AP eventually returned, the Basques did not, setting the stage for years of bitter relations between central governments (of the UCD and PSOE) and Basque politicians. Nevertheless, the constitutional project moved swiftly out of committee and through the Cortes plenum. The resulting document reflected a genuine compromise on a wide range of issues. The Socialists ceded on such issues as their preference for a republic (Spain's political system was called a "constitutional monarchy"), for constitutional approval of abortion, and for no constitutional mention of the Catholic Church (the constitution recognized the special importance of the Catholic Church). But the final document reflected some Socialist preferences. It abolished the death penalty, reduced the voting age to eighteen, and left the door open for nationalization of private enterprise and the legalization of abortion and divorce.

Negotiating Class Compromise

Elite-level negotiations were also crucial to the temporary containment of a very serious emergency. Spain's transition to democracy had coincided with an economic crisis that, though similar in its causes to its European neighbors (especially higher oil prices), was far more severe. By 1977, Spain was experiencing stagflation—steadily rising unemployment (over 800,000 Spaniards were out of work by 1977), declining growth rates (down from averages over 7 percent during the economic "miracle" of the 1960s and early 1970s to under 3 percent in 1977), and rapidly rising inflation (over 25 percent in 1977, almost double that in other OECD countries).[34] Spain's balance-of-payments deficit reached an alarming $5 billion, and low rates of productivity and capital investment were potential harbingers of an economic catastrophe during a crucial period of political consolidation.

During the transition to democracy, Suárez had avoided taking action to confront the growing crisis. Political compromise clearly took precedence over economic matters, and economic issues were put on the back burner until after the first democratic election.[35] When, in July 1977, the Suárez government proposed its first set of economic measures, it became evident that elite-level negotiations would be essential to combat the economic malaise. Much of Suárez's program smacked of a traditional austerity program (devaluation of the currency, wage restraints, restrictions on the money supply, higher prices for energy), and these measures threatened to provoke opposition from the parliamentary left and from the trade unions. In September 1977, a wave of strikes protesting the high cost of living worried both the government and the leftist opposition: neither side desired a rise in popular mobilization given the still fragile state of Spanish democracy and the persistence of significant threats to democratic rule (a growing presence of terrorism and continuing discontent within the military).[36] The PSOE was especially aware that worker unrest would not rebound to the benefit of the Socialists or to the Socialist trade union (UGT).

Other features of the reform package, especially the extensive fiscal reform, angered the Spanish right and much of Suárez's own coalition. The UCD liberals and Christian democrats were angered over the apparent influence of the social democrats (notably the vice-president for Economic Affairs, Fuentes Quintana, and finance minister Fernández Ordóñez, who later joined the PSOE and became a Socialist foreign minister) in the drafting of tax reform legislation, and they called on Suárez to take a more conservative position.

To a very large extent, the desire to reach an intraparty elite consensus on political-economic matters was the result of the insecurity of the leadership of *both* UCD and the PSOE. In early October 1977, the leaders of the major parties met with Suárez in his Moncloa Palace residence. Suárez was able to convince party leaders of the left to accept his austerity program, including a restriction on credit, a 17-percent limit on monetary growth, and a 20-percent limit on wage hikes. The parties of the left pledged to contain worker unrest to the extent possible. In return, the prime minister promised a 22-percent limit on price increases, implementation of a serious fiscal reform, an increase in unemployment benefits, and the creation of new jobs. The left also linked its acceptance of the austerity program to the further consolidation of the democratic regime and exacted promises regarding educational, agricultural, and syndical reforms.

The consequences of these important agreements, dubbed the "Moncloa Pacts," has been a subject of debate. The government gained crucial parliamentary support for its controversial reform package, and the consensus reached in the political-economic arena clearly facilitated the compromise over the writing of the constitution. The PSOE sought, first and foremost, to avoid political polarization and mass unrest over economic issues, and the Moncloa Pacts did successfully dissipate this danger in the short run. The Socialists sought good relations with Suárez and realized that their agenda partially coincided with his in a number of key areas (the writing of the constitution and the passing of tax reform, among others). Moreover, the PSOE leadership was well aware of the precariousness of Suárez within his own coalition, and the Socialists were not yet ready to see the centrist coalition disintegrate or turn to the right.

However, the pacts were also quite costly to the PSOE. The austerity measures were highly successful in reducing inflation, restoring balance-of-payments surpluses, and promoting an increase in exports. Nevertheless, they were not able to stem the rise in unemployment or increase the overall rate of economic growth. Except for their contribution to a climate of political compromise, they did not deliver most of the left's portion of the bargain. While wages were contained, inflation and unemployment exceeded the targets, and most of the promised reforms were simply not delivered.[37] Preston concludes that the Moncloa Pacts were "in many respects the culmination of the policies of moderation and self-sacrifice pursued by both the Socialists and Communists throughout the transition period," though he notes that "the government fulfilled few of its promises and, in consequence, the Spanish working class bore the brunt of the economic crisis."[38]

THE 1979 ELECTIONS

Approval of the Constitution in the December 1978 referendum marked the end of the Spanish transition to democracy, although the process of regime consolidation was far from over. Persistent terrorism, threats of a military coup (deemed especially serious should the PSOE take power), and economic crisis were real obstacles still to be overcome. For the Socialists the future looked bright. The party had worked to achieve what it deemed a progressive constitution. It had been bolstered by the integration of the PSP and, based on a number of opinion polls, expected to increase its percentage of the vote in the next elections. The entry into the electorate of eighteen- to twenty-one-year-olds for the first time was a promising sign. Felipe González enjoyed a high level of popularity, whereas Suárez's image was beginning to tarnish. Suárez had promised to hold the first democratic municipal elections in 1979, and the PSOE expected to do especially well in large and middle-sized cities where political change had been minimal since the death of Franco. These elections could then catapult the Socialists into power.

Perhaps sensing the danger of holding municipal elections first, Suárez caught the opposition off guard by calling early general elections for March 1979 (with municipal elections to follow in April).[39] As in 1977, the PSOE attempted to make use of both its long pedigree and its modern and youthful outlook. It portrayed the portrait of Pablo Iglesias, the party founder, with the slogan "100 Years of Honor." The Socialists also sought to project a moderate and responsible image through slogans such as "A Strong Government for a Secure Nation" and through an emphasis on the party's maturity (González was made to appear older) and competence.[40]

However, unlike 1977, the contradiction between this moderate image and the PSOE's radical party platform was successfully exploited by Suárez and the UCD during the entire electoral campaign. The UCD hammered away at the resolutions of the PSOE Twenty-seventh Congress, especially the references to Marxism and worker self-management.[41] Suárez's election-eve television address accused the PSOE of duplicity and raised fears about the consequences of a Socialist victory. The Catholic Church, a relatively innocuous political actor during the transition, reemerged in the 1979 campaign to indirectly attack the PSOE.[42] The Socialists had underestimated the charisma, shrewdness, and aggressiveness of Suárez, but they had also failed to assure enough voters that a PSOE government would not take serious political risks.

Given the high expectations, the electoral results of March 1, 1979 were especially disappointing for the Socialists. In general the elections produced little real change in the strength of the major parties. The PSOE vote increased only 1.22 percent, far less than the PSP's 4.46 percent in 1977. The Socialists were able to increase their presence in the lower house by only three seats (half of the six seats that the PSP won in 1977). UCD remained the largest political force in terms of seats and percentage of the vote, although it dropped two seats and lost about one half of a percentage point in the vote. The Socialists gained more votes than the UCD but were hurt by high levels of abstention in areas of PSOE strength, the resurgence of regional parties in Andalusia and the Basque Country, and a failure to capture even half of the 1977 PSP vote.[43] The PSOE suffered severe setbacks in the Basque Country, Valencia, and Andalusia, where its weakness among eighteen- to twenty-one-year-old "new voters" and workers was especially damaging.[44]

THE CHALLENGE AND DEFEAT OF THE PSOE LEFT

Ideological Crisis: The Twenty-eighth Congress

The 1979 elections gave rise to different interpretations within the PSOE and led to different prescriptions for strategy. The party left noted that the PSOE had been hurt badly by high levels of abstention in traditional Socialist strongholds, and this was viewed as its constituency's punishment for having pursued such a conciliatory policy vis-à-vis the government. Party leaders González and Guerra, prompted by a number of prominent social scientists affiliated with the party, clearly disagreed. They viewed the electoral results as an indication that the PSOE must further moderate its image if the Socialists were to have any chance of winning elections.[45] González argued that the PSOE must widen its appeal to include "all repressed people, whether manual or intellectual workers."[46] José Félix Tezanos, the party's chief social science analyst, warned:

An incorrect definition of the class nature of the PSOE that fails to take into account the new social realities, or that looks down at or ignores the importance of new social sectors, could not only lead to a dangerous isolation, preventing the achievement of an electoral majority, but could also cause serious political setbacks.[47]

By mid–1978, González had targeted the PSOE's radical party program for change. He observed,

There can be no democratic social transformation without a majority. And in order to obtain a majority it is essential to represent a much wider spectrum than originally planned. An example will suffice to illustrate what I am saying: There are twenty-six million voters in this country, out of thirty-six million citizens. Of these voters, thirteen, or fifty percent, are not in the active population, but this half can decide the future of our country with their votes.[48]

The PSOE's Twenty-eighth Congress was held in May 1979, the first legal party event in over forty years, and it was geared toward celebrating the Socialists' one-hundredth anniversary. Since the last congress the PSOE leadership, strengthened by the Socialist electoral performance in 1977 and its role in important elite-level negotiations, had gained increasing power within the party and had alienated much of the party base. Many party militants resented the concentration of power in the hands of the Sevillian-based clique dominated by González, Guerra, and others.[49] This concentration of power was especially resisted by a Madrid-based group of PSOE veterans who viewed the Sevillian leadership as opportunistic, personalistic, and ideologically unsophisticated. The integration of an ideologically diverse set of cohorts from smaller socialist parties into the top ranks of the PSOE leadership was resented by many veterans of the party and was taken as further evidence of the opportunism of the Felipistas. Attempts by Alfonso Guerra, González's hard-nosed number-two man, to strengthen the party and to impose his own organizational framework angered many local PSOE leaders. Guerra's manipulation of the selection of candidates and the ordering of party lists before the 1979 general elections was strongly resented, especially given the new "federal" nature of the PSOE that had resulted from the integration of regional socialist parties in 1978: throughout early 1979, a bitter center-periphery struggle was waged within the PSOE.[50]

Taken together, these sources of dissatisfaction caused a severe internal party crisis to explode at the Twenty-eighth Congress. Supporters of the party leadership (known as *oficialistas* or Felipistas) confronted more radical delegates (the so-called *críticos*, or critics) on three crucial issues.[51] The first issue concerned the party's ideological self-characterization. Since May 1978, González had advocated the removal of the term "Marxist" from the PSOE program; the *críticos* opposed such a change. The overt references to Marxism, approved in the 1976 Twenty-seventh Congress, were a clear deviation in the context of the Socialist Party's history, although, as has been noted in chapter 2, there had almost always been Marxist sectors in the party.

Second, the *críticos* called for a system of proportional representation for all party posts to allow their voice to be heard within the leadership. Pablo Castellano, a *crítico* leader, noted that the PSOE leadership had increasingly dominated the politics of regional and provincial organizations, and he called for a "deepening of internal democracy in the party and ... a truly federal character."[52] González and Guerra were especially eager to avoid any form of proportional representation that might encourage party factions, weaken the central leadership, and anchor the party too far left.

Finally, there was a serious debate about alliance strategy. The *críticos* generally supported a more confrontational relationship with the UCD and favored an alliance with the PCE in order to obtain a parliamentary majority. This argument was bolstered by the success of a postelectoral municipal-level pact that had allowed the left to govern Spain's largest cities (Madrid, Barcelona, Valencia) as well as twenty-seven of the fifty provincial capitals. However, the leadership rejected any such national electoral alliance (pre- or postelectoral) with the PCE, fearing the creation of another Popular Front and negative repercussions for the PSOE's image. The leadership was also unwilling to give the PCE any additional legitimacy, as numerous studies had shown that the PCE and the PSOE were competing for similar space in the party system.

At the Twenty-ninth Congress the *oficialistas* won narrow victories on the organizational and alliance strategy issues, but they were dealt a stunning defeat on the ideological issue. González's compromise proposal to define the PSOE as a "social bloc" lost to an openly Marxist definition. Since the spring of 1978, the leadership's decision to remove what was viewed as an antiquated and counterproductive label from the party program had created an unanticipated internal rebellion, and a number of party locals and regional branches, and even some top PSOE leaders, openly opposed the proposal. The huge influx of inexperienced members (70.6 percent of delegates had fewer than four years' experience in the party) had radicalized many local party organizations.[53]

Francisco Bustelo, a Madrid economics professor and a leading *crítico* spokesperson, predicted that "if today we add a little water to the old wine, tomorrow we'll add a little more and in five years' time there will be no more wine."[54] Tierno Galván used his position as mayor of Madrid, honorary party president, and the PSOE's "elder statesman" to denounce the leadership. He warned that "we defined our party very clearly as Marxist at the 27th Congress and this cannot be altered."[55] As a further attack on the leadership's attempted moderation and on what was perceived as the leadership's heavy-handedness, delegates defeated González's choice for party president and a well-known moderate, Gregorio Peces-Barba, in favor of José Federico Carvajal. The charged atmosphere of the congress reaffirmed the delegate's commitment to the radical platform adopted in 1976. References to Marxism were far more enthusiastically received than González's call for pragmatism.[56]

Faced with these rebukes, a clearly angered González refused to run for reelection as PSOE secretary general, complaining that "the country cannot wait ten years for the Party to mature. The Party cannot afford the luxury of immaturity."[57] By refusing to run for reelection, González and Guerra revealed the weakness of the PSOE left. The *críticos* had no intention of unseating the party leader, and therefore they had no candidate to present as an alternative to González. Most party members realized that the charismatic González was the PSOE's chief electoral asset, and he was well regarded within the party. González's resignation speech was greeted by the delegates with an impressive demonstration of support for the leader who had rebuilt the PSOE and who had led it to the brink of electoral victory. The *críticos* had hoped only to force some important internal changes in PSOE organization and ideology.[58] The party left tried to put together an alternative leadership slate but could not come up with a single candidate willing to replace the *oficialistas*.

Unwittingly, the *críticos* had thrown the party into complete chaos, but the crisis would ultimately rebound to the benefit of González and Guerra.[59] Because no alternate party leadership could be agreed upon, the Twenty-eighth Congress was suspended, a temporary PSOE steering committee was formed, and an extraordinary congress was called for the following September. Effective control of the party during the summer of 1979 was passed to the Socialist group in parliament, led, of course, by Felipe González. In a sense, this arrangement bought time for González and Guerra to canvass support from party members and to make sure that the *oficialistas* used the new party electoral rules to control the selection of delegates to the Extraordinary Congress.

Crisis Resolution: The Extraordinary Congress

The new party rules adopted by the Twenty-eighth Congress had been largely overshadowed by the ideological dispute, but they established an indirect, strictly majoritarian, winner-take-all electoral system for delegates to congresses, as well as a bloc-voting provision during congresses. Delegates to federal congresses had historically been elected by *agrupaciones* (party locals), thus producing a diverse and often ideologically fragmented set of delegates. The new rules adopted an indirect electoral system whereby delegates were "filtered" through both the provincial and regional party levels, where *oficialistas* usually had more than enough strength to control the delegate selection process. While it is estimated that the *críticos* were supported by as much as 40 percent of PSOE members, the new electoral norms resulted in the election of only about 10 percent of delegates.[60] Voting during congresses was now performed by eighty-six heads of delegations, virtually ensuring that *oficialistas* would control huge blocs of votes. For example, Andalusia, the largest regional delegation (with about one quarter of all votes), was represented by a single person (Alfonso Guerra) in all votes during the congress. Taken together, these provisions meant that only the majority view within the PSOE would be represented at congresses and that dissenters within delegations at party congresses would have almost no voice. By placing more power in the hands of provincial and regional PSOE organizations, the *oficialistas* could more easily control the party as a whole.

By September 1978, when the Extraordinary Congress convened, it was clear that the leadership had used González's charisma, the fear of continued intramural strife, subtle international pressures, political hardball, and the new electoral rules to produce a vastly more compliant set of delegates.[61] Compared with the Twenty-eighth Congress, there were far fewer delegates (420 compared with 1,000), fewer than half as many manual workers, students, and office workers, and a dramatic increase in bureaucrats, technocrats, professionals, and PSOE employees.[62] Delegates elected to the congress had far more experience as PSOE members.[63] The *críticos*, while effectively embarrassing the PSOE leadership, lacked the coherence, skill, and leadership to have successfully confronted the *oficialistas*. The "new" delegates voted overwhelmingly to support a moderate leadership slate led by González and Guerra, and the *críticos* won no seats on the party Executive Committee.[64] The leadership's stampede of the left was so successful that it became embarrassing, and according to Nash, "even González's most loyal supporters were uncomfortably aware that his return had been overeffectively guaranteed."[65] Luís Gómez Llorrente, the only *crítico* who had formed part of the outgoing Executive Committee, was offered a spot on the new one as a peace offering, but he turned it down.

Although the Party platform acknowledged Marxism as "a critical, non-dogmatic, theoretical tool" (the only victory for the PSOE left), it also vowed to "include a variety of contributors, Marxist and non-Marxist, who have helped to make socialism the greatest liberating alternative of our time." The PSOE was now defined as a "class party, of the masses, democratic and federal," with the word "Marxist" conspicuously absent.[66]

By comparing the resolutions adopted at the Twenty-eighth Congress and the Extraordinary Congress, it is possible to detect a change in the PSOE's outlook that would guide party strategy in the future. According to Richard Gunther, this change entailed a shift from a party of mobilization to a "catch-all" party.[67] The Twenty-seventh Congress had clearly viewed the PSOE as an agent of mass mobilization and the streets as a crucial arena for political conflict. At the Twenty-eighth Congress the PSOE advocated strategies of both parliamentary struggle and popular mobilization, but by the Extraordinary Congress all reference to mass mobilization had been dropped. In reality, there had been little mass mobilization led by the PSOE during the transition, and the party had become increasingly electoralist in orientation since the general elections of 1977.

The most important outcome of the Extraordinary Congress was its impact on the internal politics of the Socialist Party. González, Guerra, and the *oficialistas* achieved a definitive consolidation of their control over the PSOE machine. Through the electoral changes, political wheeling and dealing, and González's threat of resignation, the *críticos* had been reduced to a purely testimonial force. Where the previous two congresses had been lively affairs, full of ideological and strategic polemics, the Extraordinary Congress, like all subsequent ones, became a drab forum for the approval of the *oficialista* agenda. Many PSOE members appreciated the return to "order" established by González and Guerra after the Twenty-eighth Congress, remembering well the PSOE's tragic history of factional quarrels. Others complained that order had been restored only at the cost of extinguishing party democracy and establishing authoritarian control over the party.

In fact, after the 1979 crisis the PSOE became a remarkably disciplined party. The *oficialista* victory at the Extraordinary Congress was replicated in most of the federation congresses in 1979 and 1980. Surprisingly harsh punishment for dissent was meted out by the leadership, and the *críticos* experienced constant harassment. As will be discussed later, only in 1983 did the PSOE leadership accept a partial loosening of its iron grip on internal party politics. By then the PSOE was in government and had undergone a thorough ideological metamorphosis. The *críticos* abandoned all hope of influencing party decisions, but they did manage to sustain a precarious existence within the party. In November 1981, they formed a "study group" called the Socialist Left, modeled on the French CERES, and it was grudgingly tolerated by the leadership.

Reflecting back on the party crisis at the Twenty-eighth Congress, González compared it with a later crisis (and eventual split) within the Communist Party. "In the 28th Congress," noted González, "pragmatism collided with the accumulated ideology of the party. This collision became virulent, just as in the PCE, where Carrillo played exactly the same role [as the PSOE leadership], but the PCE didn't have the *same mechanisms* to allow him to exploit the situation."[68] González was expressing the deep-seated conviction, supported by PSOE history, that intramural struggle could only bring electoral disaster.

SOCIALIST RESPONSE TO CRISIS AND THE DISINTEGRATION OF THE CENTER

Somewhat ironically, after the PSOE leadership defeated the party left and consolidated a more moderate party program, the Socialist Party stepped up its attack on the UCD government. Ever since the 1979 elections, when Suárez stirred up fear regarding a Socialist victory, the PSOE had abandoned the unwritten code of political conduct that had prevailed during the first years of the transition and had begun to perform more as a true opposition party. In April 1979, Suárez won a vote of investiture by only one vote after an emotional and somewhat *ad hominem* attack on the prime minister-elect by an embittered González.[69] Throughout the fall of 1979, the PSOE sustained an aggressive attack on Suárez and skillfully exploited the growing internal crisis of the UCD by siding with UCD social democrats on a number of issues (even raising the possibility of a coalition between the PSOE and UCD social democrats). In May 1980, the PSOE presented a motion of censure that was defeated by fourteen votes, but it provided a forum from which a confident González could attack a beleaguered Suárez, and it showed the increasing isolation of the UCD.

The increased pressure of the PSOE on the Suárez government was in part a result of the successful completion of the constitution (and the end of cautious "transition politics"), in part a product of the resentment caused by Suárez's betrayal of the PSOE in the 1979 electoral campaign, and in part closely related to the process of disintegration plaguing the centrist coalition. Since the formation of the UCD coalition, there had been serious divisions among the leaders of the constituent parties (the so-called barons). Suárez demonstrated considerable skill as he held together the unwieldy coalition during the first years of the transition, but the writing of the Spanish constitution, the political economic pacts, the regional devolution process, and other equally divisive issues weakened the ideological unity of the coalition and debilitated the leader who had served as its major unifying force.

From the perspective of this study, it is important to note that the weakening of Suárez's position within the UCD was in large part a result of the strengthening of the UCD right. Within the PSOE, González emerged from a party crisis greatly fortified, and he had forged a unified and relatively tranquil organization. The growing chaos within the UCD and its move rightward thus opened up an important political space for the Socialist Party, and it is this factor that best explains the growing hostility of the PSOE toward the UCD coalition. The PSOE increasingly had a weaker and more conservative opponent to attack, and it was thus more eager to do so.

For most of 1980, the UCD continued to self-destruct. Suárez's attempt to dominate this coalition once and for all and to weaken the party barons failed, and the UCD government's inept handling of the regionalization process intensified the crisis.

The PSOE's policy of confrontation ended abruptly with the unexpected and somewhat mysterious resignation of Adolfo Suárez on January 29, 1981, and it was permanently shelved after the attempted coup of February 23, 1981. The Socialists were aware that Suárez had been victim of an attack not from the left as much as from the right. The attempted coup underscored the reality that the Spanish right still harbored antidemocratic intentions, and the fear it generated among PSOE leaders cannot be underestimated. The PSOE offered to join a coalition government with the UCD, now led by Leopoldo Calvo Sotelo, a more conservative centrist than Suárez. To the chagrin of the Catalans and Basques, the PSOE and UCD jointly supported the Law for the Harmonization of the Autonomy Process, a measure that was widely viewed as slowing down the devolution process. The Socialists played down all talk of military reform. Nash notes that

in the immediate aftermath of the coup... the PSOE effectively abandoned its role as parliamentary opposition and took a much more cooperative attitude towards the government. Politicians of all hues were severely unnerved by 23 February; they closed ranks in a remarkable fashion and moved smartly to the Right.[70]

The PSOE's brief and relatively mild experience as a true party of opposition was thus aborted by a crisis that threatened to undermine democratic rule. It was now faced with a familiar problem: how to support a weakening UCD government while maintaining an image as an opposition force and as a *socialist* opposition force.

As part of an effort to enhance the PSOE's role as a serious opposition party, the Socialist leadership orchestrated its first mass mobilization campaign since the transition. The PSOE chose as its target the Calvo Sotelo government's decision to join the North Atlantic Treaty Organization (NATO). While rejecting a policy of neutrality in the East-West conflict, the Socialists opposed NATO membership, arguing that it did not serve Spain's interests. The Socialists contended that a minority government should submit such an important issue to a referendum, and pledged to hold such a referendum should they win the next elections. The anti-NATO membership campaign was well organized and highly visible, and it gave the PSOE a high profile at a moment of real weakness for the UCD government. Several years later the anti-NATO membership campaign would become a source of embarrassment for PSOE leaders.

The Twenty-ninth Congress: A Spanish Bad Godesburg

Given the coup attempt and the accelerating internal crisis of the UCD, the Socialist leadership viewed the Twenty-ninth Congress, scheduled for October 1981, as an opportunity to show the public that the PSOE was a united and mature party. In terms of unity, the coherence and discipline of the "new" PSOE were to be contrasted with the disarray and squabbling of the UCD and the PCE (and, perhaps most important, the PSOE of past congresses). With the majoritarian delegate selection process and the bloc voting system for congresses, the leadership had little to fear from the *críticos*. As for maturity, González sought to paint the PSOE as the guardian of democracy and as the only party capable of picking up the pieces after the February coup attempt. Moreover, the leadership thought it essential to convince the public that there would be no radical experiments from a Socialist government.

On both counts, the Twenty-ninth Congress was a success.[71] The image of unity was so absolute that it evoked much criticism. As with the Extraordinary Congress of September 1979, there was an increase in white-collar, professional, and highly educated delegates.[72] The entire Executive Committee, led by González, was reelected almost unanimously. The concentration of leadership power was enhanced by a decision to create a nine-member permanent committee to run party affairs in lieu of the larger Executive Committee. Outraged by the effects of the delegate selection process, the *críticos* boycotted the congress, although even had they appeared, their influence would have been negligible. In fact, the entire congress had an eerie air of dullness that led some commentators to compare it with franquist or East European political gatherings.[73]

PSOE leaders made it clear that no radical socialist platform would be adopted. Carmen García Bloise, Executive Committee member (secretary of organization), argued that the PSOE had changed since 1979 because "we are not going to promise anything we cannot deliver. We will keep our socialist goals in mind, but meanwhile we will adjust our program to reality."[74] Felipe González told the Spanish press that "the PSOE has to carry out a bourgeois revolution, as a first step toward a socialist program, since the bourgeoisie in this country has yet to create one."[75]

The political resolutions of the Twenty-ninth Congress reiterated this moderate image. The party vaguely defined its vision of socialism as "the creation of social conditions that will allow people to be happy." It called on a variety of socialist and nonsocialist sectors to support the PSOE project, and appeared to exclude only the far right. Although the party program did call for the implementation of some social democratic policies (nationalization of some banks and private firms, creation of 800,000 new jobs in four years, redistribution of income, labor law reform), the Socialist economic platform was imprecise and ambiguous. Nash notes that "the aim of the program was to give hope to everyone, and antagonize no one."[76] Preston argues that

the PSOE's program could not have been more moderate. Long-term ambitions for the creation of a just and egalitarian society were subordinated to immediate practical tasks like the restructuring of Spanish industry, the stimulation of employment, the reform of Spain's cumbersome civil service and the elaboration of a more positive and independent foreign policy.[77]

The Collapse of UCD

The internal consolidation and ideological moderation of the PSOE were necessary but not sufficient preconditions for the Socialist victory in 1982. It was the final disintegration of the UCD that permitted the PSOE to take power in 1982, even though the moderation and unity of the Socialist party made an alternation in government far less traumatic than it might otherwise have been.

The UCD had failed to find a resolution to the crisis that had forced Adolfo Suárez to resign. The decay of UCD unity was exacerbated by continuing setbacks for the government in regional elections, the devastating effects of the "toxic oil syndrome" (a food poisoning scandal), and the abandonment of key UCD leaders. The lackluster Calvo Sotelo was even less able than his predecessor to stem the decline. In late August 1981, the leader of the UCD social democratic sector, Justice Minister

Fernández Ordóñez, resigned from the government, protesting the government's rightward drift. In November a group of social democrats bolted from the governing coalition to join Fernández Ordóñez's new Democratic Action Party (PAD). In May 1982, the conservative UCD Christian democrats abandoned ship, and the final blow came in July, when Suárez left to form his own party, the Democratic and Social Center (CDS). Faced with an almost total erosion of support within his own coalition, Calvo Sotelo called early elections for October 1982.

NOTES

1. Statements made in an interview with Fernando Claudín, *Zona Abierta* 20 (May–August 1979): 8.

2. Edward Malefakis, "Spain and Its Francoist Heritage," in John H. Herz, ed., *From Dictatorship to Democracy* (Westport, Conn.: Greenwood Press, 1982), p. 223.

3. Among those forces joining the Platform with the PSOE were the Basque Nationalist Party, the Christian Democratic Left, and the Spanish Social Democratic Union.

4. The PSOE reacted to the king's first speech with the following statement: "The King's first speech in the Cortes is one more sign of the power vacuum surrounding this imposed monarch. It was a talk without structure, composed of short phrases aimed at tranquilizing the various sectors of the regime, without the least mention of any intentions of political democratization. Juan Carlos has not surprised anyone. He has fulfilled his obligations to the franquist regime. He gave a continuist speech without concrete political context. He has promised to be firm and prudent, but the Spanish people need freedom and democracy." Quoted in Federico Ysart, *¿Quién hizo el cambio?* (Barcelona: Argos Vergara, 1984), p. 35.

5. José María Maravall, "Transición a la democracia, alienamientos políticos y elecciones en España," *Sistema* 36 (May 1980): 76.

6. Raymond Carr and Juan Pablo Fusi, *Spain: Dictatorship to Democracy*, 2d ed. (London: George Allen and Unwin, 1981), p. 214.

7. For a detailed study of this process, see Donald Share, *The Making of Spanish Democracy* (New York: Praeger/Center for the Study of Democratic Institutions, 1986).

8. For a provocative leftist analysis of the failure of the PSOE's strategy in the 1976 referendum, see "Análisis de coyuntura: Dos proyectos del gobierno, dos tácticas de la izquierda," *Zona Abierta* 11 (January 1977): 12.

9. These figures hide the fact that the most spectacular growth in membership took place from December 1976, when it stood at about 8,000, to the eve of the June 15, 1977 general elections, when membership reached over 50,000. See Richard Gunther, "The Spanish Socialist Party: From Clandestine Opposition to Party of Government," in Stanley Payne, ed., *The Politics of Democratic Spain* (Chicago: Chicago Council on Foreign Relations, 1986), p. 11.

10. Many of the new PSOE members had not suffered as much from severe political repression. They were therefore more likely to embrace radical slogans

and statements and were perhaps less likely to worry about provoking a rightist coup.

11. De la Cierva argues that Willy Brandt was particularly upset with the radical program approved at the Congress, and that the German Social Democratic Party began to pressure González to deradicalize the party. See de la Cierva, *Historia del Socialismo*, pp. 250–251.

12. For all references to this congress, see *XXVII Congreso del Partido Socialista Obrero Español* (Barcelona: Avance, 1977).

13. Gunther, "The Spanish Socialist Party," pp. 11–12.

14. A good account is in Eduardo Chamorro, *Felipe González, un hombre a la espera* (Barcelona: Planeta, 1980), p. 133.

15. The leadership also requested the removal of the flag of the Second Republic when it was displayed during one of the sessions. According to Chamorro, González threatened to resign if even more radical items were added to the platform (*Felipe González*, p. 138).

16. Chamorro, *Felipe González*, p. 138.

17. Indeed, Paul Preston argues that the PSOE had decided to run in elections even had the PCE not been legalized. He suggests that the PSOE feared abstaining from electoral participation because such a strategy might enhance the electoral prospects of the PSP, the FSM, and the PSOE-H, thus challenging the PSOE's hegemonic position on the socialist left. See his *The Triumph of Spanish Democracy* (London: Methuen, 1986), p. 103. At the same time, the PSOE did successfully integrate the Madrid Socialist Confederation and was able to form an electoral alliance with the Catalan Socialist Party before the elections. The PSP and the FPS ran together in a coalition called Socialist Unity.

18. In fact, the PSOE-H was the first of 160 parties to be legalized before the elections.

19. Carr and Fusi, *Spain: Dictatorship to Democracy*, p. 228.

20. On the other hand, it is important to note that the D'Hondt system of counting votes and allocating seats strongly favored the parties that received the most votes, thus benefiting the PSOE and UCD and hurting the smaller socialist parties.

21. The PSOE failed to win a seat in the two poorest provinces of Galicia, in Suárez's native province of Soria, and in Spain's two North African enclaves. The Socialists placed first in five Andalusian provinces, two provinces in Levante, and in Barcelona and Oviedo. See the excellent analysis by Mario Caciagli, *Elecciones y partidos en la transición Española* (Madrid: CIS, 1986), pp. 56–64, on which this discussion draws heavily.

22. According to Diego Armario, the PSOE leadership expected to win, at best, about 70 seats in the lower house. Instead the Socialists won 118 seats. See his *El triángulo: El PSOE durante la transición* (Valencia: Fernando Torres, 1981), p. 42.

23. The PSP success was confined largely to Madrid, where Tierno Galván had a large following. The PSP was hurt by the electoral law and by a lack of resources and organization.

24. The main exception to this strategy was the PSOE's alliance with the Catalan Socialist Party (PSC). The PSC formally joined the PSOE in July 1978.

25. Bonifacio de la Cuadra and Soledad Gallego-Díaz, *Del consenso al desencanto*

(Madrid: Editorial Saltés, 1981), p. 20. Their account of the writing of the Constitution is among the most useful treatments.

26. An excellent discussion of the constitution of the Second Republic is provided by Juan J. Linz, "From Great Hopes to Civil War: The Breakdown of Democracy in Spain," in Juan J. Linz and Alfred Stepan, eds., *The Breakdown of Democratic Regimes: Europe* (Baltimore, Md.: Johns Hopkins University Press, 1978), pp. 142–155.

27. The PSOE insisted that the writing of the Constitution take place within the confines of parliament, where the Socialists' unexpected success could be wielded. The government failed to get the PSOE's support for a variety of plans involving committees of experts and one plan calling for an extraparliamentary summit of party leaders.

28. De la Cuadra and Gallego-Díaz, *Del consenso*, p. 26.

29. Ibid., p. 28. Peces-Barba was largely responsible for elaborating the working draft.

30. Quoted in de la Cuadra and Gallego-Díaz, *Del consenso*, p. 53.

31. Ibid.

32. Suárez's initiative, along with a whole series of related developments within the UCD, are explained and detailed in Share, *The Making of Spanish Democracy*, pp. 146–149.

33. De la Cuadra and Gallego-Díaz, *Del consenso*, p. 59.

34. A good overview of the Spanish economy during this period is provided by Julio Rodríguez Aramberri, "The Political Transformation in Spain: An Interpretation," in Ralph Miliband and John Saville, eds., *The Socialist Register, 1979* (London: Merlin Press, 1979), p. 190.

35. This argument is developed in Pedro Schwartz, "Politics First—The Economy after Franco," *Government and Opposition* 1 (Winter 1976): pp. 84–103.

36. On these threats see Preston, *The Triumph of Democracy*, pp. 130–131.

37. For a leftist critique of the Moncloa Pacts, see Curro Ferraro, *Economía y explotación en la democracia Española* (Bilbao: ZYX, 1978), p. 20.

38. Preston, *The Triumph of Democracy*, p. 137.

39. See Eusebio M. Mujal-León, "The Spanish Left: Present Realities and Future Prospects," in William E. Griffith, ed., *The European Left: Italy, France and Spain* (Lexington, Mass.: Lexington Books, 1979), pp. 99–100; and José María Maravall, "La alternativa Socialista. La politica y el apoyo electoral del PSOE," *Sistema* 35 (March 1980): 3–48.

40. An excellent treatment of the 1979 elections is in J. García Morillo, "El desarollo de la campaña," in Jorge de Esteban and Luís López Guerra, eds., *Las elecciones legislativas del 1 de Marzo de 1979* (Madrid: CIS, 1979), pp. 189–292.

41. See Richard Gunther, Giacomo Sani, and Goldie Shabad, "Party Strategies and Mass Cleavages in the 1979 Spanish Election," presented at the Annual Meeting of the American Political Science Association, Washington, D.C., August 28–31, 1980, p. 60. A book dedicated to exposing these contradictions is Pilar Cambra, *Socialismo no es libertad: El verdadero programa del PSOE* (Madrid: Editorial Dossat, 1979).

42. On the role of the Church in the 1979 electoral campaign, see Eusebio M. Mujal-León, "The Left and the Catholic Question in Spain," *West European Politics* 2 (April 1982): 50.

43. Gunther, Sani, and Shabad conclude that only 41.1 percent of former PSP voters voted for the PSOE in 1979. They argue that many PSP voters abstained or opted for regional parties or for either the UCD or the PCE. See *Spain after Franco*, p. 161.

44. Caciagli, *Elecciones y partidos*, p. 136.

45. Two examples of such analyses are Maravall, "La alternativa socialista," and José Félix Tezanos, "El espacio político y sociológico del socialismo Español," *Sistema* 32 (September 1979): 51–75.

46. Felipe González, "La línea política del PSOE," in Partido Socialista Obrero Español, ed., *Socialismo es libertad: Escuela de verano del PSOE, 1976* (Madrid: Edicusa, 1976), pp. 31–32.

47. Tezanos, "El Espacio," p. 57.

48. Quoted in Enrique Gomáriz, "La sociología de Felipe González," *Zona Abierta* 20 (May–August 1979): 62.

49. See José Félix Tezanos, "Estructura y dinámica de la afiliación Socialista en España," *Revista de Estudios Políticos* 23 (September–October 1981): 122; and Caciagli, *Elecciones y partidos*, p. 211.

50. In fact, a serious struggle broke out over the creation of the PSOE lists in a number of regions. Guerra was accused of imposing "his" candidates over the choices of local parties, causing a number of important resignations. The process by which candidates were approved and which contributed much to this struggle was approved in early 1979 and is described in detail by Jorge de Esteban and Luís López Guerra, "Electoral Rules and Candidate Selection," in Howard R. Penniman and Eusebio M. Mujal-León, eds., *Spain at the Polls, 1977, 1979, 1982: A Study of the National Elections* (Washington, D.C.: American Enterprise Institute and Duke University Press, 1985), pp. 71–72.

51. An excellent overview of these contentious issues is in Jorge de Esteban and Luís López Guerra, *Los partidos políticos en la España actual* (Barcelona: Planeta, 1982), p. 121. The *críticos* were led by three distinguished Madrid PSOE members: Pablo Castellano, Luís Gómez Llorente, and Francisco Bustelo.

52. Quoted in Elizabeth Nash, "The Spanish Socialist Party since Franco: From Clandestinity to Government: 1976–1982," in David S. Bell, ed., *Democratic Politics in Spain: Spanish Politics after Franco* (New York: St. Martin's Press, 1983), p. 45.

53. José Félix Tezanos, *Sociología del socialismo Español* (Madrid: Tecnos, 1983), p. 138.

54. Quoted in Nash, "The Spanish Socialist Party since Franco," p. 43.

55. *El País* (May 11, 1978), p. 11.

56. *El País* (May 18, 1979) has excellent reporting on the Twenty-eighth Congress.

57. Statements made in an interview with Fernando Claudín *Zona Abierta* 20 (May–August 1979): 8.

58. See Antonio García Santesmases (himself a *crítico*), "La dos opciones del PSOE," *Zona Abierta* 20 (May–August 1979): 41.

59. The most likely explanation for the entire crisis is that González presented the Marxist versus non-Marxist issue in an inept manner, foolishly rallying an unhappy party base behind an ideological issue that could have been agreed upon. It is possible (though less likely) that González and Guerra intentionally

provoked the dispute, either to shore up their own positions within the party or to force the PSOE to unanimously support an ideological moderation. There is at present no conclusive evidence to support either explanation.

60. Nash, "The Spanish Socialist Party since Franco," pp. 46–47.

61. See de Esteban and López Guerra, Los partidos, p. 124. It seems clear that the changes in regulations had a profound impact on the sociological composition of the Extraordinary Congress when compared with the Twenty-eighth Congress only months earlier. See José Félix Tezanos, "Radiografía de dos congresos: Una aportación al estudio sociológico de los cuadros políticos del socialismo Español," Sistema 35 (March 1980): 79–99. There were widespread reports that the PSOE leadership undertook a drive to get oficialistas to pay their dues and later excluded all those who had not paid dues from the delegate selection process. There were also suggestions that the German Social Democratic Party threatened to withhold financial aid if Felipe González were not reelected to the party leadership. See de la Cierva, Historia del socialismo, p. 263.

62. See the data supporting these assertions in Tezanos, Sociología del socialismo Español, p. 143. See also Nash, "The Spanish Socialist Party since Franco," pp. 46–47.

63. Tezanos, Sociología del socialismo Español, p. 138.

64. The moderate slate received 85.9 percent of the votes, compared with only 6.9 percent for the críticos and 7.2 percent abstentions. For a summary of the results of the Extraordinary Congress, see Fernando Ollero Butler, "El Congreso Extraordinario del PSOE," Revista del Departamento de Derecho Político 6 (Spring 1980): 205–215.

65. Nash, "The Spanish Socialist Party since Franco," p. 49.

66. Partido Socialista Obrero Español, Resoluciones Políticas, 28 Congreso, 1979 (Madrid: PSOE, 1979), p. 2.

67. See Gunther, Sani, and Shabad, Spain after Franco, pp. 155–170.

68. Emphasis added. Quoted in Pedro Calvo Hernández, Todos me dicen Felipe (Barcelona: Plaza & Janes, 1987), p. 156.

69. See El País and Diário 16 of April 6, 1979, for graphic evidence that the period of consensus had ended.

70. Nash, "The Spanish Socialist Party since Franco," p. 54.

71. All resolutions of the Twenty-ninth Congress are contained in a six-volume set of Memorias, XXIX Congreso (Madrid: PSOE, 1981).

72. Tezanos, Sociología del socialismo Español, pp. 142–143.

73. See the editorial in Diário 16 (October 22, 1981), p. 4; an article entitled "Un congreso lamentable," Diário 16 (October 27, 1981), p. 2; and "De la desunión a la unanimidad," El País (October 19, 1981).

74. Quoted in Hoja de Lunes (October 19, 1981), p. 14.

75. Quoted in Pueblo (October 20, 1981).

76. Nash, "The Spanish Socialist Party since Franco," p. 60.

77. Preston, The Triumph of Spanish Democracy, p. 223.

4

The Socialists in Power

We find ourselves in a dual role. At times we almost resemble the inquisitors of leftist thought, while other times we are more like victims of this inquisition.

—Alfonso Guerra, 1981[1]

This chapter will focus mainly on the first four years of Socialist power. Although subsequent changes in outlook and strategy occurred, the general pattern of the PSOE's behavior in power can be surmised from a look at its first term in office. After a brief description of the dimensions of the victory and the expectations that surrounded the Socialists' rise to power, the discussion will turn to two policy areas: political-economic policy and foreign policy (specifically the issue of NATO membership). A final section will provide a brief overview of the PSOE performance in some other areas of interest.

THE PSOE IN GOVERNMENT

In many ways the PSOE triumph appeared to be a harbinger of profound sociopolitical change in Spanish society.[2] Most obviously, the Socialist success spelled the end of over forty years of rightist government. The transition to democracy was led by young, reformist *políticos* of the franquist regime. The founders of the Union of the Democratic Center (UCD) clearly hoped that the transactive transition to democracy would perpetuate center-right rule for many years, but the right could retain power for only the first five years of Spanish democracy.[3] Ideological and personal tensions within the UCD led to endless political bickering, ineffective government, and, ultimately, the electoral disaster of October 1982.[4]

The PSOE victory led many to expect sweeping changes in almost every aspect of Spanish society. Without exception, the new Socialist team represented individuals unconnected with the franquist system. If the first PSOE government was less radical than anticipated, it nevertheless included many who had actively opposed authoritarian rule. The young new prime minister, Felipe González, whose *nom de querre* had been "Isidoro," had a reputation as a fiery orator. Only a year before the elections, González appeared in blue jeans before 500,000 anti-NATO protesters to berate the politics of superpower confrontation.

From the looks of the new government, there were other apparently radical changes on the horizon. For the sensitive position of defense minister, González tapped the bearded, twenty-nine-year-old ex-mayor of Barcelona, Narcís Serra. Serra, a leading figure in the Catalan Socialist Party, had been a member of the antifranquist Popular Liberation Front, and he never completed military service. The new vice-president, Alfonso Guerra, was widely viewed as representing ideological positions to the left of the president. Foreign Minister Fernando Morán had long had a reputation as a *crítico* who favored close ties with Third World countries and opposed NATO integration.

The PSOE victory was also novel because it represented a generational break. The UCD governments had constituted a break with the franquist past, ushering in a post–Civil War generation of franquist and moderate opposition bureaucrats mostly in their forties and fifties. The new PSOE team averaged only 41.5 years. Four ministers of the government were in their thirties, and Felipe González was only forty years old.[5]

Furthermore, the *dimensions* of the Socialist victory made the enactment of its program appear feasible. The PSOE won the first absolute majority in Spain's young democracy and the first single-party absolute majority in Spanish history. Moreover, the size of the Socialist mandate was impressive. On a surprisingly high voter turnout (79.6 percent), the PSOE won 48.4 percent of the valid votes and 57.7 percent (202) of the seats in the lower house of the Cortes. Unlike past elections, the Socialists drew support from virtually every area of Spain, winning a plurality of votes in 41 of Spain's 52 provinces. This position of strength was enhanced even further in the May 1983 municipal elections, which gave the PSOE control over a majority of Spain's local governments.

A final reason for high expectations, and one requiring more elaborate discussion, was the PSOE electoral platform. As will be discussed later in greater detail, the 1982 electoral program was far more moderate than either the 1977 or 1979 version. Many observers credited this new platform with assuring the PSOE's unexpectedly large capture of votes from the center-right in the 1982 elections.[6] The platform was ambiguous and flexible enough in key areas to allow numerous interpretations. Still, compared with UCD governments, especially those of Leopoldo Calvo Sotelo, the PSOE platform promised significant changes in many areas.

As their general objective the Socialists sought to "overcome the current political and economic crisis, develop more completely the democratic system and freedoms guaranteed in the constitution, and rationalize the inefficient public administration apparatus in order to combat unemployment and social inequalities."[7] In the political economy sphere the PSOE promised to create 800,000 jobs:

The policy of previous governments, based on rising prices, systematic reduction of labor costs, reduction of real salaries or work force numbers, and the transfer of the cost of inefficient productive apparati toward the poor, has not achieved a stimulation of investment, has depressed demand, and has worsened the unemployment rate.... It is absurd to think that this country will tolerate policies whose only results are the maintenance of the old power structure—economic, political and social—at the cost of unemployment, reduction of salaries and a regressive budget.[8]

In place of such conservative policies, the Socialists advocated an expansion-oriented political economic policy in which "public investment will be the motor of the economy."[9] The PSOE called for early retirement schemes, a shorter work week, and an increased minimum schooling age, all means of reducing unemployment while spreading the cost of the crisis.[10] Continued neocorporatist arrangements among government, labor, and the entrepreneurs were to be encouraged, but the PSOE promised the "maintenance of workers' purchasing power."[11] Better unemployment and pension systems were called for, as well as a complete overhaul of Spain's fiscal system.[12] Absent from the PSOE platform were any plans for massive nationalization of industry or radical redistribution of income. The party platform fully acknowledges the need for "reindustrialization," admitting that

policies aimed at overcoming the crisis in the industrial sector cannot ignore the requisites of the market.... It will be necessary to consolidate that part of the national industry that has a chance to survive, and to favor its growth.[13]

In addition, the platform recognized that increased economic growth would be necessary in order to create new employment. Nevertheless, the party's emphasis was clear: not growth per se but "the creation of jobs is the principal challenge that Spanish society must face in the near future. Therefore, employment is the first priority of the Socialist program."[14]

Many areas of the PSOE social and cultural program were even more ambitious and controversial. In educational matters, the Socialists proposed a sweeping reorganization and democratization of the Spanish university system. Private (Catholic) schools were to continue receiving state subsidies only if they adhered to state standards. The penal code would be reformed, abortion would be decriminalized, and the PSOE promised to develop constitutional provisions regarding individual rights, such as habeas corpus, and freedom of expression. The party advocated an overhaul of the judiciary, proposed the creation of the jury system, and called for the elimination of regressive judicial fees. Widespread administrative reform was slated to "make things work better."

Perhaps most controversial was a plan to outlaw rampant *pluriempleo* (multiple job-holding) by civil servants in order to improve job performance and increase job openings. Measures were outlined to democratize the fiercely autonomous and deeply entrenched administrative corps. The PSOE military reform policy called for strict limitations on the jurisdiction of the military justice system, recognition of the right to conscientious objection, a severe reduction in the number of active members of the armed forces, and reform of the overly authoritarian military educational system.

In foreign policy the PSOE favored making Spain a nuclear-free zone and advocated the elimination of nuclear missiles from "European soil." The party claimed to oppose "all forms of colonialism or neocolonialism" and openly opposed all political regimes that limit human rights.[15] Integration in the European Economic Community was proposed as a major goal; and on the touchy issue of NATO membership the Socialists stated that "the PSOE affirms its opposition to all military and political blocs, since they have effectively divided the world into zones of perpetual influence.... All negotiations concerning our military integration [in NATO] will be frozen."[16] The Socialists promised to hold a referendum to "let the people decide" whether or not to join NATO, but the platform did not state unambiguously which position they might advocate in such a referendum. Nevertheless, the tone of the PSOE foreign policy program, together with the party's high-profile campaign against NATO entry, led virtually all Spaniards to view the Socialist stand as being opposed to NATO membership.

Collectively, these proposals were referred to as "El Cambio" (The Change), a buzzword for the widespread desire for *fundamental* sociopolitical change. The novelty of a Socialist government after years of conservative rule, the significant generational change, the dimensions of the victory, and both the ambitiousness and moderation of the PSOE program helped to create expectations for many changes that had been put off during the transition to democracy. The following sections highlight a few of the most important aspects of the PSOE record, focusing on two of the most controversial and contentious areas. This necessarily cursory treatment is for illustrative purposes only and is not intended to be an exhaustive account of the PSOE's record in government.

ADVOCATING BITTER MEDICINE: POLITICAL ECONOMIC POLICY

> We have said frequently that success in addressing the problems of the Spanish economy . . . cannot be measured simply by the reduction of inflation or the national debt, but rather by the extent to which these measures are able to avoid creating massive unemployment and avoid weakening the productive structures upon which the economy will be built.
>
> —Felipe González, 1978[17]

> Our program means short term costs, not as many as our detractors would have people believing. But to avoid adopting it would mean even more costs, short and long term.
>
> —PSOE Document, 1984[18]

> We were wrong in calculating our ability to end unemployment.
>
> —Felipe González, 1986[19]

Of all the problems faced by the new Socialist government, none was more urgent than the economic crisis. The contours of this crisis were well known throughout the industrialized world in the early 1980s, but its impact in Spain was particularly harsh. The successful political transition from authoritarianism to democracy exacted a high economic price: a long delay in taking politically unpopular economic measures to cope with the growing economic crisis.[20] A syndrome of rising prices and wages, declining productivity, and balance-of-payments deficits was exacerbated by this procrastination. The most alarming symptom of the economic crisis was unemployment. By November 1982, Spain's National Statistics Institute reported that 2,134,000 Spaniards, or 16.4 percent of the active population, were unemployed.[21]

These economic disequilibria were compounded by the historical weight of a particularly outmoded economic structure. Spain's history of delayed, regionally insolated capitalist development, together with an unstable political system in the nineteenth and early twentieth centuries, distorted the process of economic development. Industrialization almost always took place under the aegis of the Spanish state, whether behind high protective tariffs, through direct government investments and ownership, or as a result of government-induced demand.[22] Forty years of authoritarian rule increased the dependence of the Spanish economic structure on the state and, after the mid–1950s, its dependence on foreign capital. Interest groups were weak and dependent on the state.[23]

During the transition to democracy, party and union elites adopted "defensive positions." Most leaders of political parties, trade unions, and entrepreneurial organizations lacked the organized, coherent, mobilized, or experienced constituencies to successfully confront a much stronger government on fundamental political economic issues.[24] Their primary concern was to complete and consolidate the transition to democracy, to protect the nascent democracy against threats from terrorists and military conspirators (*golpistas*), and to buy time in order to strengthen their own constituencies.[25] The result of this "mutual insecurity" was five years of government-sponsored political economic pacts involving the major political parties (and their affiliated trade unions) and entrepreneurial organizations.[26] Economically, the accords established the parameters for important macroeconomic questions (inflation rates, salary increases, public sector spending) and were aimed at preserving social peace during a crucial period of the political transition. Politically, they served to legitimate the role of all actors involved in the negotiations, and the political economic pacts paralleled the emerging process of political consensus surrounding the writing of the Spanish Constitution. The Moncloa Pacts of 1977 made an important contribution, at least on a symbolic level, to the subsequent constitutional compromise, and they were renewed in a similar form (but with a modified set of participants) in 1979, 1980, and 1981.[27]

The political economic pacts attempted to keep rapidly growing salaries close to the rate of inflation and to avoid any drastic (and politically unsavory) change in the archaic and inefficient franquist labor relations edifice, while promising moderate reforms in such areas as the fiscal system. They also helped to legitimate democratic capitalism in the eyes of a working class rendered somewhat suspicious after forty years of authoritarian capitalism.[28] Although political economic accords were an essential ingredient of the successful political transition, the "social procrastination" they fostered ultimately damaged Spain's economy. Essential reforms were postponed and the productivity of the Spanish economy suffered. Consequently, employment growth stagnated, creating a distribution of income toward employed workers that was, however, detrimental to the work force and the economy as a whole. Spain's gross domestic product (GDP) grew at an average of only 1.7 percent between 1975 and 1982 compared with 7.5 percent from 1960 to 1970.[29]

After the 1982 elections the PSOE government was in a strong position to end the pacted social procrastination; it enjoyed a large, single-party parliamentary majority. Mariano Guindal and Rodolfo Serrano note that

if Adolfo Suárez and UCD had to assume the historic task of the political transition, destroying themselves in the process, Felipe and the Socialists had to carry out the economic transition, transforming a set of autarchic economic structures for the market system.[30]

The PSOE leadership contemplated two strategies to deal with the crisis, but both entailed serious risks. The "expansion-oriented" strategy, backed by the PSOE left, sought to use state investment to stimulate economic growth, create employment, and restructure industry. Strong measures to redistribute income, combined with restrictions on capital flight, would be necessary. The disastrous economic results of a similar experiment by the French Socialists, in the context of a far more vigorous economy, had been closely observed in Spain, so the risks of such a strategy were well known. The impending political costs of the French Socialist about-face were also becoming apparent by late 1982.

An alternative strategy, favored by the social democratic sectors of the PSOE, required the implementation of an economic austerity program designed to curb inflation by limiting wages and reducing state spending. A reindustrialization program would eliminate inefficient industries and redirect resources toward healthier enterprises. An overhaul of the fiscal system would help the government contend with the difficult readjustment period. The short-term risks of this strategy were obvious: an increase in unemployment, potentially irreparable damage to the Spanish industrial structure, increased dependence on foreign capital, and the possible failure of Spanish entrepreneurs to react to the austerity program with increased investment. The political costs of such a strategy might have to be paid in 1986 at the next general elections. Meanwhile, the PSOE ran the risk of alienating its trade union allies and further antagonizing its internal critics.

As noted earlier, the 1982 electoral program carefully avoided unequivocal commitment to either strategy. However, the program's emphasis on combating unemployment in the short term and its apparent dedication to expansion-oriented economic policies placed the party closer to the first strategy. Nevertheless, the González government, after an initial reaffirmation of its desire to expand the economy and create more jobs, rejected any flirtation with the French model. Instead, it implemented an economic austerity program more akin to the supply-side policies of Ronald Reagan and Margaret Thatcher, albeit with minor "socialist" correctives. To the surprise of many observers, the PSOE implemented the first genuine economic stabilization program since 1957.[31] Julio Alcaide Inchausti discusses why the new government abandoned the 1982 political economic program:

From the start it was clear that the authors of the socialist economic program had not really understood the seriousness of the economic crisis. The good will of its proposals would necessarily run up against the reality of inherited problems. It was impossible to magically avoid the obstacles that the crisis presented without applying tough medicine.[32]

The two main thrusts of the new PSOE economic policy were economic austerity (limiting wages and government expenditures) and reindustrialization of heavy industry (immediate layoffs of 65,000 workers and gradual reduction of the work force subsequently). The Socialist government's first acts as the start of a program of economic austerity were to devalue the peseta 8 percent and to enact large increases in the price of gasoline, electricity, and public transportation. The first Socialist budget, presented in April 1983, was far more austere than expected. Although budgets continued to rise during the four years of Socialist government, only three budgetary categories did not suffer cutbacks in their percentage of the total: public sector debt, social security, and regional expenditures. The Socialists proposed measures to deal with each of these unruly categories. The public sector debt was to be offset by salary limits in the public sector, a large increase in taxes (an income tax hike of 20 percent was announced in September 1983), and an overhaul of the tax system. Spiralling social security costs would be controlled by cutting pensions, tightening the rules for pension recipients, and increasing worker and business contributions to the system. The unwieldy regional structure and consequent growing drain on the budget was originally to be countered by the LOAPA, a law designed to curtail some of the autonomy of Spanish regions but subsequently ruled unconstitutional.

Among the most controversial reforms implemented by the PSOE involved Spain's costly social security system. In January 1983, the government raised pensions in order to encourage early retirement. Increased outlays, elevated by the costs of reindustrialization, strained the social security system, so the government passed measures to limit costs: it capped payments for injured, sick, and elderly; tied pension increases to cost-of-living adjustments; and (the most controversial measure) increased the minimum number of working years required to earn a pension from two to eight. The social security reform was bitterly opposed by the trade unions, including the socialist UGT. Nicolás Redondo, UGT secretary general, voted against his own party in parliament when the measure was introduced, complaining that "the government wants to streamline the economy on the backs of the workers."[33] The unions were angered over the cutback in some benefits and the new restrictions on receiving pensions. They were also miffed at what they considered the unilateral decree of these measures by the government without appropriate consultation with union leaders.

The Socialists' decision to pursue reindustrialization at the cost of short-term employment was apparent as early as January 1983 but was articulated publicly only in May 1983, when Carlos Solchaga, minister of Industry and Energy, announced that the creation of 800,000 new jobs would be impossible.[34] Begun timidly by UCD but implemented far more vigorously by the Socialists, the program had cost 72,000 jobs by late 1984. The targeted sectors were textiles, metallurgy, and shipbuilding. The closing of the huge steel works at Altos Hornos del Mediterraneo in Sagunto (near Valencia) created the worst and most prolonged labor conflict of the Socialist term in office. Similar closings throughout Spain, but especially in the north and northwest, created an almost endless series of demonstrations and factory occupations.[35] Working-class resistance caused constant embarrassment for the PSOE, but Economics Minister Miguel Boyer and Industry Minister Carlos Solchaga were able to implement the reindustrialization plan without significant setbacks or compromises.

The PSOE strategy had as its basis the continuation of *pactismo*, or pact-making, but this time toward the less savory end of implementing an austerity program, reducing government spending, and effecting a rapid and thoroughgoing reindustrialization plan.[36] The Inter-confederation Accord (AI), signed in 1982 by the government, both major trade union confederations, and the Spanish Confederation of Entrepreneurial Organizations (CEDE), was a major success. However, as the government pursued its reindustrialization and austerity programs, the AI began to break down. When the accord was abandoned definitively in early 1984, the government began a long and frustrating search for a new social pact. Labor opposition to the reindustrialization program, which peaked in the "hot" spring, summer, and autumn of 1984, further obstructed any new accord. The announcement of a cut in pension benefits in January 1984 also damaged relations between the government and the trade unions. In October 1984, the government was finally able to get the Socialist UGT and the CEOE to sign a two-year accord, the Social and Economic Accord (AES). The Communist Workers Commissions (CCOO) refused to sign the agreement, and confederation leader Marcelino Camacho called the AES "a clear sellout that eliminates almost all gains won to date by the working class."[37] The AES limited wage increases to between 5.5 and 7.5 percent, well below the predicted rate of inflation for 1985 and 1986. It called for spending cuts by the government and, most abhorrent to the unions, a reform of employment regulations that would facilitate part-time hiring and ease franquist-era restrictions on layoffs and firings.

The results of this package of economic measures were dramatic. Most alarming was the sharp rise in unemployment during the PSOE government, as shown in Table 4.1. The rates were especially high for first-time job seekers (55.7 percent for sixteen- to nineteen-year-olds and 45.5 percent for twenty- to twenty-four-year olds). Spain had the highest unemployment rate in Europe, double the average for the EEC (11

Table 4.1
Selected Economic Indicators in Spain, 1982–1986

Indicator	1982	1983	1984	1985	1986	1987
Unemployment (% active population)	16.2	17.7	20.6	21.9	21.5	20.6
Unemployment (millions)	2.1	2.3	2.7	2.9	2.9	2.9
Inflation (% rise in prices)	14.4	12.2	11.3	8.8	8.8	5.3
Real growth rates (GDP)	1.0	2.2	2.2	1.7	2.0	4.8
Public Debt (% of GDP)	-5.3	-5.3	-5.0	-4.8	-4.6	---
Balance of payments current account (billions of dollars)	-4.1	-2.5	+2.3	+2.5	+4.9	+1.2

Source: Anuário El País, 1988 (Madrid: El País, 1988); *Diário 16,* May 24, 1986, p. 19.

percent).[38] A total of 734,300 people lost their jobs during the PSOE's four years in power.[39] By the end of 1987, over three million Spaniards were unemployed (20.94 percent).[40]

At the same time, the percentage of the work force covered by unemployment insurance dropped under the PSOE government.[41] According to the AES signed in 1984, the government was supposed to extend coverage to 42 percent of the unemployed by the end of 1985 and to 48 percent by 1986. Data released by the National Institute of Employment revealed that by October 1987, only 27.01 percent of unemployed workers were covered by insurance.[42] Moreover, the data showed that recipients were, on average, receiving fewer benefits.

Despite the Socialist pledge to maintain purchasing power, workers lost ground between 1982 and 1984. Real salaries dropped 1.5 percent in 1982, .3 percent in 1983, and 3.9 percent in 1984, the harshest year of the austerity policy. Moreover, in order to reduce the deficit and promote reindustrialization, the PSOE raised taxes considerably, and the impact on lower incomes was especially harsh. In only three years, taxes increased from 30.8 to 34.3 percent of Spain's GDP. The PSOE increased taxes on households more than on businesses, on income more than consumption, and on salaries (payroll taxes) more than on capital.[43] In addition, with Spain's entry into the European Economic Community, the government was obliged to implement a value-added tax on January 1, 1986.[44] As is to be expected, personal and regional income inequality were also worsened by these economic policies.[45] The Spanish public was shocked in October 1986 when a prominent charity organization published a report stating that eight million Spaniards were poor and about four million of these were categorized as extremely poor.[46]

By 1987, much of the other macroeconomic data were more positive for the Socialists. Inflation was reduced to a manageable 4.7 percent, reserves increased, the balance of payments improved dramatically, and the economy was growing at over five percent. The government was able to boast that its policies had led to the creation of almost 800,000 jobs (although many of these were part-time) even if the unemployment rate was not dropping.

The government was far less successful limiting the increase of state expenditures, mostly because of a large increase in public sector debt (up from 5.2 percent of GDP to 6.2 percent of GDP). It was able to limit the damage of spending increases due to a large increase in tax intake. On the whole, the government effectively streamlined the Spanish economy and created a good climate for foreign and domestic investment. A boom in the Spanish stock markets and a flurry of important direct foreign investments were widely interpreted as an entrepreneurial vote of confidence in the government's political economic policy. Although concern about the large budget deficit persisted, major international economic institutions continued to give the PSOE economic policies their seal of approval.[47] Indeed, 1987 was the best year of the decade in terms of the standard economic indictors. Rapid growth, low inflation, and a significant reduction of the public sector debt all contributed to considerable optimism regarding the future of the Spanish economy.[48]

Notwithstanding these accomplishments, the persistence of unacceptably high levels of unemployment cast considerable doubt on the overall success of the PSOE strategy and has raised questions about its ultimate consequences.[49] When it abandoned the pledge to create 800,000 jobs, the PSOE argued that the streamlining of the economy would create the basis for future job growth, but a substantial increase in employment has yet to be observed. In the words of one critic:

Short-term sacrifice and streamlining of the economy are acceptable. The PSOE did it with more honesty and austerity than the right could have. But what long term vision does the PSOE have that is different from that of Reagan or Thatcher? What future gain will justify the undeniable decline in real salaries under the PSOE government?[50]

Table 4.2
Number of Work Days Lost to Strikes, 1978–1987 (In Thousands)

YEAR	DAYS LOST
1978	11,550.9
1979	18,916.9
1980	6,177.5
1981	5,153.8
1982	2,787.6
1983	4,416.7
1984	6,357.8
1985	3,223.5
1986	2,280.3
1987*	4,412.5

*Through November

Source: *Anuário El País, 1988* (Madrid: El País, 1988), p. 422.

Moreover, the government's decision to channel scarce resources into the most technologically advanced and most highly competitive industries cannot be realistically reconciled with the desire to absorb the unemployed 20 percent into the work force. The PSOE made the Spanish economy more efficient, but "efficiency, as an end, is the main characteristic of neoliberals and neoconservatives."[51] Critics within the party, on the communist left, and even to the right were noting by 1986 that the PSOE had become obsessed with efficiency and had lost the traditionally socialist emphasis on equality.[52]

As illustrated in Table 4.2, the number of work days lost to strikes was, with the exception of 1984, lower under PSOE governments than during the preceding conservative governments. The most conflictual years were 1984 and 1987. Between January and March 1987, a wave of strikes crippled the Spanish economy and cost an estimated 40 million lost labor hours.[53] During the second week in April, over a million Spaniards were on strike, including teachers, students, and doctors. The most shocking and graphic example of popular unrest occurred during that same time in the town of Reinosa, when a near stage of siege was required to quell striking workers who were protesting proposed plant closures. The brutal confrontation between police and strikers was shown live on television and created a national outcry.

At the height of the labor unrest, the long-standing feud between Economics Minister Carlos Solchaga and UGT leader Nicolás Redondo also exploded on national television. During a widely viewed television debate concerning the prospects for negotiated political economic pacts, Redondo accused Solchaga of having jumped into the enemy bunker and suggested that his relationship with the owners was "almost one of

cohabitation."[54] Solchaga, along with CEOE (the main employers confederation) president José María Cuevas, bitterly counterattacked by
labeling the unions irresponsible. The spectacle of a Socialist minister
engaged in a vicious squabble with the leader of a Socialist trade union
was only one of the many contradictions resulting from the PSOE's
adoption of neoliberal economic policies.

Throughout 1988, strike and protest activity continued among workers and professionals. These events, occasionally violent in nature, were
increasingly coordinated by *both* trade union confederations. For example, on April 22, 1988, over 100,000 Spaniards were protesting government policy. Ranchers blocked roads throughout Spain to protest
low prices; thousands of teachers in Madrid protested low wages; and
a strike in the shipbuilding sector in Vizcaya resulted in two serious
injuries. A general strike in El Ferrol protested the government's slow
implementation of policies designed to offset the impact of reindustrialization. Nicolás Redondo, UGT secretary general, warned that "the Government will pay a high price if it doesn't alter its economic policies."[55]

SOCIALIST FOREIGN POLICY: FROM "NATO NO" TO "NATO SI"

> NATO is nothing more than a military superstructure built by the
> Americans to guarantee the survival of capitalism. It is not only
> directed against the communist countries, as officially stated, but
> against all possible revolutionary transformations in the capitalist
> countries themselves.
>
> —Felipe González, 1976[56]

> To break our relations with the Atlantic Alliance would create a
> trauma, with consequences I cannot foresee.
>
> —Felipe González, 1985[57]

The Socialist foreign policy platform had been far more ambitious
than its more moderate domestic program.[58] But as was the case with
political economic policy, Socialist foreign policy once the party was in
office involved far less change than had been advocated by party leaders
during the electoral campaign. But unlike the political economic sphere,
where a consensus in favor of austerity and reindustrialization quickly
emerged within the government, foreign policy matters divided the Socialist leadership during much of the PSOE's first years in office. Moreover, the government's earlier foreign policy image (for example, its
opposition to NATO membership, Felipe González's meeting with Ar-
afat, and his controversial parley with Qaddafi) contrasted markedly with

its more conservative hue later in its mandate (support for integration in NATO, reversal of its policy toward the Polisario guerrillas in the Sahara).[59] González's early interest in Latin America gave way to a more distanced Spanish policy toward the region.[60] Fernando Morán's resignation as minister of foreign affairs in July 1985, and his replacement with ex-UCD cabinet member Francisco Fernández Ordoñez, marked the definitive abandonment of all vestiges of PSOE's earlier attraction to Third World ideologies (*tercermundismo*).

No foreign policy issue was more visible or controversial than that of Spain's integration into NATO. Spain had been denied entry into NATO during the franquist regime, and the NATO question remained secondary during the first two years of Spanish democracy. Integration into NATO was first proposed as part of the UCD's 1979 electoral platform, largely at the insistence of the Christian democratic sector of the governing coalition, but Adolfo Suárez and his foreign minister, Marcelino Oreja, resisted formal application procedures until early 1981. When the more conservative Leopoldo Calvo Sotelo was inaugurated in February 1981, he pledged to make Spain a member of the Atlantic Alliance. The government formally applied for NATO entry in September, and the Cortes approved NATO entry on October 27, 1981, over the opposition of the PSOE and the PCE.[61] Spain became a member of NATO in the spring of 1982, shortly before the convocation of the October general elections.

The decision by the UCD government to join NATO provoked the PSOE's first genuine attempt at mass mobilization since Franco's death. The PSOE's passionate anti-NATO campaign in the fall of 1981 was clearly viewed as an opportunity to flex its political muscle and to mobilize the electorate for the next general elections. The theme of the campaign, "OTAN, de Entrada No" (NATO, No to Entry, or NATO, Not at the Outset), was viewed by critics as purposely ambiguous.[62] The Socialists called for a referendum to decide the issue while not explicitly calling for withdrawal. Nevertheless, there is no question that most of the PSOE leadership opposed NATO membership per se, and not just the government's method of entry.[63] During his parliamentary opposition to NATO membership, Felipe González pledged to hold a referendum with the stance of "de salida sí" (exit from NATO, yes). The October 1981 Twenty-ninth PSOE Party Congress, while endorsing a generally moderate party platform, called for withdrawal from NATO.[64] At that time the Socialists argued that NATO did not suit Spain's defensive needs, that it increased the risk of nuclear war, and that it encouraged a dangerous bipolarization of the world. The visible presence and participation of the top PSOE leadership at a November 1981 rally in Madrid (drawing 500,000 demonstrators) left no room for doubt about the Socialist position.

Of all the potential political issues around which to mobilize, the NATO issue was an awkward choice for the Socialists. Only since the twilight of franquism had the PSOE been particularly attached to the idea of neutrality. Ironically, the PSOE's alternative to NATO membership was the maintenance of the U.S.-Spain Bases Agreement, but this bilateral arrangement, begun in 1953, was a crucial source of legitimacy for the diplomatically isolated franquist regime. The younger generation that had assumed control of the PSOE in the 1970s had a sentimental attachment to anti-imperialist positions, but they were also extremely critical of the USSR and its allies. Moreover, the PSOE had close ties with socialist and social democratic parties that had long since accepted NATO. Thus "this was not an old issue, long a concern of the party (as were agrarian reform, secular education, or regional autonomy) but was rather a very recently and artificially created issue, and one which the PSOE very much created for itself."[65] It was, however, an issue of great popular appeal. The PSOE, bolstered by opinion polls, used the NATO issue to rally popular support against the crumbling UCD government and to enhance its image as a party of change.[66]

The initial policy of the socialist government was to freeze negotiations over Spain's integration into the military organization of the alliance while publicly pledging to hold a referendum only after Spain had joined the Common Market. To that end, in early December 1982, Foreign Minister Morán refused to sign a joint NATO statement regarding the placement of nuclear missiles in Europe.[67]

By the spring of 1983, there were signs of division within the Socialist government over the NATO issue. A June 1983 anti-NATO rally called by the PCE drew many Socialist Party militants and a number of top PSOE leaders, and this reportedly angered González. Vice-President Guerra and ministers Morán, Lluch, Solana, Maravall, and Campo continued to advocate withdrawal from NATO. The "austerity technocrats," Miguel Boyer and Carlos Solchaga, both favored membership in the alliance, fearing that withdrawal could hurt Spain's image among the developed nations, scare off investors, and hinder its integration into the Common Market. Defense Minister Serra and the party's leading expert in defense matters, Enrique Múgica, also favored membership in NATO.[68] They were well aware that among the democratic sectors of the military pro-NATO sentiment was strong, and they wanted nothing to spoil the honeymoon between the armed forces and the Socialists.

González remained undecided on the NATO question, but by mid–1983 his genuine hostility toward NATO was quickly eroding. From approximately June 1983 to October 1984, González and his government assumed a position on NATO widely referred to as "calculated ambiguity." In May 1983, speaking in the German Bundestag, González spoke of the NATO alliance in a conciliatory tone. Speaking to the Socialist group in parliament on June 29, 1983, he stated:

[T]he government is not in favor of Spain's entry into the military structure of NATO, but the government does not intend to campaign for or against it. The government will be neutral with respect to the referendum, although it would be the government's position to defend non-integration, because the Party position has not changed on this matter.[69]

In October 1983, the president pledged to stand behind the decision of NATO members regarding the placement of nuclear missiles in Europe. In early 1984, speaking in Denmark, González said that he opposed any notion of unilateral disarmament or a nuclear freeze. In May he called for the restoration of a broad foreign policy consensus, which he claimed had been shattered when UCD unilaterally took Spain into NATO. In June he told the press that a future referendum must raise the question of the overall defense policy of the government, and not merely the NATO issue. González also pointed out that referenda, according to the constitution, were not binding. During the remainder of 1984, previously recalcitrant members of the government softened their positions on NATO. Alfonso Guerra, widely viewed as the chief governmental opponent to NATO, stated in July 1984 that "it would not be honest to say that NATO limits Spanish sovereignty or that it increases the danger of a nuclear war."[70] However, two months later he told the Spanish weekly *Interviu*, "The truth is that I continue to believe, and I insist, that Spain would not benefit from membership in NATO."[71]

Foreign Minister Morán, widely respected within the party, proposed in September 1984 that Spain leave only the military command of NATO. In the spring and summer of 1984, Morán had prepared a document aimed at restoring the foreign policy consensus advocated by González. The Morán document was presented as the definitive compromise plan on NATO, and it was used by González to rally his government, party, and the public behind this new definition of Socialist policy. In late October 1984, González and the cabinet finally agreed to accept the "compromise solution." As a concession to pro-NATO forces, the government now proposed continued membership in NATO (now referrred to more benignly as the Atlantic Alliance). For opponents it called for nonintegration in the military command of the alliance, a ban on nuclear weapons on Spanish territory, and a reduction of U.S. troops based in Spain.

Despite the change in policy of the top PSOE leadership, large sectors of the Socialist Party and a solid majority of the Spanish public continued to oppose NATO membership. Within the PSOE, González easily imposed the new party line during the PSOE Thirtieth Congress in December 1984.[72] Public opposition to NATO remained more resistant to change and was strong until the March 12, 1986 referendum, a constant source of anxiety for the PSOE leadership. A poll published by *El País* in October 1984 showed that 52 percent opposed NATO membership, and another survey appearing in the same publication in November 1985 showed that 49 percent were in favor of withdrawal from the alliance, whereas only 19 percent favored remaining in NATO.

In February 1985, González finally announced that his government would call a referendum after Spain's entry into the Common Market and would campaign in favor of NATO membership. The text of the question, kept secret until shortly before the referendum, was designed to make its defeat virtually impossible. It forced voters to give a yes or no response to a complex compromise proposal:

The government considers it appropriate for the national interest that Spain stay in the Atlantic Alliance according to the following terms:

1. Spain's participation in the Atlantic Alliance shall not include its incorporation into the military command.
2. The installation, storage or introduction of new nuclear arms in Spain will continue to be forbidden.
3. There will be a progressive reduction of U.S. military presence in Spain.

Do you think it appropriate for Spain to remain in NATO under these conditions?

Politically, the text of the referendum was a stroke of genius, despite its obviously confusing and somewhat unscrupulous wording. Parties of the right could hardly oppose a referendum question calling for continued membership in NATO, even if the conditions were distasteful. The largest conservative opposition party, the Popular Alliance, was thus forced into the awkward position of advocating abstention in the referendum, a posture that could easily be portrayed as disruptive, indecisive, and antidemocratic. Moreover, given the breadth of the question and AP's decision to call for abstention, the Socialist government had little trouble turning the referendum into a popular vote of confidence on González's leadership. The referendum had been put off until after the worst period of reindustrialization was over and after Spain had joined the European Community (EC). PSOE leaders harped on the relationship between EC entry and participation in NATO. These factors, plus the disarray of the opposition, made the gamble of winning the referendum appear worthwhile. As José Oneto observed,

[N]ow it was a matter of holding a referendum not to withdraw from the Atlantic Alliance, from the military bloc of NATO, but to determine whether the . . . extremely honest Socialist Party, after 100 years of honor and integrity, had the right or not to change its mind overnight.[73]

To make sure that the gamble paid off, the PSOE launched an effective campaign to sell its NATO policy. The campaign theme stated "Vote

Table 4.3
Results of the March 12, 1986 NATO Referendum

	VOTERS	PERCENTAGE
In favor	9,042,951	52.53
Opposed	6,859,977	39.84
Spoiled/blank	1,314,362	7.63
Total	17,217,290	100.00
Abstention rate		40.26

Source: El País, March 14, 1986, p. 13.

Yes, in the Interest of Spain." A typical electoral advertisement run by the PSOE during the campaign warned Spaniards that

> to break with the Atlantic Alliance is to obstruct our exports; to break with the Atlantic Alliance is to hinder our industrial and technological development; to break with the Atlantic Alliance is to diminish capital investments we need in order to create new industries; breaking with the Alliance would take us back to the past, to the exclusive bilateral relationship with the USA; breaking with the Alliance would . . . create problems without any advantages in return. Your "yes" vote will be a realistic and effective one, because it will consolidate a positive situation.

Despite the fact that last-minute opinion polls showed pro- and anti-NATO forces to be almost even, the text of the NATO question won an absolute majority of the vote, and yes votes outdistanced no votes by almost twelve percentage points (see Table 4.3).[74] However, the abstention rate of over 40 percent, by far the highest rate of the new democracy, appeared to reflect deep popular resentment of the PSOE's handling of the NATO issue and bitterness over the shrewd referendum text. The government position lost by huge margins in the Basque Country and in Catalonia, and the text was rejected by a narrower margin in Madrid.

The government viewed the NATO victory as a strong popular endorsement of its first term in office, and González decided to capitalize on his momentum by calling early elections for June 1986. Thus almost overnight the PSOE turned a potentially disastrous foreign policy issue into a source of strength that proved capable of assuring four more years of PSOE rule.

OTHER ISSUES: A MIXED RECORD

In the political economic and foreign policy arenas, the first years of Socialist government were characterized by a steadily more conservative set of policies. But what about some of the many other areas in which the Socialists had promised to promote change? In fact, the Socialists promised to implement an impressive panoply of reforms during their first term. The pace of legislation and reform in the first PSOE term of office was without precedent in Spanish history. While many of these reforms fell victim to the overall political economic orientation of the administration, as well as to the generally conservative approach of the Socialist government, many important changes were put into effect.

Democratization of the Armed Forces and Police

The PSOE's moderation has most often been justified as a necessary means to shore up a fragile democratic regime. Indeed, the Socialists assumed power in the aftermath of a frightening military coup attempt aimed against a UCD government.[75] Plans for a coup d'état scheduled to take place before the October 1982 elections emphasized the urgency of dealing with the military problem. The Socialist caution in government, especially in the area of foreign policy, might be explained by a desire to definitively "constitutionalize" the armed forces. The Socialists argued that modernization and reorganization of the Spanish armed forces was a prerequisite to the creation of a more democratic military. To a considerable extent, the Socialists have been remarkably successful in this area.[76]

González's new minister of defense, Narcís Serra, appeared at first an unusual choice, but in retrospect appointing him was a wise decision. Serra had never completed military service (because of flat feet) and had a history of antifranquist activism. Nevertheless, his professionalism and decisiveness, especially when compared with his UCD predecessors, soon gained him widespread support within the armed forces.

From the start the Socialists employed a mixture of suasion and force-fulness in their dealings with the military. The principle of civilian control of the military has been emphasized by PSOE governments. Several days after Serra took office, he refused to allow Alvaro Lacalle, the top official of the armed forces, to give the customary speech in honor of the Pascua Militar, a traditional holiday occurrence. Instead, Serra insisted that as head of the armed forces, he himself should give the speech.[77] In early 1983, the government asked the Supreme Court for strong sentences for the convicted *golpistas* from the February 23 attempted coup despite intense pressure from the top military brass.[78] After some of the chief conspirators received stiff sentences, González refused to consider any pardon. The Socialists successfully united the branches of the armed forces under a single command and made the entire military structure more accountable to the head of government. The government reduced the overall size of the military (especially the officer corps), scaled back the number of military regions, and implemented plans to move troop concentrations away from major civilian centers and has oriented the military more toward defense against foreign foes. Under the Socialists an ambitious rejuvenation of the top leadership has been affected, and in early 1984 the top four leaders of the military were replaced. Promotion based on merit rather than seniority has made inroads within the armed forces. Military courts, which once enjoyed wide jurisdiction in Spain, have been strictly limited. A law governing conscientious objection was approved by the government in November 1983. Legislation submitted to the legislature in March 1986 attempted a further consolidation of these reforms.[79] In 1988, the government initiated a wide-ranging reform of the military educational system, long a bulwark of authoritarian ideas.[80]

Vocal opponents of these changes have met strict discipline. However, if the Socialists were generally forceful in their dealings with the military, they were also careful not to antagonize the armed forces. Early in the Socialists' first term the government appeared unwilling to act on demands for recognition and integration into the military of two groups that had been persecuted by the franquist regime: Republican members of the armed forces (from the Second Republic) and the Democratic Military Union (UMD, a democratic group within the military). The military vocally opposed any reconciliation with these groups. In June 1983, a Socialist military amnesty bill covered the Republican soldiers but excluded UMD members. Only in 1985 did the government announce its intent to make good on its promise to allow UMD members to rejoin the armed forces, but implementation of the reform dragged on much longer and was not completed until after the 1986 general elections.

In addition to its support of NATO membership, much favored among the more democratic sector of the military, the PSOE has been careful to provide the armed forces the means with which to modernize. During a time of economic crisis, the Spanish military received steadily rising budget allocations, making the armed forces a privileged sector. The Socialists have vigorously promoted the development of a defense industry, raising criticisms regarding arms sales to such officially condemned regimes as Iran and South Africa.[81]

In its reform of the military organization the Socialists have taken great care to avoid mistakes and antagonisms that were made during the Second Republic. Upon taking office Serra chose to work with much of the existing staff at the defense ministry rather than attempt a full sweep of personnel. The reform has been gradual and was based on early retirement and incentives rather than drastic cuts. Such measures as the approval of a conscientious objection law have been tempered with many restrictions in order to appease the military hierarchy. The government actively pursued a hard line for those accused of participation in the February 1981 coup attempt but took a much softer approach with regard to those accused of participation in the October 1982 incidents. While the Socialists' largest success may have been the elimination of *golpismo* within the military, it is apparent that such a victory has had some associated costs.[82]

Given the unusual nature of Spain's police forces, police reform also became an issue affecting the armed forces. Spain's three police corps are officially under the direction of the Interior minister but remain subject to military law. The Socialist program called for demilitarization of the police, the legalization of a police trade union, and consolidation of the three forces. The police trade union was legalized and some reforms were implemented, but during 1984 and 1985, members of the three corps staged numerous demonstrations protesting the government's reluctance to act quickly on the matter.

Terrorism plagued the entire first term of the PSOE, beginning with the murder of General Victor Lago Román on November 4, 1982. However, the number of terrorist attacks appeared to have peaked during the PSOE's first term, and the Socialist government made important progress in the fight against terrorism, especially in the area of cooperation with the French government. During 1987, the government scored significant victories in the war against the Basque terrorist organization ETA. Perhaps most important, the first real negotiations between the government and ETA were initiated, although the results were initially disappointing. The PSOE's general success in the war against terrorism has raised questions about illegal police tactics, the use of torture, and the power of the intelligence apparatus. The Antiterrorist Law supported by the Socialists (although since rescinded) came in for special criticism from organizations such as Amnesty International because it severely limited the rights of the accused. Overall, perhaps the greatest success in this area is that terrorist attacks, though aimed largely against military targets, no longer appear to incite antidemocratic reactions within the armed forces, as was the case during the early years of the transition.

Perhaps the single most worrisome aspect of the PSOE's record regarding security issues was the spectacular growth of crime in Spain during the first Socialist term.[83] The causes for the rising crime rate are multiple but likely included the PSOE's penal code reform (which released thousands of criminals from Spanish jails in an effort to ease the overload of the Spanish penal and legal systems) and the growth of unemployment. The persistence of the crime and terrorism problem made the police corps more invaluable to the government precisely at a time when the government was attempting to implement controversial reforms in the security forces' organizational structure.

Health Care and Education

The Socialists took power with a strong commitment to improving the quality of health care and education. During their first term, health care expenditures fell victim to the PSOE's emphasis on cutting the budget. Thus although social security expenditures were 3.84 percent of the GDP in 1982, by 1986 they had fallen to 3.43 percent.[84] Francesc Raventós, director of Insalud (Spain's main provider of health care), resigned midway through the first Socialist term in protest over the low budgetary allocations for health care. Socialist attempts to end the practice of *pluriempleo* (multiple job holding) within the state health sector by forcing state sector doctors to actually work all hours they were paid for provoked fierce resistance from physicians. Although the Socialists have introduced a popular extension of health care coverage (which now more effectively applies to unemployed workers), a reduction of the cost of some medicines, and more individual choice of physicians within the state health care system, one expert concluded that "after four years, the essence of the health structure remains practically unchanged."[85]

No health care issue was more controversial than the legalization of abortion. The Socialists' 1982 program was officially committed to the legalization of abortion. In early 1983, as part of the reform of the penal code, the government decriminalized abortion. Massive demonstrations followed, both in favor of a more genuine legalization of abortion and against any type of legalization. In October 1983, the legislature approved the decriminalization measure by an ample margin, but in April 1985, the Supreme Court struck down part of the law. When a revised law was finally approved, abortion was legal only when the pregnancy was a result of rape, the mother carried a deformed fetus, or the pregnancy posed a significant health threat to the mother. According to one account, only about 20 percent of all abortions in Spain fall into one of these three categories.[86] In the first four years of Socialist government, only a tiny fraction of abortions were performed legally.

The Socialists' plans for educational reforms were equally controversial and, ironically, provoked the first massive mobilization against the PSOE government. In June 1983, the government proposed a set of measures designed to regulate the relationship between private (mostly Catholic) schools and the state. The Socialist plan did not end state subsidies to private schools, as was favored by some sectors of the PSOE, but it did attempt to standardize the curriculum for all schools receiving state financing. Even this moderate measure provoked a huge reaction from the right (mainly the Popular Alliance) and the Church. In December 1983, a wave of demonstrations against the reform swept Madrid, but the measure passed in the legislature. Surprisingly large demonstrations continued throughout 1984.

Socialist Education Minister José María Maravall embarked on an ambitious overhaul of the Spanish public educational structure that attempted to modernize and democratize the schools and universities. Despite these efforts, a major student upheaval in early 1987 shocked the nation and was aimed primarily at the low level of state educational funding (especially scholarships).

Judicial and Administrative Reform

Upon taking power, the PSOE viewed as its principal task the completion of democratization, and the Socialists had ambitious plans for an overhaul of Spain's inefficient and conservative judiciary. The judicial reform immediately became politicized and was in general stubbornly resisted by the right and by judges. Legislation regulating the judiciary was approved by parliament in early 1984, implementing habeas corpus, reducing the age of retirement for judges (from seventy-two to sixty-five), allowing judges to be appointed from outside Spain's tightly regulated legal corps, and giving the legislature more direct control over the judiciary. These reforms drew heated protest, as the PSOE was accused of politicizing the judiciary and was viewed as compromising its independence. Once again, the PSOE's resolve to pursue a tight budgetary policy has limited possible solutions to the tremendous backlog and incredible inefficiency that plagues the legal system. An editorial in *Diário 16* complained that "the government has been more interested in extending its tentacles into the judiciary than with correcting its grave defects."[87] The public outcry over the backlog of cases in the Spanish court system finally convinced the government to raise the Justice Ministry budget by 28 percent for 1988.

The government's effort to reform Spain's lackluster public administration was somewhat more successful. Immediately after taking power, the PSOE made the almost revolutionary announcement that all ministries and public offices would have to be open during the afternoooon, and threatened to punish all workers who arrived late for their jobs. The government announced an overall administrative consolidation and pledged to end the rampant *pluriempleo* in the public sector: in January 1985, a law prohibiting multiple job holding went into effect and was expected to create 2,000 additional jobs in the public administration.

Despite these notable successes, one specialist concluded that "consumers of bureaucracy, the citizens, have hardly noted any improvement in the administration, except on rare occasions."[88] An equally pervasive criticism has been that the reform of the Spanish state has provided the Spanish Socialists an opportunity to pack the administration with PSOE supporters. During 1988, major questions were raised regarding the *pluriempleo* of some top PSOE officials, and more serious charges of influence-peddling were brought against top Socialist ex-officials, including ex-minister Miguel Boyer.

The Regional Record

Failures by the UCD to efficiently meet the growing demands of Spain's regions were an important cause for its calamitous defeat in the 1982 elections. The new government oversaw the completion of the regionalization process, begun by the UCD. During the Socialists' first term the complex web of regional, provincial, and national institutions that resulted from Spain's transition to democracy proved beyond reform. During the transition the PSOE had abandoned its traditional centralism and had eagerly supported regional devolution. As Shabad has noted, it successfully used the regional issue to enhance its image among voters on the periphery and to launch a final assault on the moribund UCD.[89]

After the attempted coup of February 1981, the PSOE began to back off from its support of further devolution of power to the regions. In 1982, together with UCD, it introduced the Organic Law for the Harmonization of the Autonomy Process (LOAPA), designed to curtail and rationalize the devolution process. The LOAPA evoked fierce opposition from regional politicians and set the stage for future conflicts between the regions and the Socialist government.

Much of the LOAPA was declared unconstitutional in August 1983, frustrating the PSOE's desire to gain control over the unwieldy proliferation of bureaucracies and budgets. Attempts by the Socialist government to reign in rapidly skyrocketing regional budgets that were the result of newly assertive regional governments inevitably created tensions between the center and the periphery.[90] Ironically, these problems were present even where the PSOE controlled regional government, as demonstrated by the case of Andalusia, where a bitter struggle broke out between the central government and Andalusian President Rafael Escuredo in early 1984.

The Socialist reversal on NATO also appears to have exacerbated the regional cleavage. Given that the PSOE did not control the regional legislatures of the Basque Country or Catalonia, it is hardly surprising that relations between center and periphery were often acrimonious. The central government's decision to prosecute Catalan President Jordi Pujol in relation to a bank scandal and tensions regarding the creation of a Basque police force were examples of center-periphery conflict. Ironically, however, the PSOE's decision to remain in NATO (supported by both non-Socialist regional governments) may have most effectively crystallized opposition to the central government. In the NATO referendum Catalan voters registered the most opposition to the government of any region; in Basque voters handily rejected the governmental measure.

At the Thirty-first Congress the PSOE officially accepted the position of the Catalan branch of the party, advocating a federal system for Spain, as a means of resolving the ambiguous and overlapping arrangements currently in place. It is unlikely, however, that this novel position will revitalize the PSOE's image in the most important autonomous communities.

CONCLUSION

In the two issue areas highlighted earlier in this chapter—political economic and foreign policy—the PSOE almost completely abandoned its program of 1982. In a host of other areas, a few of which were briefly discussed earlier, the PSOE's record reveals far more success. Even in these areas the Socialist attempt to restructure, reorient, and democratize elements of Spanish society were ultimately limited by the conservative budgetary policies that resulted from its overall political economic orientation. In two areas—regional and defense expenditures—the government was politically unable or unwilling to impose austerity, but elsewhere (health care, the legal system, education, social security) the budget axe was the dominant constraint.

NOTES

1. Alfonso Guerra, et al., *El futuro del socialismo* (Madrid: Editorial Sistema, 1986), p. 15.
2. The public reaction to the PSOE victory is described in Sergio Vilar, *La década sorprendente, 1976–1986* (Barcelona: Planeta, 1986), p. 135.
3. On the vision of the founders of UCD, see Eduardo Chamorro, *Viaje el centro de UCD* (Barcelona: Planeta, 1981).
4. An excellent analysis of the demise of UCD is in Richard Gunther, "Democratization and Party Building: Contradictions and Conflicts Facing Party Elites in the Spanish Transition to Democracy," presented at the 1985 Annual Meeting of the American Political Science Association, New Orleans, La.: August 29–September 1.
5. This average was greatly inflated by Fernando Morán, who at age 56 was the senior citizen of the PSOE government. The ministers in their thirties were Almunia (Labor and Social Security, 34), Barón (Transportation, Tourism, and

Communication, 38), de la Cuadra (Territorial Administration, 36), Serra (Defense, 39) and Solchaga (Industry and Energy, 38).

6. For example, see Elizabeth Nash, "The Socialist Party since Franco," p. 31.

7. See the Preamble of the *1982/1986 PSOE Manifiesto Electoral* (Madrid: PSOE, 1982).

8. Ibid., preamble.

9. Ibid., section I, part 1.

10. Ibid., section II, part 3.4.

11. Ibid, section I, part 1.

12. Ibid, section II, part 1.2.

13. Ibid., section II, part 3.3.

14. Ibid., section II, part 1.1.

15. Ibid., section V, part 4.5.

16. Ibid., section V, introduction.

17. Felipe González, *España y su futuro* (Madrid: Cuadernos Para el Diálogo, 1978), p. 53.

18. Partido Socialista Obrero Español, *El Gobierno ante la crisis económica: Explicación de la política económica e industrial de los Socialistas* (Madrid: PSOE, 1984), p. 2.

19. Quoted in *Cambío 16* (February 3, 1986), p. 7.

20. An overview of the political economy of the transition is in Pedro Schwartz, "Politics First—The Economy after Franco," *Government and Opposition* 1 (Winter 1986): 84–103.

21. José María Carrascal, *La revolución del PSOE* (Barcelona: Plaza & Janes, 1985), p. 138.

22. For an overview of Spanish economic development, see José A. Moral Santín, et al., "La formación del capitalismo industrial en España (1855–1959)," in R. Caballo, et al., *Crecimiento económico y crisis estructural en España* (Madrid: Akal, 1981).

23. The best treatment of Spanish interest group history is in Juan J. Linz, "A Century of Politics and Interests in Spain," in S. Berger, ed., *Organizing Interests in Western Europe* (New York: Cambridge University Press, 1981), pp. 367–415.

24. Victor Pérez Díaz, "Políticas económicas y pautas sociales en la España de la transición: La doble cara del neocorporatismo," in Juan J. Linz, ed., *España: Un presente para el futuro*, vol. I (Madrid: Instituto de Estudios Económicos, 1984), pp. 32–33.

25. It should be noted that trade unions and political parties were still unsure of their real strength in society. The UGT, for example, was only one of two major socialist confederations, and it needed time to consolidate its organizational strength. Low levels of mass mobilization and the weakness of interest groups appear to constitute a condition for successful transitions through transaction. For an overview of this argument, see Donald Share and Scott Mainwaring, "Transitions through Transaction: Democratization in Brazil and Spain," in Wayne A. Selcher, ed., *Political Liberalization in Brazil* (Boulder, Colo.: Westview Press, 1986), pp. 175–215.

26. For an overview of the pacts, including their content and time framework, see *Anvário El País, 1984* (Madrid: El País, 1984), p. 381.

27. For a critical analysis of the Moncloa Pacts, see Curro Ferraro, *Economía y explotación en la democracia Española* (Bilbao: ZYX, 1978).

28. See Pérez Díaz, "Políticas económicas," p. 43, for data in support of this statement.

29. Julio Alcaide Inchausti, "La distribución de la renta en España," in J. Linz, ed., *España*, p. 129.

30. Mariano Guindal and Rodolfo Serrano, *La otra transición: Nicolás Redondo y el sindicalismo Español* (Madrid: Unión Editorial, 1986), p. 128.

31. Julio Segura, "La estrategia socialista de política económica," *El País* (May 30, 1986), p. 59.

32. Julio Alcaide Inchausti, "Balance económico de cuatro años de gobierno Socialista," *Cuenta y Razón* 25 (1986): 62.

33. Carrascal, *La revolución del PSOE*, p. 36.

34. Vilar, *La década sorprendente*, p. 138.

35. See R. Serrano and R. Cullell, "La reconversión de nunca acabar," *El País* (June 12, 1986), p. 18.

36. González and Guerra met with Ferrer Salat and Cuevas, who represented the entrepreneurial organizations, on November 6 1982, to assure the business elite of this plan.

37. Carrascal, *La revolución del PSOE*, p. 45.

38. Vilar, *La década sorprendente*, p. 121.

39. Gustavo Matías, "La mayoría de los españoles ha perdido capacidad adquisitiva," *El País* (June 12, 1986), pp. 18–19.

40. See *El País*, International Edition (January 18, 1988), p. 28. The actual rate of unemployment was probably closer to two million. Of this figure, 30 percent consisted of first-time job seekers. The official figure was somewhat inflated because of the large underground economy in Spain. See *Cambio 16* (May 26, 1986), p. 14.

41. Ibid., pp. 18–19.

42. The data are published in *Cambio 16* (February 2, 1988), p. 45. Part of the reason for the drop in coverage was the increase in the use of part-time workers, who do not receive coverage when laid off.

43. Matías, "La mayoría, pp. 18–19.

44. For a critique of PSOE tax policy, see César Albiñana, "Cuatro años de impuestos Socialistas," *Cambio 16* (June 6, 1986), p. 30. In all fairness, the PSOE also launched a major attack on tax fraud, raising penalties and passing laws to "make taxpayers tremble." A study by the Instituto de Estudios Fiscales concluded that professionals and entrepreneurs hide an average of 70 percent of their income.

45. Matías, "La mayoría," pp. 18–19. More data on income inequality can be found in *El País* (May 17, 1987), p. 12.

46. *El País* International Edition (October 13, 1986), p. 16.

47. Alcaide Inchausti, "Balance económico," p. 62.

48. *Anuário El País* (Madrid: El País, 1988), p. 349.

49. See Segura, "La estrategia," p. 59, for a presentation of some of these questions.

50. Ibid., p. 59.

51. Ibid., p. 60 (May 31, 1986, continuation).

52. A good example of this criticism from the right was a televised interview with Adolfo Suárez on May 22, 1986, on TVE1. The ex-president claimed that the PSOE had ignored the redistributive aspects of its program, while big business enjoyed its largest profits ever.

53. As reported in *Cambio 16* (April 13, 1987), pp. 60 ff.

54. The events are reported in *El País* International Edition (February 22, 1987), p. 29.

55. Quoted in *El País* International Edition (May 2, 1988), p. 1.

56. Quoted in Antxon Sarasqueta, *Después de Franco, la OTAN* (Barcelona: Plaza & Janes, 1985), p. 98.

57. Quoted in *Cambio 16* (February 17, 1986), p. 19.

58. See Eusebio M. Mujal-León, "Foreign Policy of the Socialist Government," in Stanley G. Payne, ed., *The Politics of Democratic Spain* (Chicago Council on Foreign Relations, 1986), pp. 197–245.

59. *El País* editorial (June 11, 1986), p. 12.

60. The change in Socialist Latin American policy culminated with González's controversial decision not to attend the inauguration of Alain García in Peru. Instead, he took a cruise on Franco's yacht, the *Azor*, creating a storm of protest.

61. The vote was 186 in favor, 146 against. Six members of the mixed parliamentary group voted with the opposition.

62. Later a parody of the slogan became, "de Entrada No, de Salida Tampoco!" (No entry, but no exit either!).

63. Mujal-León, "Foreign Policy," p. 216, describes the PSOE foreign policy at the time, "unabashedly neutralist."

64. See *Resoluciones, 29 Congreso PSOE* (Madrid: PSOE, 1981), p. 34.

65. José Oneto, *El secuestro del cambio* (Barcelona: Plaza & Janes, 1984), p. 159.

66. Mujal-León, "Foreign Policy," pp. 217–218.

67. Mujal-León, "Foreign Policy," p. 219, argues that González had "probably discarded this option [calling for a referendum immediately after the election] before coming to power."

68. Oneto, *El secuestro*, p. 160.

69. Vilar, *La década sorprendente*, p. 170.

70. Ibid.

71. Quoted in *El País* (July 27, 1984).

72. See the discussion of internal party opposition below for more on the Thirtieth Party Congress.

73. Oneto, *El secuestro*, p. 159.

74. For an overview of the NATO referendum, see Anthony Gooch, "A Surrealistic Referendum: Spain and NATO," *Government and Opposition* 3 (1986): 300–315.

75. A good description of these events is in Paul Preston, "Fear of Freedom: The Spanish Army after Franco," in C. Abel and N. Torrents, eds., *Spain: Conditional Democracy* (New York: St. Martin's Press, 1984), pp. 161–185.

76. For an overview, see Stanley G. Payne, "The Role of the Armed Forces in the Spanish Transition," in Robert P. Clark and Michael H. Haltzel, eds., *Spain in the 1980s* (Cambridge, Mass.: Ballinger, 1987), pp. 79–95; and Payne, "Modernization of the Armed Forces," in *The Politics of Democratic Spain* (Chicago: Chicago Council on Foreign Relations, 1987), pp. 181–196.

77. Oneto, *El secuestro*, p. 41

78. Oneto claims that Serrá threatened to fire any member of the armed forces who publicly pressed for lighter sentences. See his *El secuestro*, p. 43.

79. A good overview of the PSOE's military record is found in *Cambio 16* (March 3, 1986), and *El País* (March 4, 1986).

80. *El Globo* (May 16, 1988), p. 26.

81. On the PSOE's defense industry policy, see Carlos Yarnoz, "Potenciación de la industria militar Española," in *Anuário El País, 1984* (Madrid: El País, 1984), p. 133.

82. For a critical look at the PSOE's military record, see Fernando Reinlein, "Un precio demasiado alto," *Diário 16* (May 23, 1986), p. 13. For a more positive view, see Jesús M. de Miguel, "El balance sanitorio Español," in *Anuário El País, 1988* (Madrid: El País, 1988), pp. 173–174.

83. For data on the rising crime rate, see J. L. Guardia, "La inseguridad ciudadana ha sido un de los cánceres que más minaron al gobierno," *Diário 16* (June 6, 1986), p. 16.

84. Cited in Milagros Pérez Oliva, "El 'cambio' apenas ha tocado la estructura sanitaria," *El País* (June 10, 1986), p. 18.

85. Pérez Oliva, "El 'cambio,' " p. 18.

86. See Christina Almeida, "La despenalización del aborto, un tímido intento," in *Anuário El País, 1984* (Madrid: El País, 1985), p. 151.

87. *Diário 16* editorial (June 1, 1986), p. 2.

88. See Carlos Gómez, "La reforma de la administración se limitó a cambios superficiales," *El País* (June 6, 1986), p. 18.

89. See Goldie Shabad, "After Autonomy: The Dynamics of Regionalism in Spain," in Payne, *The Politics of Democratic Spain*, p. 120.

90. By 1984, 130,000 million pesetas of debt had been accumulated by sixteen regional governments, seriously threatening the PSOE's desire to cut budget expenditures. In May 1984, the government reluctantly approved a special credit to cover some of the deficit. See Vilar, *La década sorprendente*, pp. 154–156.

5

From Social Democracy to Neoliberalism: Explaining the Socialists' Behavior in Government

PARTY HISTORY AS A PARTIAL EXPLANATION: A RECAPITULATION

Any attempt to explain the PSOE's moderate behavior in government must take into account the dramatic evolution of the party's ideology between 1977 and 1982 that was the focus of the preceding chapter. The process of social democratization had been largely completed before the Socialist government took power, although once in office the PSOE leadership acted far more moderately than called for by the party platform. Moreover, the same logic that propelled the PSOE toward a more social democratic posture while in opposition continued to influence the Socialist government, although its direct importance may have diminished. The evolution of the PSOE's ideology between 1977 and 1982 was outlined in chapter 3, but the main ingredients of this evolution can be summarized as follows.

In the early 1970s, the PSOE was rebuilt under the direction of a young, less conservative PSOE leadership based inside Spain rather than in exile. The Socialists had been virtually extinguished during franquism, but the accession of a young generation of militants to the leadership marked the start of the party's rebirth. The young and inexperienced leaders waged a semiclandestine struggle inside Spain to rejuvenate the Socialist left, and they emerged from authoritarian rule armed with a combative, pseudo-revolutionary ideology and rhetoric. Under González the "new" PSOE used its radicalism to rebuild the party, to mobilize its supporters, and to help consolidate the Sevillano leadership. As a party dominated by youth, it espoused a form of crude Marxist ideology and rejected any type of democratization negotiated with the authoritarian leadership. However, the radical zeal so successful in party building contradicted the harsh realities of Spain after Franco's death and obstructed the party's ability to participate in the building of a democratic regime.

The franquist regime succeeded its founder without any collapse or power vacuum. While the franquist families struggled for power, the regime maintained order and proved capable of sustaining itself against all threats. Adolfo Suárez, appointed in 1976, implemented a transition through transaction that presented the Socialists with a painful dilemma: they could either accept democratic change initiated by the franquist political class or oppose such a process by refusing to collaborate. The former decision was tantamount to admitting the organizational and ideological inferiority of the Socialist opposition, and it involved democratization without any control over or formal participation in the process. The latter option ran the risk of contributing to an authoritarian involution—or worse, promised to relegate the PSOE to the position of testimonial opponent to a new democratic regime.

The Socialists chose to collaborate with Suárez's strategy for several reasons. First and foremost, most party leaders valued a return to democracy despite objections to the way in which democracy was restored. Second, the organizational weakness of the Socialist Party made any failure to collaborate an overly risky prospect. Third, the ideological hard line adopted by the inexperienced PSOE leadership, which might have prevented such collaboration, was only skin deep; it had been developed during the turbulent 1960s and during a period of clandestine struggle, but it was patently out of place among the realities of Spain in the 1970s. Moreover, the radicalism of the party was increasingly out of sync with the values and priorities of most of the PSOE's prospective voters.

As the PSOE entered the electoral arena in the democratic regime, these incongruities became more evident and costly. The Socialist support of transition through transaction, and the concomitant acceptance of the monarchy and other limits imposed during the transition process, hardly fit with the party's revolutionary and combative ideology or its leaders' rhetoric at electoral rallies. The radical party programs in effect from 1977 to 1979 appeared to contradict the PSOE's concern for the consolidation of democracy and worked against the party's increasingly moderate electoral strategy. These contradictions were exploited by the UCD during the 1979 electoral campaign, and the PSOE leadership viewed them as a chief cause for the party's failure to win power. On the one hand, the PSOE's impressive performance in both elections gave the Socialist leadership a greater stake in the new democratic system. On the other hand, the remnants of the party's earlier radicalism haunted the PSOE's public image and sabotaged its electoral prospects.

The decision to abandon socialist ideology and rhetoric and replace it with a more social democratic program and image was made by the party leadership after the 1979 general elections. The showdown between the advocates of this decision (González and his supporters) and the party left (the so-called *críticos*, or critical left) occurred at the Twenty-eighth PSOE Congress in May 1979. After a serious internal party crisis, the leadership proposed the elimination of the Marxist definition of the party, and it introduced organizational reforms to solidify a more moderate majority within the party and to prevent factionalism. The 1982 electoral program, while retaining much socialist flavor, represented a dramatic ideological shift to the right. In addition, Felipe González and his supporters had gained firm control of the party apparatus and used this new position of strength to marginalize the party left.

Between 1979 and 1982, party leaders often explained this ideological evolution as an attempt by the PSOE to consolidate Spain's new democracy. The ongoing terrorist violence, the deteriorating economy, and, most important, the failed *golpe de estado* (coup d'etat) of February 1981 made this a credible justification. Socialist leaders *were* genuinely more concerned with preserving democracy than with adhering to socialist doctrine. However, the party's continuing ideological moderation after its victory in 1982 is more difficult to explain simply in terms of a desire to consolidate democratic rule. Terrorism, economic crisis, and military unrest all continued after 1982, but these factors no longer appeared as a direct threat to the democratic regime. Although the PSOE's record in office helped to consolidate the democratic regime against a variety of threats, there are other equally compelling explanations of the party's moderation, which will be explored in the following sections. These explanations focus less on the Socialists' desire to protect the democratic regime and place more emphasis on the PSOE's position within the party system, on its sources of societal support, and on its internal politics. Taken together, they portray the PSOE in terms very familiar to students of democratic politics: as a party seeking to maximize its political power vis-à-vis other parties and guided by a party leadership eager to consolidate its internal control.

THE SPANISH PARTY SYSTEM

After the 1982 general elections, the constellation of political forces in the party system strongly favored the social democratization of the PSOE. As shown in Table 5.1, the 1982 elections were unusual because of the virtual elimination of the center-right and the communist left. The first democratic elections in 1977 placed the PSOE in a strong but difficult position. The party won 29.3 percent of the vote and 33.7 percent of the seats, but it was faced with a strong Communist Party to its left and the largest vote-getter, the UCD, to its right. The situation was made even more difficult by the fact that the PCE was perhaps the

Table 5.1
Results of Spanish General Elections, 1977, 1979, 1982, and 1986

	PCE/ PSUC	PSOE	UCD	AP/ CD/CP	OTHER	TOTAL
JUNE 1977*						
% Valid votes	9.4	29.3	34.4	8.3	18.6	100.0
Seats (deputies)	20	118	165	16	31	350
MARCH 1979**						
% Valid votes	10.8	30.5	35.0	6.0	17.7	100.0
Seats (deputies)	23	121	168	9	29	350
OCTOBER 1982***						
% Valid votes	4.1	48.4	6.7	26.5	14.3	100.0
Seats (deputies)	4	202	11	106	27	350
JUNE 1986****	(IU)		(CDS)			
% Valid votes	4.6	44.0	9.3	26.2	15.9	100.0
Seats (deputies)	7	184	19	105	35	350

*1977 Elections:	"Other" category includes socialist PSP/US, regional parties, and all other parties not winning seats (in vote column)
**1979 Elections:	"Other" category includes regional parties, the rightist UN, and all other parties not winning seats (in vote column)
***1982 Elections:	"Other" category includes regional parties, Suarez's CDS, and all other parties not winning seat (in vote column)
****1986 Elections:	"Other" category includes centrist PRD, the Carrillo's Unidad Comunista, regional parties, and all other parties not winning seats (in vote column)

Source: 1977–1982 elections: Howard R. Penniman and Eusebio M. Mujal-León, eds., *Spain at the Polls, 1977, 1979, and 1982* (Washington, D.C.: American Enterprise Institute, 1985), pp. 319–334. 1986 elections: *El País* International Edition, June 23, 1986, p. I.

most moderate communist party in Western Europe. Its behavior in the first years of Spain's democracy often placed it to the right of the PSOE on a number of issues. This phenomenon tended to make the PSOE appear more radical in the eyes of the electorate than might otherwise have been the case, and it obliged the Socialists to face stiff competition from the PCE for votes of the center-left.

The 1979 elections reconfirmed this troublesome scenario. The UCD under Suárez recaptured a plurality of votes, and the PCE increased its percentage of the vote. In office, Suárez and the UCD social democrats gave the governing coalition a centrist and occassionally center-left hue. More than ever, the UCD clearly distinguished itself from the forces to its right with its fiscal and social policies. At the same time, it successfully portrayed the Socialists as a revolutionary party, and as a party occupying the left of the party system rather than the center-left.

Between 1979 and 1982, both the UCD and the PCE virtually self-destructed in what must have appeared as a godsend to PSOE leaders. The heterogeneous personal and ideological forces comprising the UCD coalition initiated an increasingly overt struggle for control of the government and coalition leadership. Suárez's inability to impose discipline and order in the coalition forced him to resign as party leader and head of government. He was replaced by Leopoldo Calvo Sotelo, a drab politician with closer ties to UCD Christian democrats and liberals, but Calvo Sotelo had even less success managing the unruly governing party. Ultimately, the intramural squabbling led the Christian democratic and social democratic sectors to abandon the coalition, and the electorate increasingly viewed the government as too weak and too involved in petty infighting to deal with a number of impending crises.

In the 1982 elections, the UCD received one of the worst electoral drubbings of any governing party in history. It declined from 168 to 12 seats, and from almost 35 percent of the vote to just over 7 percent. The governing coalition failed to carry a single province, and only two of the cabinet members were able to win reelection. The UCD not only lost the right to govern, it ceded the leadership of the opposition to the conservative Popular Alliance, which had obtained only 9 seats in the previous parliament. In early 1983, after only five years of existence as a party, the UCD formally disbanded.

In the wake of the UCD's disappearance there remained a number of centrist politicians with plans to fill the void. Adolfo Suárez, who had abandoned UCD in protest over its rightward drift under Calvo Sotelo, formed the Democratic and Social Center (CDS) in July 1982, shortly before the genereal elections. His party polled only 2.8 percent of the votes and won only two seats in the legislature. UCD social democrats, led by Francisco Fernández Ordóñez, had formed the Democratic Action Party (PAD) in November 1981 but ultimately decided to run some candidates on PSOE lists in the 1982 elections. In early 1983, the PAD dissolved and formally joined the PSOE, thus eliminating another possible occupant of the political center. Finally, the Liberal Democratic Party (PDL) of Antonio Garrigues tried to assemble the remains of UCD together for the 1982 elections but was unsuccessful.

The absence of any viable centrist alternative characterized the entire four-year term of the first Socialist government. Suárez's CDS, with only two seats, could hardly claim to occupy center ground, and even less given the reclusive behavior of the ex-president. As the 1986 elections approached, a new attempt to reconstruct the center took place under the prominent Catalan centrist Miguel Roca. As one of seven "fathers" of the Spanish Constitution, and as a leader of the governing Catalan party, Convergence and Union (CiU), Roca appeared to have impeccable credentials for the task. However, Roca's Democratic Reform Party (PRD) suffered from the start from a lack of clear identity. The Socialists had firmly occupied center ground in the party system during their first term in office, inhibiting the rebuilding of a centrist party. This factor, together with Roca's inability to transcend his image as a regional politician, doomed the project from the start, and the PRD received no seats in the 1986 election.

In light of the PRD disaster, the recent political comeback of Suárez and his CDS may appear paradoxical. At the time of this writing, data on the 1986 election were insufficient to allow any definitive analysis of the CDS performance. Nevertheless, it seems safe to hazard a guess that the CDS's 9.31 percent of the vote and its nineteen seats were a result least in part of a protest vote *against* the Socialists' centrist drift. This analysis seems at least plausible given the CDS's image as a populist party and Suárez's consistent attacks on the PSOE for having abandoned its commitment to equality. Suárez's reputation as a politician who fulfilled his promises during the transition, his charisma, and his ability to exploit the role of political underdog made his party the likely respository of antigovernment protest votes from all but the most leftist of ex-PSOE supporters.

Even so, with nineteen seats in parliament, the CDS hardly constitutes a serious centrist challenge to the PSOE. The CDS increased its percentage of the vote to almost 10 percent in the 1987 municipal/European parliament elections, but despite the meteoric comeback of Suárez, some real obstacles to his return to power remain. Suárez will be embraced by conservative sectors in Spain only with great reluctance. His unpredictable behavior while president (in both domestic and foreign affairs) and his turbulent relationship with the armed forces and financial elite make him far less appealing than González in the eyes of the Spanish right. The bulk of votes in the Spanish electorate are anchored on the center-left of the ideological spectrum, where the PSOE has become well anchored. Suárez's attempt to create a separate identity for his party has been and will continue to be wrought with contradictions. Suárez's "populist-socialist" attacks on the PSOE's record in government do not mesh with his recent attempts to identify with West European liberal parties. As of late 1987, opinion polls gave the CDS the support of only 8.1 percent, compared with 27 percent for the PSOE.[1]

The disintegration of the communist left was equally important for the PSOE's move rightward. In the early years of Spanish democracy, the PCE had established a reputation as a competent, democratic party.[2] Its consensual behavior during the transition and its willingness to accept the monarchy and sign the Moncloa Pacts was rewarded with about 11 percent of the vote in 1979. The party enhanced its reputation when, after April 1979, it entered into a pact with the PSOE allowing for the formation of municipal-level governments of the left. Many prominent intellectuals and artists were members of the PCE, and party leader Santiago Carrillo was considered a chief spokesperson of modern Eurocommunism.

However, as has occurred with other European communist parties, the PCE's desire to embrace Eurocommunism conflicted with the more traditionally hierarchical and centralized party structure.[3] Santiago Carrillo appeared especially unwilling to tolerate the internal democratization of his party advocated by a younger generation of party activists. In late 1981, a group of such advocates, which included a number of well-respected intellectuals and a number of Madrid city council members, was expelled from the party for insubordination. A subsequent wave of protests by party militants was followed with more expulsions, and after a year of internal struggle the party had succeeded in damaging the modicum of respectability it had established during the transition.

The exodus from the PCE of many influential intellectuals and the continual reports of intrigue and counterintrigue were directly responsible for the PCE's alienation of its usually reliable electorate. The decline of the PCE parliamentary bloc from twenty-three to four seats and its loss of votes, from 10.8 percent in 1979 to only 3.8 percent three years later, led to the long overdue resignation of Carrillo from the party leadership. His replacement with Gerardo Iglesias did little to stem the party's decline. The infighting continued, this time between the party left and the Eurocommunist leadership. In October 1984, the leftist wing of the party, led by Ignacio Gallego, split off to form the rival Communist Party of the Spanish Peoples (PCPE). Carrillo, who remained on the PCE Executive Committee and Central Committee, continued to attack his successor for failing to confront the PSOE government's policy shifts. Carrillo was finally expelled from the party in May 1985, along with eighteen of his supporters, but the PCE's public image was irreparably damaged. If this continued disunity were not sufficient to seal the Communists' electoral fate, their division vis-à-vis the 1986 elections seemed designed to do so. The PCE of Iglesias formed a coalition, United Left (IU), with a bizarre array of political *grupúsculos*, (tiny groups) including the Humanist Party and the Carlist Party. Carrillo refused to accept this alliance and formed his own coalition under the rather audacious name of Unidad Comunista (Communist Unity). Given the disarray of the communist left, the performance of IU in the 1986 election was surprisingly strong. The PCE-dominated coalition won 4.61 percent of the vote and seven seats in the lower house, constituting an improvement over the 1982 debacle. In the municipal/European parliament elections of 1987, the IU again improved its percentage of the vote to almost 7 percent. But the Communists are still far from digging out of the hole they had dug for themselves, and the PCE cannot claim to represent a serious threat to PSOE. Like the CDS, the IU will continue to be hurt by an electoral law that favors the larger and regionally concentrated parties. Internal political squabbles continue to debilitate the communist left, and a recent leadership change portends an immediate future of continuing turmoil.

The PSOE has been an important beneficiary of the disintegration of the parties to its left and its right. According to a study conducted by the Centro de Investigaciones Sociológicas, in 1982 the Socialists picked up 48 percent of those voting PCE in 1979.[4] Although the PSOE's moderation might have caused a loss of votes to its left, the disarray of the PCE apparently prevented such an outcome: only 2 percent of those voting PSOE in 1979 moved left to the PCE in 1982. About a third of UCD voters in 1979 voted for the PSOE in 1982, abandoning the moribund centrist coalition and opting instead for a rapidly moderating Socialist Party.

After the 1982 elections, the only credible parliamentary opposition to the Socialist government was the conservative Popular Alliance. However, AP was handicapped by a number of factors. First, it was widely perceived as a "franquist" party, located too far right in the party system for a majority of the Spanish electorate (see Tables 5.2, 5.3, and 5.4 for data on this point). The destruction of the UCD, the entry of conservative UCD sectors into AP, and the remarkable AP electoral performance in 1982 (106 seats and 25.3 percent of the vote) all helped the rightist coalition to assume a more centrist image, but it could not completely overcome its franquist legacy. AP leader Manuel Fraga had an authoritarian reputation, and his prominent role as cabinet minister during the franquist regime reminded many Spaniards of the past. Although Fraga's charisma and energy were the unifying force of AP, his impetuous behavior at times damaged its image.

Second, the right suffered from internal disunity. The Popular Alliance was the first party to be formed during the transition, but it had run with a different set of parties and under a different name in each election. The influx of Oscar Alzaga's UCD Christian democrats (PDP) after the demise of UCD only intensified the personal and ideological conflicts within the coalition, which now calls itself the Popular Coalition (CP). Since the 1982 elections the right has suffered from an internal struggle between those who want to modernize its image and rejuvenate its leadership and those who continue to view Fraga as the coalition's chief asset. Shortly after the June 1986 elections, Fraga's coalition part-

Table 5.2
Spanish Public's View of Pragmatism versus Idealism in Politics
(percentages)

"With which of the following statements do you feel most in agreement?"

	ALL RESPONDENTS	PROSPECTIVE PSOE VOTERS
"PRAGMATIC"		
In politics it is better to try to make the best of every situation than to defend one's own principles.	12	12
In politics it is best to reach agreements and practical compromises even if principles are sacrificed.	51	53
"IDEALISTIC"		
In politics, you must always be true to your own ideals, regardless of other considerations.	27	27
Didn't know	9	7
No response	1	1
Total	100	100

Source: Data supplied by the Centro de Investigaciones Sociológicas, published in *Revista Española de Investigaciones Sociológicas* 28 (October–December 1984): 328.

ners announced their plan to leave CP and to form separate parliamentary groups.[5]

Third, the social democratization of the PSOE was so profound between 1982 and 1986 that the right was hard pressed to find fault with the Socialist government.[6] Although it attacked the huge increase in unemployment and the PSOE's handling of the NATO issue, the right essentially agreed with PSOE policy in both areas. CP could distinguish itself only on traditional issues of the Spanish right, such as abortion, private education, and the increase in public "disorder," but its ability to harp on these issues was limited: they countered the coalition's attempt to appeal to centrist voters. Recent attempts by the Popular Alliance to raise charges of influence-peddling against the government have failed to improve the right's image.

Table 5.3
Spanish Public's View of Pragmatism-Idealism of Parties (percentages)

"Would you say that each of the following parties tries to impose its principles and ideals above all other considerations, tries to make the most out of all situations without worrying too much about principles, or tries to reach agreements and practical compromises even if it has to give up its ideals?"

	ALL RESPONDENTS					PROSPECTIVE PSOE VOTERS		
	AP	CiU	PCE	PNV	PSOE	AP	PSOE	PCE
PRAGMATIC								
Tries to make the most of all situations without worrying too much about principles	22	15	21	15	19	24	13	21
Tries to reach agreement and practical compromises even if it has to give up its ideals	16	14	19	10	40	9	59	22
IDEALISTIC								
Tries to impose its principles and ideals over any other consideration	40	11	28	18	19	49	13	29
Didn't know or no response	22	60	32	57	22	18	15	28
Total	100	100	100	100	100	100	100	100

Source: Data supplied by the Centro de Investigaciones Sociológicas, published in *Revista Española de Investigaciones Sociológicas* 28 (October–December 1984): 329.

The failure of CP to improve its performance in 1986 (it lost one seat) and the coalition's subsequent unravelling suggest that these obstacles may be more serious than Fraga imagined. The Popular Alliance will continue to exercise its role as the opposition leader, but it will now have to contend with Adolfo Suárez's resurgent centrists. The presence of a centrist group in parliament, together with the exit of the most centrist sectors from the coalition, may help sustain AP's image as a rightist rather than a center-right party.

The replacement of Fraga as party leader promises both to facilitate and to complicate the AP's future. The stepping down of Fraga, the last Spanish party leader with a thoroughly authoritarian image, paves the

Table 5.4
Spanish Public's View of Class Support for Political Parties (percentages)

"I will read you a list of the major parties represented in parliament. Could you tell me if in your view people who vote for the party tend to be upper class, middle class, working class, or from all classes?"

CLASS	PNV	PSOE	PCE	AP/PDP	CDS	CiU
Upper	8	1	1	62	20	11
Middle	22	14	4	14	46	26
Working	7	53	75	1	2	3
All classes	14	27	10	17	17	11
Didn't know	46	5	9	6	15	46
No response	3	0	1	0	1	3
Total	100	100	100	100	100	100

Source: Data supplied by the Centro de Investigaciones Sociológicas, published in *Revista Española de Investigaciones Sociológicas* 23 (October–December 1984): 336.

way for a more complete "democratization" of the AP, but it also deprives the party of its most charismatic and experienced leader. Fraga's successor, Antonio Hernández Mancha, a young Andalusian, has had to struggle externally with a popular image of being a political neophyte and internally with a number of contending leaders and a number of elder statesmen (including Fraga). One prominent party baron, Alfonso Osorio, was criticized in mid-1988 for predicting that Hernández Mancha would not be ready to govern for at least ten years.[7] A serious rift between the AP and its traditional ally, the Spanish Confederation of Entrepreneurial Organizations, has further complicated the future for AP.[8] Ironically, AP leaders complained that the CEOE had fallen under the influence of the Socialist government. The results of the 1987 municipal/European parliament elections, a drop of nearly six percentage points, suggest that the AP's woes are not over and point to the fact that the conservatives have not been able to benefit from a decline in electoral support for the PSOE.

In summary, the party system after the 1982 elections was unusually conducive to the PSOE's centrist drift. The party's social democratization and the government's moderation in office took place with the prospect of few political costs and many benefits. Punishment from the party's leftist supporters was unlikely given the extreme disarray of the Communist camp. At the same time, the party's move toward the center of the political spectrum lessened the prospects of a resurgence of the center and prevented the right's attempt to present a more centrist image. According to one conservative author:

The objective of the PSOE under Felipe is to replace the center, eliminate the possibility of another center, and to "be in" the center without actually becoming the center or acting like it. That is, to succeed the UCD but avoid its fate.[9]

However, the PSOE's abandonment of its electoral platform does appear to have exacted an electoral price. In the 1986 elections, the Socialists lost 18 seats, more than any other party, and the PSOE vote dropped almost two percentage points, losing over one million votes. The PSOE's performance in major cities was especially disheartening (for example, the PSOE vote dropped 11 points in Madrid). Still, the Socialists preserved their absolute majority by nine seats in the lower house and by eighteen seats in the upper house. Higher abstention rates appeared to hurt a number of parties and did not punish the PSOE disproportionately.[10]

The municipal/European Parliament elections of 1987 delivered a far more severe blow to the Socialists.[11] The PSOE's percentage of the vote dropped over seven points to 37.16, a loss of over one and one half million votes. Since 1983, the PSOE had dominated municipal and regional government, enjoying a majority in twelve of seventeen autonomous communities and controlling the mayor's office in 67 percent of Spanish municipalities. Of the thirteen autonomous communities holding elections during 1987, the PSOE was able to retain an absolute majority in only three. The Socialists lost over 5,000 elected positions at the local level and lost its absolute majorities in twenty-one provincial capitals, including Spain's four largest cities.

However, given the controversial political economic and foreign policies pursued, and given the persistence of high unemployment, the PSOE did not suffer as much at the polls as could be expected. While the PSOE lost about three million votes since 1982, it retained an absolute majority in the legislature. Moreover, even had the PSOE lost its parliamentary majority, it would still have been the largest and most coherent political force in a badly fragmented party system. Either in a minority government or in coalition with some assortment of centrist forces, it is unclear whether and how the PSOE would have to moderate its policies. Thus even if the PSOE has paid a price in votes for its behavior in government, the beneficiaries were not national parties capable of mounting an effective challenge to the Socialists. While small gains were registered by the CDS and the communist left, the biggest increases were registered by regional parties and by abstainers.

IDEOLOGICAL MODERATION AND PUBLIC OPINION

The Advantages of Pragmatism and Flexibility

The PSOE's move toward the center of the party system was not only profitable in electoral terms; it was also supported by the bulk of popular opinion. The ideological moderation of the Socialist Party while in government may have disappointed many party militants, but there is ample evidence that the PSOE was perceived as pragmatic and flexible and was therefore congruent with the general perspective of the Spanish population regarding the correct behavior of political parties.

A study conducted halfway through the Socialist term in office supports the view that the PSOE's moderation in office was broadly compatible with public opinion.[12] Respondents were asked to agree with one of three general statements about politics, two of which can be characterized as "pragmatic" and one that is more "idealistic" (see Table 5.2). Of the respondents, 63 percent agreed with the two pragmatic approaches to politics; 27 percent took a more idealistic view. This relationship held up across all educational, demographic, and partisan categories.

The CIS data make it possible to estimate roughly how supporters of each party view their preferred party's adherence to the pragmatic or idealistic approach (see Table 5.3). Of all parties, the PSOE was seen as the most pragmatic: 59 percent of respondents viewed the Socialists as either willing "to reach agreement and practical compromises even if it has to cede some of its ideals" (40 percent) or as a party that "tries to make the most of each situation without worrying too much about principles" (19 percent).[13] Prospective Socialist voters viewed their own party as even more pragmatic than did the public at large (72 percent), whereas they saw the AP as the least pragmatic of all parties (49 percent), far more so than the public at large. These data suggest that the popular image of the PSOE was closer to the more pragmatic preference of the Spanish electorate. They may support the argument that voters endorsed the pragmatism of the PSOE on the NATO issue even though most Spaniards opposed membership per se. It may also partly explain why the Socialists remained very popular despite major policy reversals in key areas.

A related point is that Spaniards viewed the PSOE as having contributed to the stability of democracy. Not only did respondents feel that the PSOE government had weakened the traditional authoritarian bulwarks of the military, the Church, and the bureaucracy, but a large segment of PSOE voters in 1986 chose the Socialists because they felt the party "guaranteed the continuation of democracy."[14]

Public Opinion and the Autonomy of the Socialist Government

The PSOE's ability to deviate from its program once in government was facilitated by the Spanish public's clear preference for pragmatic politics. Data collected in numerous surveys suggest that the government's need to pursue "leftist" policies in order to appeal to an ideological support group was minimal. Although many scholars have noted the weakness and volatility of party identification in democratic Spain, left-right identification has been shown to be stronger and more stable.[15] However, the Spanish public was very unclear about the precise meaning of the term "left."[16] When asked to give meaning to the concept, only 32 percent defined it in class terms (saying it meant the defense of working class). Even among PSOE supporters, only 38 percent gave any class content to the term. Another 13 percent identified "left" with the term "progressive," whereas 26 percent were unsure of the meaning of "left."

If the weakness of party identification and the ambiguities of the left-right dimension gave the PSOE considerable room to maneuver, class consciousness also failed to constrain the Socialist government. The PSOE was still viewed by the public as a party supported by the working class (see Table 5.4), but it was also perceived as having the most cross-class support of all parties (27 percent). By comparison, AP was seen far more as a single-class party. The data collected by Gunther, Sani, and Shabad revealed that about 70 percent of the Spanish public felt that political parties should represent all classes.[17]

Like party identification, Spaniards' class consciousness has been found to be weaker than is often assumed. Gunther et al. found that only four of ten Spaniards said that they belonged to a social class.[18] As is suggested in Table 5.5, the PSOE drew well in 1982 from all occupational groups, although the Socialists did especially well among skilled workers. The PSOE received substantial support from upper- and middle-level occupations. As shown in Table 5.6, the PSOE received a respectable portion of entrepreneurial votes and a plurality of votes from upper-, middle- and lower-level white-collar workers, sales and supervisory personnel, skilled workers, and unskilled workers. Similarly, Gunther et al. concluded that "[a] more detailed classification of voters in different occupational strata reveals that no party enjoyed a monopoly of support from any one social group," a conclusion echoed by McDonough, Barnes, and López Pina.[19] In terms of income groups, the CIS data (one illustration is presented in Table 5.7) suggest that in the 1986 elections the PSOE did well across all categories and its support roughly mirrored the makeup of the population at large. The Socialists thus enjoyed relative autonomy from any single group within Spanish society. In the words of Gunther et al., the complexity of modern social

Table 5.5
PSOE Vote in the 1982 General Elections, by Occupation (percentages)

OCCUPATION	PSOE VOTERS	TOTAL SAMPLE
Entrepreneurs	2	3
Upper level	3	4
Middle level	13	15
Sales	5	4
Lower level	5	5
Independent	10	16
Supervisory	3	2
Skilled workers	32	25
Unskilled workers	24	21
No response	5	5
Total	100	100

Source: "Post-electoral, 1982," conducted by the Centro de Investigaciones Sociológicas (Madrid), study number 1327, November 1982. The sample included 12,451 respondents over eighteen years of age.

structures mean that "no single social group can provide a sufficiently large bloc of voters to allow a party to play a major role."[20]

Other public opinion data appear to support the argument that the Spanish public supported the compromise and moderation of the PSOE government *even while strongly opposing many of the specific policies pursued by the government.* It is important to recall that the PSOE came to power, in large part, on a wave of discontent about the economy: by 1981, 41 percent of respondents felt that the economy had worsened.[21] Chief among the public's concerns was unemployment, mentioned by 62 percent of those surveyed as the chief problem facing the nation.[22]

As has been discussed, unemployment subsequently skyrocketed under the Socialist government. After two years of Socialist leadership, 60 percent of respondents said that they "hoped government policy would have been more progressive during the last two years," compared with 10 percent who favored a more conservative set of policies.[23] Whereas 43 percent felt that "the group that has benefited most from the government's political economic policy" was big business, only 6 percent said that peasants and workers benefited the most.[24] The distribution of taxes under the Socialists was seen as "less fair" by 48 percent of respondents

Table 5.6
PSOE Vote among Occupational Groups (percentages)

OCCUPATION	PSOE VOTERS
Entrepreneurs	28
Upper level	27
Middle level	34
Sales	44
Lower level	35
Independent	25
Supervisory	55
Skilled workers	49
Unskilled workers	43
No response	39

Source: "Post-electoral, 1982," conducted by the Centro de Investigaciones Sociológicas (Madrid), study number 1327, November 1982. The sample included 12,451 respondents over eighteen years of age.

Table 5.7
Income Group Composition of PSOE Voters in 1986 General Elections (percentages)

	MONTHLY INCOME (Pesetas)					
	UNDER 30,000	30,000–50,000	50,001–75,000	75,000+	NO ANSWER	TOTAL
Total Sample	10	19	21	26	24	100
PSOE	12	22	24	23	19	100

Source: "Post-electoral elecciones generales 1986 y autonómicas Andalucía," conducted by the Centro de Investigaciones Sociológicas (Madrid), study number 1542, July 1986. The sample included 8,236 respondents over eighteeen years of age.

and judged "more fair" by only 36 percent.[25] Spaniards also tended to side with striking workers against the Socialist government. A survey published in May 1987 reported that 58 percent of Spaniards supported the workers during the hugh wave of strikes that engulfed the nation in early 1987, and 53 percent felt that the government was not helping to resolve the crisis.[26] About half of the respondents viewed strikes as "the only way to get the government to pay attention to problems."[27]

Despite these negative assessments of the PSOE policies, the Spanish public appeared to judge the overall Socialist performance in comparison with previous governments, the perceived ability of available political alternatives, and their rather realistic expectations. When, in 1985, Spaniards were asked to compare social inequalities with inequality in 1975, 42 percent of the respondents claimed there was less inequality, whereas only 16 percent felt there was more.[28] McDonough et al. report that Spaniards favorably compared the performance of the PSOE government during its first years with that of previous UCD governments, or the Franco regime, on all issues except law and order.[29] Even without the benefit of comparison, the PSOE government received generally positive ratings. As demonstrated in Table 5.8, midway through the PSOE's first term (and a year before the 1986 elections), a majority of respondents felt the PSOE government had contributed to the creation of equality, the improvement of health care, and a better educational system. Large percentages also rated the government favorably on its reform of the public administration and its handling of terrorism. Only on the question of reducing unemployment and inflation did the government receive very negative ratings.

The Socialist record on redistribution of wealth, (hampered by rising unemployment) might appear to be the most vulnerable to public criticism given that the Socialists themselves made a call for redistribution of wealth a central campaign issue in 1982. However, McDonough et al. conclude that "plainly, redistributive demands are not central to Spaniards who support the PSOE government."[30] Their data led them to assert that the Socialists could "play many variations" on the distributive theme, although they doubted that the PSOE could totally abandon distributive goals without paying a severe price.[31] While identifying a strong desire for social and economic policy "skewed toward the left," McDonough et al. also note a "certain shallowness and softness to the opinions themselves. It is unclear whether they form a coherent message for policy-makers."[32] They conclude that "the constellation of beliefs about economic and social policy in Spain is patterned but not polarized. There is a socialist-populist ethos more than a clear cut mandate for rigorous socialism."[33] Indeed, the abandonment of the social democratic bent of the PSOE's 1982 platform meant that "Spaniards who favor a

Table 5.8
Public Perception of PSOE Government Performance on Selected Issues (1985)

	TOTAL	EMPLOYED	UNEMPLOYED
Percentage of respondents who felt that the PSOE government had worked to:			
Promote equality	55	57	55
Reduce inflation	28	32	28
Improve public administration	45	49	44
Improve medical care	53	53	54
Reduce unemployment	20	20	20
Improve education	58	60	60
Improve individual security	42	44	44
Combat terrorism	40	43	41

Source: "3 años de gobierno Socialista," conducted by the Centro de Investigaciones Sociológicas (Madrid), study number 1492, November 1985. The sample included 12,451 respondents over eighteen years of age.

capitalist ethic see little contradiction between their views and those of the incumbent Socialists."[34]

Yet given the alarmingly high rate of unemployment, it is still surprising that the PSOE did not suffer a severe electoral backlash. At the very least, one could expect that unemployed workers would themselves be hostile toward the government. Surprisingly, there is relatively little evidence of such a backlash. As demonstrated in Table 5.8, unemployed and employed respondents gave roughly similar assessments of the PSOE's record in government, with only a slightly more hostile assessment coming from unemployed respondents. Nor were unemployed workers notably more pessimistic about the government's prospects for success in the future (see Table 5.9). In general, the data suggest that the opinions of the unemployed on a host of issues are roughly similar to those of the public at large.

Moreover, there is little evidence to support the contention that the PSOE had ever depended significantly on the votes of unemployed workers. In a postelectoral survey conducted in November 1982, the largest single group of unemployed respondents said they had abstained (34

Table 5.9
Public Perception of Prospects for Future Performance by the PSOE
Government on Selected Issues (1985)

	TOTAL	EMPLOYED	UNEMPLOYED
In the future, the PSOE government is likely to work to:			
Promote equality	52	55	53
Reduce inflation	40	43	40
Improve public administration	47	52	48
Improve medical care	54	55	55
Reduce unemployment	38	40	39
Education	55	59	57
Improve individual security	48	51	50
Combat terrorism	47	50	48

Source: "3 años de gobierno Socialista," conducted by the Centro de Investigaciones Sociológicas (Madrid), study number 1492, November 1985. The sample included 12,451 respondents over eighteen years of age.

percent); the next largest group voted for the PSOE (27 percent), followed by the UCD (11 percent). Thus the percentage of unemployed voters who supported the PSOE in 1982 was far lower than the 48.4 percent of the overall vote obtained by the Socialists.[35]

The broad cross-class support enjoyed by the PSOE, as well as the weakness of contending parties, may help to explain the government's initial willingness and ability to pursue its controversial political economic policy. Even so, the rapid increase in unemployment might still have led to a popular backlash against the government in the 1986 general elections. However, Table 5.10 suggests that in 1986, the PSOE actually did better among unemployed than employed Spaniards. It is true that the PCE (IU) also fared better among unemployed voters; however, the communist left was trounced by the Socialists among this category of voters. If the PSOE suffered any backlash, it appears to have been from students, who voted in higher proportions for the conservative right and for the communist left, and from abstainers, a result that will be discussed further.

When the PSOE government's relative autonomy from public opinion is considered together with the party system factors discussed earlier in

Table 5.10
Party Support among Unemployed versus Employed and 1986 Election (percentages)

VOTE IN 1986	TOTAL SAMPLE	OCCUPATIONAL CATEGORY				
		WORKS	UNEMPLOYED	RETIRED	STUDENT	NO ANSWER
CP	14	16	7	12	17	18
CDS	9	9	8	4	7	7
IU	5	5	9	3	13	0
UC	1	1	2	1	0	0
PRD	1	1	1	1	2	0
PSOE	44	43	49	49	33	46
CiU	4	5	3	6	5	5
PNV	1	1	1	3	12	4
Others	5	5	7	3	12	4
Didn't know	17	15	14	20	8	15

Key:

CP: Popular Coalition (Popular Alliance)
CDS: Democratic and Social Center
IU: United Left (PCE)
UC: Communist Unity
PRD: Democratic Reform Party
CiU: Convergencia i Unió
PNV: Basque Nationalist Party

Source: "Post-electoral elecciones generales 1986 y autonómicas Andalucía," conducted by the Centro de Investigaciones Sociológicas (Madrid), study number 1542, July 1986. The sample included 8,236 respondents over eighteen years of age.

this chapter, the PSOE's political success—despite many unpopular policies—is more easily understood. The point that a lack of credible political alternatives (especially on the left) shielded the PSOE from a potential voter backlash is nicely illustrated by the data presented in Table 5.11. When respondents were asked which party they had most seriously considered as an alternative to their own in the 1986 election, a large plurality (45 percent) of 1982 PSOE voters said they had considered the centrist CDS, whereas only 19 percent said they had considered voting

Table 5.11
Major Party Alternative Considered by PSOE Voters in the 1986 General Election

DEBATED BETWEEN VOTING PSOE AND:	PERCENTAGE VOTING
IU	19
UC	4
CDS	45
PRD	4
CP	16
Others	6
Didn't Know	1
No response	5

Key:

CP: Popular Coalition (Popular Alliance)
CDS: Democratic and Social Center
IU: United Left (PCE)
PRD: Democratic Reform Party

Source: "Post-electoral elecciones generales 1986 y autonómicas Andalucía," conducted by the Centro de Investigaciones Sociológicas (Madrid), study number 1542, July 1986. The sample included 8,236 respondents over eighteen years of age.

for a leftist alternative (only three percentage points higher than those who considered voting for the conservative CP). Thus in 1986 (as in 1982), the left presented no significant threat to lure Socialist voters. The still amorphous political center offered the greatest potential threat to the PSOE, a fact that is not surprising given that the PSOE had a political base that was strikingly similar to that of the defunct UCD.[36]

In summary, it is clear that the identity of the PSOE was not based exclusively or even largely on its ideological image or on its working-class ties, and that the "catch-all" appeal of the Socialists—especially given the lack of serious political contenders—was a source of strength for the Socialist government.

Public Opinion and the NATO Paradox

Among the most perplexing phenomena of the Socialist experience in power was the government's dramatic victory in the March 1986

Table 5.12
Views on Spain's Membership in NATO, on the Eve of the March 1986
NATO Referendum (percentages)

OPINION REGARDING SPAIN'S MEMBERSHIP IN NATO:	TOTAL SAMPLE	PSOE VOTERS	18- to 25- YEAR-OLDS
Strongly favor	9	10	7
Favor	29	34	24
Oppose	20	19	35
Strongly oppose	13	10	19
Didn't know	25	24	12
No response	4	3	3
Total	100	100	100

Source: "Alianza Atlántica 12a," conducted by the Centro de Investigaciones Sociológicas (Madrid), study number 1521, March 10–11, 1986. The sample included 1,118 respondents over eighteen years of age.

referendum on NATO. As discussed in Chapter 4, González reversed the PSOE's official opposition to NATO and now asked voters to endorse Spain's continued membership in the Atlantic Alliance (though without military integration, and with other provisions designed to placate the party left and the peace movement). Opinion polls consistently showed strong public opposition to the government's new position up until the day of the referendum, although the resistance to NATO membership eroded as the referendum date approached. A study conducted on March 10, 1986 (see Table 5.12), two days before the referendum, revealed that the public was roughly divided between supporters (those strongly in favor and those in favor, 38 percent), opponents (those strongly opposing and those opposing, 33 percent), and undecided voters (25 percent). Socialist voters were far more supportive of the governmental position than the population at large, although a majority were still either opposed to NATO or undecided about it.[37] The data suggest a potential for political backlash among the eighteen- to twenty-five-year-old voters, who opposed NATO by a clear majority, strongly diverging from the makeup of the general population.

In fact, a postreferendum study (see Table 5.13) clearly shows that votes against the NATO proposal were heaviest, and votes in favor of the proposal weakest, among the eighteen- to twenty-five-year-old category. Abstention rates were the highest of any election since the estab-

Table 5.13
Vote on the NATO Referendum, by Age Groups (percentages)

VOTE IN NATO REFERENDUM	TOTAL SAMPLE	AGE GROUPS				
		18 – 25	26 – 40	41 – 60	60+	NO RESPONSE
Yes	34	26	36	38	35	46
No	28	37	33	26	15	1
Didn't vote	25	30	21	22	29	25
Spoiled ballot	0	0	0	1	0	0
Didn't know	6	2	4	6	12	14
No response	7	5	6	7	9	14
Total	100	100	100	100	100	100

Source: "Post-electoral elecciones generales 1986 y autonómicas Andalucía," conducted by the Centro de Investigaciones Sociológicas (Madrid), study number 1542, July 1986. The sample included 8,236 respondents over eighteen years of age.

lishment of democracy (40.26 percent), and young voters were the most likely to abstain in the referendum, effectively weakening the strength of opposition to NATO among the most hostile sector of the electorate.

Given the undercurrent of NATO opposition among the electorate in general and among youth in particular, the results of a 1986 study, conducted shortly after the June 1986 general elections, are particularly instructive. Table 5.14 shows that the PSOE received one fifth of its votes from those who had voted against NATO only three months earlier. The PSOE's support from NATO opponents was lower than the percentage of NATO opponents among the total respondents, and is especially lower than the percentages of NATO opponents who voted for the two parties of the left and the largest regional parties. Nevertheless, the amount of support is still substantial and suggests that the PSOE did not suffer as severe a backlash from NATO opponents as could have been expected. Moreover, the data presented in Table 5.15 suggest that in 1986, the PSOE more than held its own among the youngest category of voters. It easily drew its largest percentage of the vote from eighteen- to twenty-five-year-olds and actually received a higher percentage of votes from the youngest age cohort than from any other age group. Finally, the PSOE actually captured a higher percentage of the young vote than in 1982. In short, the sector of the national electorate most opposed to the PSOE about-face on NATO did not punish the Socialists in 1986.

Table 5.14
**PSOE Voters in the June 1986 General Election and Their Vote in the
March 1986 NATO Referendum (percentages)**

VOTE IN NATO REFERENDUM	TOTAL SAMPLE	PSOE VOTERS JUNE 1986
Yes	34	60
No	28	20
Didn't vote	25	13
Spoiled ballot	0	0
Didn't know	6	5
No response	6	2
Total	100	100

Source: "Post-electoral elecciones generales 1986 y autonómicas Andalucía," conducted by
the Centro de Investigaciones Sociológicas (Madrid), study number 1542, July 1986. The
sample included 8,236 respondents over eighteen years of age.

Once again, it appears that the diversity of demographic, generational,
and ideological support for the PSOE facilitated the Socialist government's abandonment of its 1982 campaign pledge regarding NATO.
When asked to explain their votes in the NATO referendum, only opponents to the government's position had a clear motive (see Table 5.16):
81 percent of the total sample and 83 percent of 1982 PSOE voters
stated that they opposed NATO membership. Among supporters of the
government a variety of explanations were given. The largest group of
respondents said they voted yes because their party advocated such a
vote, whereas substantial percentages believed that Spain should participate in the defense of Europe, professed long-standing support for
NATO, stated that the government had convinced them, or wanted to
avoid giving the government a defeat. The PSOE thus garnered a mixture of support from "utilitarians," those with strong convictions about
the issue, recent converts to the government's position, and party
loyalists.

The public's favorable view of the PSOE's moderation and compromise
in office, the lack of credible alternatives, and the diverse base of Socialist
support among the electorate made controversial policy decisions, like
the NATO reversal, more feasible and less costly in terms of public
opinion and electoral results. The last but by no means least important
factor in the PSOE's success among public opinion was the public's generally favorable assessment of González's leadership.[38]

Table 5.15
Vote in 1986 General Elections by Age Group (percentages)

VOTE IN 1986 GENERAL ELECTION	AGE GROUP				
	18 - 25	26 - 40	41 - 60	60+	No Response
CP	11	12	17	16	0
CDS	8	9	11	5	10
IU	9	6	3	2	1
UC	1	1	1	1	1
PRD	1	1	1	1	1
PSOE	48 (25)	47 (53)	40 (46)	44 (42)	53 (51)
CIU	3	3	4	6	0
PNV	1	1	1	1	6
Others	9	6	4	2	0
No response	9	14	18	24	30
Total	100	100	100	100	100

*Figures in parentheses represent the figure from the 1982 General election.

Key:

CP: Popular Coalition (Popular Alliance)
CDS: Democratic and Social Center
IU: United Left (PCE)
UC: Communist Unity
PRD: Democratic Reform Party
CiU: Convergencia i Unió
PNV: Basque Nationalist Party

Source: "Post-electoral elecciones generales 1986 y autonómicas Andalucía," conducted by the Centro de Investigaciones Sociológicas (Madrid), study number 1542, July 1986. The sample included 8,236 respondents over eighteen years of age.

The Felipe Factor

In early 1986, when opinion polls continued to show a majority of Spaniards opposed to NATO membership, González remained the most popular politician in Spain.[39] González's consistently high levels of popularity may appear paradoxical given controversial and unpopular policies pursued by his government. Yet in the context described earlier, in which a government feels relatively autonomous from class, ideological, and other types of constituencies, leadership factors take on added

Table 5.16
Reasons for Votes in the March 1986 NATO Referendum (percentages)

	TOTAL SAMPLE	PSOE VOTERS
VOTED "YES" IN THE REFERENDUM BECAUSE:		
It is the position of the party I usually vote for.	28	33
Spain should participate in Europe's defense.	29	25
I have always supported Spain's membership in NATO.	15	13
The government convinced me.	23	26
Did not want the government to lose on the issue.	13	13
Other	6	6
No response	3	2
VOTED "NO" IN THE REFERENDUM BECAUSE:		
It was the position of the party I usually support.	4	4
I support full integration in NATO.	2	1
I wanted to protest against the PSOE government.	7	6
I oppose NATO membership.	81	83
I oppose the current regime	6	4
Other	7	8
No response	2	3

Note: Columns do not total 100 because respondents were allowed to give two reasons.

Source: "Post-Referendum Alianza Atlántica," conducted by the Centro de Investigaciones Sociológicas (Madrid), study number 1522, March 23–26 1986. The sample included 2,587 respondents over eighteen years of age.

weight.[40] Where "catch-all" electoral appeals are likely to capture votes from the inchoate political center, the importance of a charismatic and popular leader becomes enhanced. Where political parties are weak and where levels of political organization and political involvement are low, electoral appeals depend increasingly on mass media images and, in modern Spain, largely on television images.[41] As ideologoical messages and adherence to the party program become less important, the role of political leadership and image is amplified in what has often been referred to as an "Americanization" of Spanish politics. Hans-Jürgen Puhle has also attributed the importance of personalism to González's lack of rivals within the PSOE, the prime ministerial focus of the Spanish parliamentary system, and the weak tradition of political "localism" in the Spanish party system (only about half of Spaniards know who heads their Party list in their district).[42]

Similar in some ways to Margaret Thatcher's image as an iron lady able to impose her will first on her party and then on the nation at large, González emerged strengthened from the internal party struggles of 1979 and the policy reversals of the early years of his government. Like Thatcher and Mitterrand, González has won admiration for his ability to impose unpopular policies on recalcitrant party members. Francisco Bustelo, a former member of the PSOE Executive Committee and a leading critic of *Felipismo,* nevertheless attributes to González an almost mythical power. He notes González's *barraca,* or divine gift for persuading others to change their minds:

How else does one explain the President's many and often counterintuitive victories? For example, how can one explain the popular support for him when his political economic policies, inevitable as they may be, favor the powerful over the needy? Or the risky referendum victory? Or his undisputed leadership of the party that he has turned inside out like a sock? Or the disappearance of all forces opposed to him?[43]

Since the advent of parliamentary democracy, González has gradually cultivated an image that is acceptable to a majority of Spaniards. According to data collected under the direction of Juan Linz, relatively small percentages of the 1978 electorate viewed González as "responsible" (36 percent), "honorable" (28 percent), "experienced" (23 percent), or "skilled" (40 percent).[44] By 1982, a majority of the electorate viewed González as responsible and honorable, whereas the PSOE leader was still poorly rated on experience and skill (somewhat understandably given González's lack of governmental experience).

Although the popularity of the leader (and especially of his government) has oscillated during the PSOE's two terms in office, and despite assorted scandals, González has always been the most popular politician in Spain. His popularity cuts across the most common demographic categories (class, income level, and education), and his appeal is surprisingly strong among devout Catholics and the elderly.[45] Even during the mass unrest in early 1987, González maintained a large lead over his nearest rival, CDS leader Adolfo Suárez. Indeed, the emergence of the CDS in the 1986 elections as a serious electoral contender was significant not mainly because of the organizational or ideological challenge that the new party presents, but rather because PSOE leaders considered Suárez the only potential rival to González's charisma and popularity.

The unique relationship between González and Vice-President Alfonso Guerra has also contributed to the former's insulation from criticism. Compared with the more aloof González, Guerra has been portrayed as carrying out the dirty work of party discipline, and his relationship with the Spanish press and public is clearly more conflictual and erratic. Guerra appears to thrive in his position as a public opinion "shield" for González, even though the two leaders are very close friends and inseparable political allies. González, meanwhile, has cultivated an interest in foreign affairs and international diplomacy, showing less interest in domestic issues. The relationship between González and Guerra has helped to prevent a more rapid political exhaustion of *Felipismo*.

The importance of Felipe González for the electoral success of the PSOE was not lost among the leadership or membership of the Socialist Party. As will be discussed later, González's value as an electoral asset and the feeling that the PSOE would be little without him helped him to win some crucial battles within his own party.

SOCIAL DEMOCRATIZATION AND INTERNAL PARTY POLITICS

One of the most important characteristics distinguishing the PSOE from all other Spanish parties was its high degree of internal cohesion.[46] The PSOE's incomparable success in limiting the impact of intramural struggles over ideology and power is at the heart of any explanation of why the Socialists effected such a rapid change in the party program with so few electoral costs. As Fernando Jauregui has observed:

It became an obsession to avoid a repetition of the UCD's experience, in which different sectors of the party aired their differences in the press. The new government, especially Alfonso Guerra, was constantly concerned about avoiding any kind of rumors that could weaken the image of the Socialists.[47]

Given the dramatic shifts in policy during the first four years of Socialist government, the party's internal unity certainly requires explanation.

Internal PSOE opposition to the Socialist government was centered in two sectors: the leftist opposition current known as Socialist Left (IS), also referred to as the *críticos*, and the Socialist trade union confederation, UGT. Nevertheless, the party leadership weathered the storm of dissent unscathed, and internal opposition never acted as more than a "testimonial" force.

As explained in chapter 3, the defeat of the most serious *crítico* challenge to the PSOE leadership occurred in May 1979 at the party's Twenty-eighth Congress. The left's attempt to retain a more unambiguously Marxist image was defeated, although not until an Extraordinary Congress held four months later, when it became clear that any challenge to the Socialist leadership constituted an unwelcome challenge to party leader Felipe González. Although the PSOE left enjoyed considerable support on ideological and policy issues, it stood no chance of rallying party supporters against the leadership of the popular and charismatic González. Moreover, by the time the Extraordinary Congress was convened, a number of crucial rule changes had been implemented that established strict majoritarian procedures for party elections at all levels. These two factors—the unassailable leadership of González and the use of majoritarian electoral mechanisms—remained the essential ingredients of the PSOE's internal unity during its first term in office.[48] According to one prominent IS member:

Felipismo is not only a matter of a pro-NATO foreign policy or a neoliberal political economic policy, but involves a new organizational model within the party, in which superpersonalized leadership and unconditional support are more important than pluralism.[49]

A good illustration of this new organizational model was the PSOE leadership's maintenance of strict discipline among members of parliament. Stiff fines were deducted from paychecks for all missed parliamentary sessions and committee meetings, a move designed to prevent absenteeism from turning into a form of silent protest against the government.[50]

The effectiveness of the leadership's control was put to a strong test during the first years of Socialist government. If the Socialist left ever hoped to mount a successful challenge to the Socialist leadership, the NATO issue was its golden opportunity. Were the UGT to oppose the government on political economic policy, the austerity and reindustrialization programs were also an ideal rallying point.

The internal struggle over the leadership's "Copernican" reversal of the party's official NATO policy assumed full force in the spring of 1984.[51] In May the leadership began an "educational program" to convince the skeptical membership of the advantages of continued NATO membership.[52] Party leaders warned anti-NATO members that "a defeat of Felipe in the 30th Congress would have to be considered a personal defeat, and could lead to a dissolution of the parliament."[53] This line of reasoning proved especially effective in a congress of delegates composed largely of PSOE officeholders, PSOE-dependent bureaucrats, and other political appointees.[54] Meanwhile, IS began a campaign to win as many anti-NATO delegates as possible to the party's Thirtieth Congress, scheduled for December 1984. The battle was fierce, as the party had mobilized against NATO only two years earlier, and the Juventudes Socialistas (Socialist Youth, JJSS), the UGT, and many important regional PSOE organizations were on record as opposing membership in the Atlantic Alliance.

Despite the impressive strength of the anti-NATO campaign during the delegate selection process, previously approved rules limited the impact of IS and greatly reduced its presence at the Thirtieth Congress. Party rules limited the number of IS delegates from each regional party organization. For example, IS received 33 percent of the vote in the Madrid delegate selection process but only 25 percent of the delegates.[55] This scenario was repeated throughout Spain; and although IS often obtained a majority of votes for anti-NATO amendments, the PSOE left could not convert the opposition on this single issue into delegates at the national level.[56] With few exceptions, the "officials" list of delegates won out over IS representatives. IS fell short of the 20 percent of the total delegates required to gain official status as a party current, receiving about 15 percent of the total. The leadership's control over the most powerful regional federations (Madrid, the Basque Country, and Andalusia) made any upset virtually impossible.

The Thirtieth Congress, convened during December 1984, transpired without surprises. The delegates adopted the new government policy on NATO and approved statements aimed at justifying the PSOE's austerity policy. The new Federal Executive Committee included only four new members, all individuals close to González and Guerra. Thoroughly defeated, the critical left was given a small consolation prize: the delegates approved a new system of proportional representation for elections to the party's Federal Committee, but not for the highest policymaking organ of the party, the Federal Executive Committee.[57] Nevertheless, the conciliatory treatment of the Socialist left faction could not hide the fact that IS had been excluded from the major decisions of the leadership. Pablo Castellano, a leading IS spokesperson, warned that "if the PSOE does not tolerate greater discrepancy of opinion, the party runs the risk of creating a new *nomenklatura,* and it will encourage all dissenters to leave the party."[58] However, the disarray of the communist left, the attractiveness of membership in the governing party, and the rightward drift of the PSOE government diminished the impact of the threat.

The leadership's ability to marginalize IS and avoid defeat on the NATO issue or its political economic policy was facilitated by the structural weakness of the PSOE. In 1984, the Socialist Party had only about 155,000 members, far fewer than its counterparts in smaller countries such as Belgium or Austria. The PSOE had one of the lowest ratios of members to voters of any European socialist or social democratic party.[59]

In the 1982 municipal elections for 8,039 municipalities, the PSOE could field candidates in only 5,629.

Over 50 percent of the membership either held party or government posts or appeared as candidates for office on Socialist lists.[60] The very low ratio of members to voters and the high ratio of PSOE-dependent position holders to party members gave the leadership tremendous leverage over the rank and file. Consequently, a large portion of the delegates at party congresses depended directly on the leadership. The unwillingness of the membership to attack this leadership, especially when such an attack might weaken the government, is easy to comprehend. The paucity of membership and the personalized leadership of Felipe González limited the ability of the PSOE to maintain autonomy from the government. As an *El País* editorial observed, shortly after the 1984 Thirtieth Congress, the PSOE had become a support organization for the González government:

Despite its 100 years of existence, the PSOE is a recently "re-created" party, newly founded in the 1970s. It lacks sufficient membership or cadres to continue as a socially rooted party, especially after thousands of its supporters were recruited by the state apparatus. The hemorrhage of cadres destined for the public administration left the party headquarters with a small group of leaders to defend, halfheartedly, the party's autonomy.[61]

Shortly before the NATO referendum, Txiki Benegas, the PSOE's top organizational man, affirmed that "the party can disagree with the government, but this discrepancy must never be made public."[62]

After the Thirtieth Congress, the PSOE left's "testimonial" criticism of the government and party continued. The leadership continued to hold all the cards and responded with a mixture of tolerance and discipline.[63] The NATO referendum, held only three months before the general elections, gave the party leadership a perfect opportunity to punish members who failed to toe the party line. The IS decided not to campaign against NATO membership in the referendum, but a number of its leaders complained about the government's tactics and the text of the referendum. Many prominent PSOE and UGT members joined the Movement for Peace and Disarmament in October 1985, angering top party officials. The party leadership sent an official reprimand to all party members who signed the movement's declaration of principles. The case of José Luis Sánchez, a popular and well-respected PSOE deputy from Huesca, exemplifies the leadership's intolerance of public criticism. Sánchez published an article in February 1986 in which he complained:

To link the national interest exclusively to a "yes" vote in the NATO referendum is a marketing tactic, and is wrong. The national interest is also a matter of respecting the popular peace movement, which is vital for the future of our party.[64]

Sánchez was later excluded from the PSOE lists as punishment for his criticism of the government.

Others, like Pablo Castellano, IS's most prominent spokesperson and a member of the General Council of Judicial Power, decided to exclude themselves rather than face the embarrassment of being left off party lists.[65] The JJSS, consistently the most outspoken sector of the PSOE in its opposition to NATO membership, ultimately decided to remain silent vis-à-vis the referendum. Unlike the PSOE congress, the last Socialist Youth Congress had overwhelmingly opposed NATO membership. On the eve of the NATO referendum all but five members of the JJSS Federal Committee voted to oppose membership. Nevertheless, the JJSS leadership refrained from taking an active role against the party. The leader of the JJSS stated:

Due to a basic sense of political prudence, which we have displayed throughout, we will take a wait and see attitude [about the NATO issue].[66] . . . We stand where we have always stood, but we are not going to enter the campaign.[67]

The strong position of the party leadership and the unenviable tactical and moral dilemmas facing IS began to take their toll on the PSOE left. By March 1986, serious tensions were evident within Izquierda Socialista centering on whether or not IS should join other anti-NATO forces during the referendum campaign. When a majority of IS members rejected such participation, the most radical group, led by Fernando Gascón, bolted.

Despite the presence of such testimonial opposition, the leadership had little trouble rallying the party behind the new NATO policy. There were many anecdotal examples of the leadership's success, but perhaps the best example was Juan Barranco, the PSOE mayor of Madrid. In 1982, Barranco had organized a contest in the Socialist Federation of Madrid aimed at collecting the most signatures on anti-NATO petitions. Less than four years later, he once again served his party in Madrid, but this time he organized the local campaign to remain in NATO! According to an Executive Committee member, "the party respond[ed] like nobody could have dreamed."[68] Since the defeat of IS on the NATO issue and the victory of the government in the March 1986 referendum, there was relatively little public criticism of the government and party leadership from the PSOE left. The government's calling of elections soon after the NATO referendum led to a period of calm within party ranks as the Socialists attempted to preserve their absolute majority. The Federal Executive Committee met on March 18, shortly after the referendum, and decided not to pursue sanctions against IS members who publicly opposed the party's NATO views, claiming that the March 12 victory had erased internal problems and calling instead for a "diplomatic reconciliation."[69]

The most worrisome opposition for the party leadership came from the Socialist trade union, the UGT.[70] Confederation General Secretary Nicolás Redondo was the single most outspoken critic of Socialist political economic policy. Although his position within UGT was strengthened during the first Socialist term, the confederation had little success altering the policies of the government.

Trade unions are notoriously weak in Spain, a fact that has limited their ability to oppose the policies of all governments since the transition.[71] Union density in Spain is very low; the unions are on thin ice financially; and the union movement is badly fragmented acording to partisan and regional cleavages.[72] Spanish unions suffer from the overall atrophy of popular organizations and low levels of citizen participation that form part of the legacy of forty years of authoritarian rule. The transition to democracy was dominated by political parties, often at the expense of trade union autonomy and power. The two major trade union confederations, especially the UGT, are closely linked to political parties even if they retain a large degree of autonomy. Union strategy has followed party lines more often than not.[73] PSOE members are required by statute to join the UGT, and it is not uncommon for the PSOE and UGT to hold joint executive committee meetings at the local level. Gunther, Sani, and Shabad note that about 90 percent of UGT members traditionally vote for the PSOE.[74]

Despite the weakness of trade union opposition, Redondo's stubborn resistance to governmental policy clearly struck an emotional chord among PSOE members. During the last plenum of the Thirtieth PSOE Congress, Redondo delivered a sharp attack on the Socialist government and was rewarded with a longer ovation than that received by Felipe González.[75] Both trade unions and the CEOE signed the Inter-confederation Accord in 1982, at the start of the PSOE term, but the honeymoon between the confederations and the government was soon over. In the summer of 1983, Redondo and the government fought over proposals to allow employers *despido libre* (unregulated layoffs), and they clashed over plans for reindustrialization. Redondo called it a "black summer" for the working class, and he threatened to mobilize his confederation against the government proposals.[76]

In 1984, the government stepped up its austerity and reindustrialization policies, seriously damaging labor relations. Work hours lost in labor conflicts rose from 2,341,000 in 1983 to 7,896,093 in 1984, a situation that only exacerbated the UGT's uncomfortable predicament. During negotiations with the government over the Social and Economic Accord (AES), in the fall of 1984, the CEOE and both trade union confederations were far apart. The entrepreneurs demanded pension reforms, spending cuts, and complete freedom in the labor market. The UGT wanted urgent government measures to employ 200,000, while CCOO called for a thirty-eight-hour week and a superfund for unemployment insurance.[77] The CCOO pulled out of the negotiations, and the UGT almost did the same. When the government tried to insert a clause into the AES allowing *despido libre*, Redondo said he would not sign it "dead or alive." A compromise text, stating only that Spain would adapt its labor laws to those of the European Community (and allowing UGT to save face), was finally agreed upon, and the UGT signed the AES on October 9, 1984.

By far the most contentious issue between the UGT and PSOE concerned the government's pension reform plan. Although most unions accepted the need for a reform of some kind, in the context of the government's austerity policy, they were in no mood to accept any scaling down of pension benefits. Redondo's outspoken criticism of the government's plan strained relations between the Socialist Party and the UGT. During the parliamentary vote on the pension reform, only two PSOE members (Redondo and a UGT senator from Badajoz) voted against the government.[78] Redondo told a Spanish weekly in April 29, 1985 that "while I wouldn't say that the government is following a reactionary policy, it does coincide in some areas with Reagan's policies. It is neo-liberalism and is thus applauded by the entrepreneurs it favors."[79] José Luís Corcuera, secretary of Syndical Action, the leading PSOE man in the UGT, resigned his union position because of his inability to stem the UGT's attack on the government pension reform. In June 1985, UGT joined with the rival CCOO to hold a major demonstration against pension reform.[80]

As with the internal party opposition to NATO membership, the UGT's attack on the party's political economic policies has been largely testimonial. Redondo's popularity within the UGT, and the UGT's limited autonomy, has shielded the Socialist confederation from more direct sanctions from the party leadership. Even after the UGT had lost on the pension reform issue, it continued to take a hard line on NATO membership. In March 1986, Redondo sent a letter to UGT members reminding them of the official UGT opposition to NATO.[81] However, in an apparent pact with the government, Redondo noted that the UGT "does not even plan to budget one peseta for an anti-NATO campaign."[82] Once again, the party leadership could not force the membership to agree with government policy, nor could it silence its affiliated trade union confederation, but it was successful in limiting the political consequences of internal opposition.

The continuing acrimony between the UGT and PSOE has its potential costs for the UGT, and these may eventually limit the UGT's ability and willingness to oppose Socialist policies. An internal dispute within the Catalan UGT between critics and supporters of government policy threatened to split the organization wide open.[83] When the UGT leadership expelled three progovernment dissenters, the PSOE defended the expelled individuals and called for more internal democracy within the UGT.[84]

In early May, the PSOE and UGT agreed to a "nonaggression" pact in which it was clearly understood that in the future the UGT and PSOE would maintain far more independence than in the past. In order to protect union interests, the UGT would no longer be a "transmission belt" for the PSOE and would feel more free to criticize the government.[85]

The Thirty-first Congress: The Continuation of a Testimonial Opposition

The Thirty-first Congress, held in January 1988, did almost nothing to change the scenario described earlier. Both sources of internal opposition, the IS and the UGT, were visible at the congress, but both failed to alter party policies or influence the selection of the top party leadership.

The congress was held against a backdrop of increasing social mobilization against the government's political economic policy and decaying relations between the PSOE and UGT. The wave of strikes and unrest that punctuated the political landscape during most of 1987 forced the top UGT leadership to step up its opposition to the government. In October 1987, the top two UGT leaders, Nicolás Redondo (secretary general) and Antón Saracíbar (secretary of Organization), resigned their seats in parliament in protest over the government's proposed budget. The UGT began to coordinate its opposition with the Communist CCOO. Agustín Moreno, UGT secretary of Syndical Action, stated:

The hour of mobilization has arrived, considering the antisocial nature of the budget. The budget does not reduce unemployment, reduces social protections, cuts purchasing power, and raises taxes.[86]

Despite a last-minute government concession to the UGT (it increased the amount allocated for pensions), tensions continued up to the Thirty-first Congress.

The Socialist Left continued to attack the PSOE leadership on the eve of the Thirty-first Congress. The IS blasted the draft of the *ponencia política* (the main policy statement to be approved at the congress), arguing that it placed the PSOE far to the right of West European social democratic parties. The IS complained that "we have been asked to approve a document that we didn't participate in," and charged that "the *ponencia* has an anti-union ring to it and seems to have been written by a chamber of commerce."[87] IS leader Antonio García Santesmases warned,

The obsession to represent the whole nation dilutes all socialist discourse into a vocabulary of "modernization, growth, productivity, and technological renovation."... I suggest that we measure these myths against the reality of modern capitalism: an increase in inequality, the persistence of high levels of workers condemned to unemployment, and conflict with the trade unions.... We must abandon *Felipismo* and begin to break ground that has been unbroken in past Congresses: What is the economic model that will fight unemployment and inequality?[88]

Unlike previous congresses, there was evidence of dissent and calls for changes from a broader sector of the party, not associated with IS or the UGT. Ricardo García Damborenea, the PSOE leader in Vizcaya, lamented that "we Socialists do not know what our role in society is," and called the *ponencia política* "triumphalist and ambiguous."[89] Joaquín Leguina, leader of the PSOE in Madrid, called for more party democracy and argued that "Felipe cannot continue to lead the party this way.... He will have to decide whether to let 1000 flowers bloom ... or whether to shut us up definitively."[90]

Despite this opposition, the PSOE leadership easily controlled the delegate selection process, and the *oficialistas* won over 80 percent of the delegates. Vice-President Alfonso Guerra proved skillful in working out arrangements with the most important regional delegations, and even with some sectors of the party that were not completely supportive of the leadership.

The Thirty-first Congress was convened under the slogan, "Ganar el Futuro" ("Win" or "Earn" the Future) and transpired with few incidents. Many observers expected the party to respond to the loss of three million voters since 1982 and the rise in antigovernment protest. But the PSOE leadership, citing a 5 percent growth rate, took the offensive, arguing that 1987 had been the best year of the decade for the Spanish economy and claiming that the promise of creating 800,000 new jobs had now been fulfilled (although somewhat belatedly, and not with a reduction of unemployment).[91] The leadership pointed with pride to its record of integration into the European Community, successful industrial reconversion, political decentralization, consolidation of democracy, resolution of the contentious bases issue with the United States, and the steady growth in party membership. Txiki Benegas, the PSOE's third-ranking leader, attacked the UGT as being "worried about increasing salaries for civil servants whose job is guaranteed for life.... I doubt they are any closer to the man in the street than we are."[92]

As in the previous three congresses, the delegates unanimously approved the leadership of González and nearly unanimously endorsed the record of the PSOE Executive Committee. For both of these crucial elections the party's bloc-voting procedure was in effect, eliminating the possibility of a protest vote by individual delegates. In the elections for a new PSOE Federal Committee, the main "legislature" of the PSOE between congresses, the *oficialista* slate won 72.9 percent of the vote, but the Socialist Left slate won a surprising 22.5 percent of the vote. The success of the IS in the Federal Committee election was possible because of the provision allowing delegates to vote individually and not as part of a regional bloc. Because the IS had only about 7 percent of the congress delegates, the result was seen by many as a mild protest against the party leadership.[93] As a result, the IS broke the 20-percent barrier and was entitled to proportional representation (nine of thirty-six seats) on the Federal Committee. Hardly anticipating such a strong showing by the PSOE left, the *oficialistas* had earlier offered the IS four seats on the Federal Committee if they would agree not to run a separate slate of candidates. Prudently, the IS rejected the offer and instead won a great moral victory.

Much of the attention at the Thirty-first Congress was directed away from ideological and political economic issues and focused instead on the leadership's decision to endorse a new party rule, reserving 25 percent of all party posts for women despite the fact that women make up only about 16 percent of the total membership. This novel measure helped to create a festive atmosphere among the delegates and attracted most of the media attention.

The moment of greatest tension occurred when UGT leader Nicolás Redondo addressed the delegates. González had offered Redondo a position on the party executive as a gesture of reconciliation, but the union leader turned it down.[94] In his remarks to the congress, Redondo doused the delegates with icy remarks, decrying the festive atmosphere and the triumphal tone of the party leadership:

Although it might seem too simple to put it this way, this party will have to think about whether the policies it has pursued up to now have benefited the rich or the poor.... The improvement of the economic indicators has not led to an improvement of the basic social indicators ... there is more unemployment, greater inequality of income, and less public protection of citizens.[95]

Redondo's comments often drew applause, but none of the PSOE Executive Committee applauded the union leader.[96]

Reflecting on the Thirty-first Congress as a whole, the daily *ABC* concluded that there was

continuity and self-satisfaction among the ranks of the PSOE at the end of a congress where everything was put in its place beforehand. . . . Minority groups were allowed the convenient gratification of some seats on the Federal Committee, in an acceptable number; Redondo gave his dignified speech without crossing the boundary of hostility toward the delegates; and women received their quota. González once more had the skill to divide up power just enough to keep most sectors of the party happy.[97]

NOTES

1. *Cambio 16* (January 18, 1988), pp. 26–29.

2. On the Spanish Communist Party, see Eusebio M. Mujal-León, "The Spanish Communists and the Search for Electoral Space," in Howard R. Penniman and Eusebio M. Mujal León, eds. *Spain at the Polls, 1977, 1979, and 1982* (Washington, D.C.: American Enterprise Institute and Duke University Press, 1985), pp. 160–187. On their disintegration, see Sergio Vilar, *Porque se ha destruido el PCE* (Barcelona: Plaza & Janes, 1986).

3. Howard Machin, "Communism and National Communism in West European Politics," in Howard Machin, ed., *National Communism in Western Europe* (London: Methuen, 1983), pp. 1–23.

4. See the data presented in Antonio Bar Cendón, "Normalidad o excepcionalidad?: Para una tipología del sistema de partidos español," *Sistema* 65 (March 1985): 3–19.

5. As reported in *El País* International Edition (July 7 and 14, 1986).

6. Vilar, *Porque se ha*, p. 132.

7. Quoted in *Cambio 16* (May 23, 1988), p. 18.

8. Juan Altable, "Cuevas Rompe con Mancha," *Cambio 16* (May 23, 1988), pp. 17–21.

9. José María Carrascal, *La revolución del PSOE* (Barcelona: Plaza & Janes, 1985), p. 57.

10. See Pilar del Castillo and Giacomo Sani, "Las elecciones de 1986: Continuidad sin consolidación," in Juan Linz and José Ramón Montero, eds., *Crisis y cambio: Electores y partidos en la España de los años ochenta* (Madrid: Centro de Estudios Constitucionales, 1986), p. 628.

11. A good overview of the 1987 elections is in Paul Heywood, "Spain: 10 June 1987," *Government and Opposition* 4 (1987): 390–401.

12. The data were based on a sample of 2,500 interviews conducted during December 6–13, 1984. The data were collected by the Centro de Investigaciones Sociológicas.

13. In response to another question asked in the sample, 47 percent of respondents agreed that the PSOE "had moderated its positions in office," whereas 32 percent said the PSOE "had maintained its positions." Of the total, 19 percent

did not know and 2 percent did not respond. See *Revista Española de Investigaciones Sociológicas* 28 (1984): 328–329.

14. The data on the perceived weakening of the military, Church, and bureaucracy were collected in a survey, "Dos años de gobierno Socialista," conducted by the Centro de Investigaciones Sociológicas, November 1984 (survey number 1439). A total of 12,293 were sampled. It asked respondents if, compared with two years earlier, the following groups had more power. For the military, 22 percent said "more," 42 percent said "less," 2 percent said "same," 30 percent did not know, and 3 percent did not respond. For the bureaucracy, the percentages were "more," 22; "less," 35; "same," 2; did not know, 38; no response, 3. For the Church, the percentages were "more," 11; "less," 57; "same," 2; did not know, 27; no response, 3.

15. On the weakness of party identification and the strength of the left-right identification, see Samuel H. Barnes, Peter McDonough, and Antonio López Pina, "The Development of Partisanship in New Democracies: The Case of Spain," *American Journal of Political Science* 29 (1985): 699–700. Left-right identification, through weaker than in most other West European nations, was stronger than in Italy or the United States.

16. See *Revista Española de Investigaciones Sociológicas* 23 (October–December 1984): 332.

17. Richard Gunther, Giacomo Sani, and Goldie Shabad, *Spain after Franco: The Making of a Competetive Party System* (Berkeley: University of California Press, 1986), p. 191.

18. Ibid., p. 199.

19. Ibid., p. 194; and Peter McDonough, Samuel H. Barnes, and A. López Pina, "The Spanish Public in Political Transition," *British Journal of Political Science* 2 (1981): 73.

20. Gunther, et al., *Spain after Franco*, p. 190.

21. Thomas D. Lancaster, "Economics, Democracy, and Spanish Elections," *Political Behavior* 4 (1984): 357.

22. Ibid., p. 356.

23. From the 1984 survey, "Dos años de gobierno Socialista," conducted by the Centro de Investigaciones Sociológicas, November 1984 (survey number 1439). A total of 12,293 were sampled; 27 percent did not know and 3 percent did not respond.

24. Ibid. The percentages were as follows: big business, 43; middle class, 6; retired people with pensions, 8; small business, 3; workers, 5; peasants, 1; none, 1; does not know, 27; no response, 7.

25. Ibid. Of respondents, 15 percent did not know and 1 percent did not respond.

26. See the data published in *Diário 16* (May 3, 1987), p. 1.

27. See the poll results published in *Cambio 16* (April 13, 1987), p. 61.

28. From the Centro de Investigaciones Sociológicas survey, "3 años de gobierno Socialista" (survey number 1492), conducted in November 1985. There were 12,451 surveys conducted; 32 percent perceived no change, 10 percent did not know, and 1 percent did not answer.

29. Peter McDonough, Samuel H. Barnes, and Antonio López Pina, "The

Growth of Democratic Legitimacy in Spain," *American Political Science Review* 3 (1986): 743.

30. Peter McDonough, Samuel H. Barnes, and Antonio López Pina, "Economic Policy and Public Opinion in Spain," presented at the Annual Meeting of the Midwest Political Science Association, Chicago, April 17–120, 1985, p. 6.

31. Ibid., p. 17.

32. Ibid., p. 10.

33. Ibid., p. 12.

34. Ibid., p. 13.

35. From the Centro de Investigaciones Sociológicas survey, "Post-electoral 1982" (survey number 1327), conducted in November 1982. There were 2,394 surveys conducted. Other percentages were the Coalición Democrática, 2; PCE, 6; regional parties, 2; other parties, 3; and did not respond, 16.

36. Gunther, Sani, and Shabad conclude that "a comparison of the social composition of the PSOE and the UCD is striking more in its similarity than its difference." See *Spain after Franco*, p. 194.

37. The ability of the PSOE to rally its constituents around such a controversial issue presents an especially intriguing puzzle, given the energy with which the PSOE had opposed NATO membership in 1981 and 1982. The answer may relate to the finding, reported by Barnes, McDonough, and López Pina, that although overall levels of party identification are low in Spain, the PSOE has been the most successful at converting its voters into identifiers. See "The Development of Partisanship," p. 15. Indeed, the CIS data presented in Table 5.16 suggest that a substantial portion (33 percent) of PSOE voters voting "yes" in the referendum did so because it was the position of their party.

38. Fernando Jauregui, "El hermetismo calculado de González," *El País* (June 2, 1986), p. 20.

39. On a scale of 1 to 10, with 10 as the most favorable, González received a 5.52. He was followed by Suárez (CDS, 4.91), Guerra (PSOE, 3.98), Roca (PRD, 3.67), Alzaga (CP, 2.92), Fraga (CP, 2.87), Iglesias (PCE, 2.65), and Carrillo (PCE, 2.50). See *El País* (March 6, 1986), p. 14.

40. A parallel argument was made with regard to the enhanced role of leadership in the transition to democracy in Donald Share, *The Making of Spanish Democracy* (New York: Praeger/Center for the Study of Democratic Institutions, 1986). With regard to the contemporary Spanish party system, a similar argument is made by McDonough, Barnes, and López Pina in "The Spanish Public," p. 71.

41. On the weakness of levels of political institutionalization, see McDonough et al., "The Spanish Public," p. 51. On the low levels of political participation, see Thomas O. Lancaster and Michael S. Lewis-Beck, "The Spanish Voter: Tradition, Economics, Ideology," Occasional Paper, Laboratory for Political Research, Department of Political Science, University of Iowa, number 16 (1985), p. 6. On the importance of television and the ability of González to use the medium, Barnes et al. note that these factors have allowed the PSOE to "achieve a great deal of electoral success with a modest level of party organization." See "The Development of Partisanship," p. 3.

42. Hans-Jürgen Puhle, "El PSOE: Un partido dominante y heterogéneo," in

Juan J. Linz and José Ramón Montero, eds., *Crisis y cambio: Electores y partidos en la España de los años ochenta*. (Madrid: Centro de Estudios Constitucionales, 1986), pp. 340–341.

43. Francisco Bustelo, "De la Barraca del Presidente," *El País*, February 24, 1987, p. 16.

44. Juan J. Linz et al., *Informe sociológico sobre el cambio político en España, 1975–1981* (Madrid: Euramerica, 1981), pp. 256–260.

45. McDonough et al., "Economic Policy," pp. 13–14.

46. Luis López Guerra, "Partidos políticos en España: Evolución y perspectivas," in García de Enterría, ed., *España: Un presente para el futuro* (Madrid: Instituto de Estudios Económicos, 1984), p. 138.

47. Jauregui, "El hermetismo," p. 20.

48. López Guerra, "Partidos políticos en España," p. 138.

49. Antonio García Santesmases, "Otra ocasión perdida," *Diario 16*, May 21, 1986, p. 6.

50. See *El País* (May 23, 1986), p. 18.

51. Term used by Pablo Castellano, in Sergio Vilar, *La década sorprendente* (Barcelona: Planeta, 1986) p. 174.

52. See the report by Fernando Jauregui in *El País* (May 23, 1984), p. 13.

53. Jauregui, in *El País* (May 23, 1984), p. 13.

54. See the *El País* editorial, "El Congreso del Presidente" (December 10, 1984), p. 10.

55. *El País* (November 5, 1984), p. 19.

56. A "war of figures" broke out between the IS and the government. Guillermo Galeote, PSOE publicity secretary, insisted that only 34 percent of the party membership opposed NATO during the delegate selection process, whereas the IS claimed that 57 percent were opposed. See *El País* (October 17, 1984), p. 14.

57. *El País*, (October 14, 1984), p. 21. The Executive Committee wrote the *ponencia de síntesis* (summary platform) that was presented to delegates at the Thirtieth Congress and was supposed to reflect the opinions expressed at regional congresses. The IS claimed the *ponencia* completely ignored opposition to the government from the party left.

58. Quoted in *El País* (October 18, 1984), p. 15.

59. Even the Popular Alliance had a higher ratio. See *El País* (October 14, 1984), p. 18.

60. López Guerra, "Partidos políticos en España," pp. 132 ff.

61. *El País* editorial, "El congreso del Presidente" (December 10, 1984), p. 10.

62. Vilar, *La década sorprendente*, p. 175.

63. See Pedro Altares's analysis in *El País* (March 15 and July 22, 1984).

64. His remarks appeared in *El Día* (February 21, 1986).

65. Andres Cebrantes, *Balance y futuro del socialismo* (Barcelona: Planeta, 1984).

66. *Cambio 16* (February 10, 1986).

67. *Cambio 16* (March 4, 1986).

68. *El País* (March 4, 1986), p. 16.

69. Reported in *El País* (March 18, 1986).

70. On the UGT, see Mariano Guindal and Rodolfo Serrano, eds. *La otra transición: Nicolás Redondo y el sindicalismo Socialista* (Madrid: Unión Editorial, 1986).

71. For an overview of the Spanish labor movement, see Gary Prevost, "The Spanish Labor Movement," in Thomas O. Lancaster and Gary Prevost, eds., *Politics and Change in Spain* (New York: Praeger, 1985), pp. 125–143. For a discussion of the reasons for union weakness, see Santos M. Ruesga, "Estrategias sindicales actuales," in *Anuario El País, 1986* (Madrid: El País, 1986), p. 402. On the generally low levels of participation in Spain, see Peter McDonough, Antonio López Pina, and Samuel H. Barnes, "The Spanish Public in Political Transition," *British Journal of Political Science* 2 (January 1981): 49–79; S. Barnes and Antonio López Pina, "Political Mobilization in Old and New Democracies: Spain in Comparative Perspective," delivered at the 1982 Annual Meeting of the American Political Science Association, Denver, September 2–5; José María Maravall, *La política de la transición, 1975–1980* (Madrid: Taurus, 1981), part 2.

72. Vilar, *La década Sorprendete*, p. 152.

73. Prevost, "The Spanish Labor Movement," p. 133; and Guindal and Serrano, *La otra transición*, p. 127.

74. Gunther, et al. *Spain*, p. 214.

75. Described in *El País* (May 26, 1986), p. 116.

76. The events are described in Vilar, *La década sorprendente*, pp. 151–153.

77. Guindal and Serrano, *La otra transición* p. 159.

78. The senator, Antonio Rosa, resigned his seat the next day in protest over the policies of his party.

79. Quoted in Vilar, *La década sorprendente*, p. 150.

80. Ibid., p. 151.

81. *El País* (March 4, 1986), p. 16.

82. Quoted in *Cambio 16* (February 10, 1986), p. 18.

83. *El País* International Edition (March 28, 1988), p. 14.

84. Ibid. (April 4, 1988), pp. 28–29. González created further tension by meeting with the three expelled union members.

85. *Tiempo* (May 9, 1988), p. 41.

86. Quoted in *El País* International Edition (October 26, 1987), p. 12.

87. From the IS amendment to the *ponencia política*, published in *El País* International Edition (October 5, 1987), pp. 16–17.

88. Quoted in *Cambio 16* (January 18, 1988), p. 20.

89. Quoted in ibid., p. 19.

90. Quoted in ibid., p. 18.

91. See the comments by Txiki Benegas on the eve of the Thirty-first Congress, reported in *El País* (January 18, 1988), pp. 14–15.

92. Quoted in *Cambio 16* (January 18, 1988), p. 21.

93. One example of this interpretation is Javier Pradera, "La cuarta parte del cielo," *El País* International Edition (January 25, 1988), p. 13.

94. As reported in *El País* International Edition (January 25, 1988), p. 11.

95. Quoted in ibid., p. 12.

96. See *Cambio 16*, (February 3, 1988), p. 118.

97. *ABC* International Edition (January 27–February 2, 1988), p. 11.

6

The Socialist Experience in Government: Evaluating the Past and Prospects for the Future

I'll tell you what a socialist society is, and everything else is a joke. To design a socialist society like a painting . . . is foolish. . . . There is no other definition of socialism than the deepening of democracy in every direction.

—Felipe González[1]

There is no use trying to weaken the criticism or soften the shock by convincing oneself that the policies of those governments will have a socialist outcome. It is clear that this is not the case and that the Socialists' policies are not even social democratic. The economic situation allows little room for social reforms, especially when the governments have been totally unable to reduce, let alone eliminate, unemployment. Without full unemployment and a high growth rate, no social democratic program can work.

—Ignacio Sotelo[2]

THE UNFORTUNATE TIMING OF THE SOCIALISTS' RISE TO POWER

Any attempt to assess the Socialists' experience in government must first consider the unfortunate historical, economic, and international environment within which the PSOE took power. Although these factors did not determine the behavior of the Socialist government from 1982 to the present, they constituted unusually severe constraints. Moreover, these factors were often employed by party leaders, in most cases sincerely, to justify policy shifts.[3]

Most important, the Socialists assumed government in a country that had never experienced a complete bourgeois revolution. The economic and political weakness of the Spanish bourgeoisie is a constant theme throughout Spanish history. The shallowness, regional marginalization, and ultimate failure of liberalism in the nineteenth century, the importance of foreign investment, the dependence on state protectionism, and the strength of authoritarian and anticapitalist forces were all classic features of Spanish society well into the twentieth century. The weakness of bourgeois political forces vis-à-vis the reactionary right and the revolutionary left was a factor contributing to the collapse of the Spanish Second Republic. The victory of franquism in the Spanish Civil War led to an initial period of antibourgeois and antiliberal autarchy (1939–1956). While most of Europe participated in the emergence of a liberal capitalist economic order, Spain's economy remained protected, isolated, and increasingly static.

Only in the 1950s was Franco forced to abandon autarchy in favor of a political economic model more open to the forces of international and domestic capitalism. The spectacular growth of the Spanish economy during the 1960s was intimately linked to the emergence of a new and more modern domestic bourgeoisie, but the political power of this group lagged in comparison with its economic role; and compared with the rest of Europe, Spain's capitalists were still outmoded, protected, and monopolistic.

The delicate political transition after Franco's death prevented a rapid remedy to this situation. Major socioeconomic reform was removed from the agenda in order to facilitate political compromise. The UCD was ill-suited to carry out a restructuring and modernization of Spanish capitalism as it was a coalition that represented both modern and more conservative sectors of Spanish capital. In fact, the unravelling of the UCD began with the protest by UCD conservatives against the Suárez government's first major fiscal reform. The constant feuding between progressive and conservative sectors of the Spanish bourgeoisie, and the fact that Suárez represented neither sector, contributed to the collapse of the center in Spain.

It is hardly surprising, therefore, that the internal bloodletting of the UCD and its turn to the right after Suárez's resignation had as a consequence the entry of many progressive and even liberal capitalists into the Socialist Party. Fernández Ordóñez and Miguel Boyer are only two prominent examples of politicians who gravitated toward the PSOE after it became clear that the Socialisty Party stood the best chance of undertaking the modernization of Spanish capitalism.

Thus although the UCD had successfully consolidated much (though not all) of the process of the political transition to democracy, it had proved incapable of completing the bourgeois revolution that was stillborn in the nineteenth and early twentieth centuries, frozen during the early period of franquism, and stunted during the late franquist period.

The need to modernize capitalism by reducing state protectionism; attacking established bastions of monopoly, privilege, and access; promoting greater competition and efficiency; and integrating Spain into the European Community were goals widely accepted by the PSOE leadership on the eve of their rise to power.

That such a "mission" would be especially difficult for a Socialist Party to carry out—indeed, it would necessarily contradict many of the short- and medium-term redistributive goals contained in the Socialist program—was not well understood within the Socialist Party at the time. The implementation of such a modernization of Spanish capitalism would necessarily entail severe sacrifices and costs, and the distribution of those costs and sacrifices could not easily be justified in traditional socialist terms.

It is within this context that the leadership's desire to prevent any and all internal dissent becomes more comprehensible. The Socialists' decision to consolidate and modernize capitalism would be impossible to implement in all but the most disciplined and complacent party.

Moreover, the contradictions, costs, and sacrifices went beyond the ironies of a Socialist Party implementing an essentially capitalist and liberal set of reforms. The Socialists attempted such a program during a period of sluggish growth and severe international economic recession. Unlike its northern European counterparts, the PSOE could not hope to contribute to the solidification of Spanish capitalism while simultaneously redistributing the fruits of an expanding economic pie.

The Socialist project was even more contradictory because of the proximity of the democratic transition and the continued fragility of the democratic system. After the twice-victorious UCD had completely disintegrated, the Socialists inherited a perilous relationship with the armed forces, a persistent and vexing problem of terrorism, and a still incomplete framework of regional autonomy. Although the most severe threat to the consolidation of democracy had passed by the time the PSOE assumed power, the new regime was hardly out of the woods: a military coup plot, planned for the eve of the Socialist victory, was discovered shortly before the elections of 1982.

Finally, the PSOE was completely inexperienced in government. The young Socialist leaders represented a new generation and were still, by and large, undergoing a process of ideological and personal maturation. Understandably, most of the top PSOE leaders lacked any real administrative experience, which helps to explain why González found it advisable to tap more experienced individuals (the neoliberal technocrats) for key cabinet posts, even when they had little previous connection with the Socialist party and in some cases clearly rejected the PSOE electoral program.

In short, compared with the postwar history of the northern European social democrats—who assumed power in the context of advanced and competitive capitalist systems, steady and rapid domestic and international economic growth, consolidated democratic regimes, and with more experienced leaders—the PSOE took power in a very inauspicious context.

SURROGATE REFORMS

In chapter 4, it was argued that the PSOE shelved much of the redistributive orientation of its program after its rise to power in 1982. In evaluating the Socialist performance in government, however, it cannot be argued that the PSOE record was one of inaction. On the contrary, the Socialists had an impressive record of accomplishments in their first six years of government. They chose to deemphasize redistributive reforms, but they did achieve several other types of reform that might be viewed, in part, as surrogates for traditionally Socialist goals. Although covered in more detail in Chapter 4, the PSOE's success in implementing five major types of reform can be summarized as follows.

Parliamentary Democratic Reform

On the whole the PSOE helped to consolidate democratic rule and strengthened the delicate political compromise that underpinned the transition to democracy. The rise to power of the Socialists caused little commotion in Spanish political life and thus assured a wide spectrum of society that political alternation was both desirable and feasible. Given Spain's previous democratic experiment during the Second Republic (discussed in Chapter 2), the Socialist leadership regarded this as a significant achievement.

As noted in Chapter 4, the Socialists achieved a *modus vivendi* with the Spanish armed forces, long an obstacle to democratic consolidation. A top adviser to Felipe González stated in the fall of 1986:

The PSOE has governed for almost four years with coherence and prudence, always preferring to be accused of excessive moderation rather than risking mistakes. Thanks to this, social tension that might favor a coup does not exist.[4]

Though some consider the price for such a peace excessive, the virtual elimination of the specter of *golpismo* was a major Socialist contribution to the democratic regime.

The Socialists also oversaw the completion of the regional autonomy process, although the chaotic and somewhat unwieldy relationship between the center and the autonomous communities will eventually require modification. The salient point is that regional challenges to the democratic regime appear to be manageable within the context of the new Constitution.

Well before the Socialists took power, many observers were predicting that the key to the consolidation of parliamentary democracy would be whether alternation from a conservative to Socialist government would be possible and whether an incoming Socialist government would be able to sufficiently moderate its program so as not to antagonize the Spanish right.[5] From this perspective the PSOE experience has been an unqualified success.

The Consolidation and Liberalization of Spanish Capitalism

Although the need to consolidate and liberalize Spanish capitalism was recognized in the 1982 PSOE program, the priority accorded this goal by the government surpassed all expectations. Much criticism has pointed to the regressive consequences of the PSOE's reform of Spanish capitalism, but there can be little doubt that the Socialists have implemented the reform with vigor.

The specifics of the reform have been noted elsewhere in this study (see Chapter 4), but its major focus has been an industrial reconversion and a reduction in state impediments to both domestic and foreign private sector investment. When assessing the results of the reform, any analysis must consider that Spain's entry into the European Community—supported by every major national political force—made significant economic restructuring imperative. The national consensus regarding Spain's integration into Europe by definition demanded a program of economic liberalization. Thus critics of the PSOE's political economic record generally cite the failure to equitably distribute the costs of such a reform across social classes but do not question the logic of liberalization per se.

Looking ahead to 1992 with considerable apprehension, the Socialists spent considerable enery creating the conditions that might facilitate a smoother transition to full EC membership: industrial reconversion, investments in high technology, and promotion of mergers among Spain's comparatively small enterprises.

Significant Social Reform

Although the Socialist record in the area of social reform has clearly been mixed, the Socialists accomplished a great deal in a relatively short period. Among many reforms, the Socialists overhauled the Spanish penal code, restructured the civil service, improved somewhat the responsiveness of the state bureaucracy to the demands of the citizenry, and reorganized the university system.

Many Spaniards have expressed a sense of deception because the reforms have not always met the expectations created by the Socialists themselves, because some reforms have not easily meshed with traditionally socialist concepts, and because PSOE budget priorities have contradicted earlier pledges. However, though it soon became clear that the *cambio* would be unable to fundamentally alter large areas of Spanish society, the Socialist record in the area of social reform was one of considerable activity.

Reforming the Political Discourse

The Socialists' total domination of national politics after 1982 allowed them to shape the political discourse and influence the political culture. The widely perceived "Americanization" of Spanish politics has been encouraged by the PSOE's behavior in government in several respects.

First, by radically severing the connection between electoral platforms and government behavior, the Socialists have downplayed the value of political programs, campaign promises, and political rhetoric. In this sense, as noted earlier, the PSOE has simply extended and exaggerated the dominant political culture and norms of the transition to democracy. The abandonment of much of the 1982 platform has not led to massive punishment by voters but, rather, has been seen as a healthy dose of political flexibility. The Socialist experience has forced the Spanish public to realize that in a modern democracy, "politicians, regardless of ideology ... are with rare exceptions just like Western public choice theory described them: they most often look out first for their own interests, and then their friends' interests. Their greatest worry is to win the next election."[6] In short, the Socialists have helped to end the political naiveté about the workings of modern polyarchies cultivated by forty years of authoritarian rule.

Second, given that the importance of platforms and campaign pledges has been downgraded, the role of leadership and political imagery has been enhanced. At the level of society and party, Felipe González has been particularly adept at marshaling his charisma and popularity to counteract potential sources of opposition to his policies. As in most advanced democracies, the role of the mass media in cultivating the importance of political image and downplaying ideology and concrete political platforms has continued to increase. As the PSOE quickly emulated the "catch-all" nature of "modern" political parties, its leaders felt obliged to respond more to the common denominator of public opinion than to the demands of Socialist interest groups, fractions, or ideological principles. At the Thirty-first Congress in January 1988, González counseled delegates, "we must remember that the voter who supports us is just as socialist as those holding party cards."[7]

Finally, the Socialist experience has once and for all ended the very notion of significant and rapid political change. As early as 1981, González warned that a future Socialist government would not attempt rapid change. At the Twenty-ninth Congress in 1981, he stated that the party needed to "elaborate a long range program of 25 years, because the transformation of society will not take place in four years, even if we win the elections."[8] At the Thirtieth PSOE Congress in 1984, Enrique Tierno Galván criticized González's cautious approach to politics, warning that "one cannot go up the stairs so slowly and with such delay that upon arrival the building is about to fall apart." González retorted to his aging colleague that "if you want to arrive at the top like a twenty year old, go up like an eighty year old."[9] By eschewing a major *cambio,* despite having won two consecutive absolute majorities, the PSOE enhanced the notion of incremental reform. As was argued in Chapter 5, such moderation caused much frustration among sectors of society and the party but was widely supported by Spanish public opinion.

A New Party Model

The PSOE provided the new Spanish party system the first example of an effective and truly modern catch-all party. Like the defunct UCD, its appeal was cross-class, based less on ideology than on image (especially that of its leader). Unlike the UCD, it remained highly disciplined and unified behind a single leader. It can be argued that the PSOE, at least after 1979, was the only unified and cohesive political party of the new democracy. After 1982, it was widely perceived as the only party capable of forming a coherent and stable government.

While in power the PSOE was plagued by few internal personality clashes, almost no internal power struggles, and relatively little political dissent. Felipe González and Alfonso Guerra dominated the Socialist Party almost completely and with little real challenge to their power. In parliament, the PSOE delegation behaved as a highly disciplined bloc. Although it is often noted that the maintenance of such high levels of internal cohesion was possible only by limiting party democracy and resorting to occasionally authoritarian methods, it is also true that the Socialists were spared the constant squabbling and back-stabbing so characteristic of their competitors.

The Socialists also added to the essentially elitist nature of Spanish politics, long a tradition in Spanish history but exacerbated by the transactive transition to democracy. Despite a steady growth in party membership, the PSOE is a minuscule party, and its members are, on the whole, best described as dependents rather than militants. The Socialist impact at the level of street politics is minimal. In the words of one observer, "Among the most noteworthy aspects of the current Spanish situation is the terror the Socialists have of all street demonstrations."[10]

The PSOE thus became a strictly disciplined party dominated by a strong leadership. Its attempt to reform the traditional Spanish party model was in part a necessary response to the contradictions created by the Socialist government's controversial policy decisions. But as Mario Caciagli argues, it was also a reflection of the societal weakness of the PSOE:

If the leadership of the PSOE was inclined toward oligarchic solutions, it appears to have done so more out of necessity, fearing that it was "floating" on a still unformed, and above all, weak and limited base.[11]

Regardless of the motives, the leadership's *ability* to carry out such a reform was never guaranteed, and the attempt was always risky: its success in this respect was remarkable.

COSTS AND POTENTIAL PITFALLS

The loss of government office and entry into opposition is frequently traumatic for political parties, particularly after a prolonged period of government, when the turn of events is interpreted as a watershed in the party's history. The breakdown of their ascendancy in the party system often signifies an adverse change in the political landscape, to which they must respond. It often also reflects the erosion of the political or intellectual credibility of their basic values and policies. Moreover, while in government, the exercise of power frequently serves as the party's *raison d'etre*. Entering opposition it must submit those values which constitute its *identity* to a thoroughgoing reappraisal.

—Stephen Padgett[12]

The preceding discussion suggests that the Socialists *did* achieve a great deal in government even though they did not emphasize redistributive goals. As was argued in Chapter 5, the PSOE's electoral record after 1982 was remarkable, and its prospects in the near future appear quite favorable. Nevertheless, it is important to inquire into the possible costs and potential pitfalls related to the PSOE's rapid ideological shift, its new party model, and its continued political success.

Substituting Power for Ideology

As with all parties that occupy government for long periods, especially in such conditions of political hegemony, the PSOE has consistently struggled with accusations that it has abused political power during its long tenure in office. Two incidents that were most damaging—at least on a symbolic level—were Felipe González's cruise on Franco's yacht, the *Azor*, in 1985, and Alfonso Guerra's use of an Air Force jet to rescue him from a traffic jam at the Portuguese-Spanish border in 1988. Many observers saw these incidents as proof that the Socialists had become overly comfortable in their position of power and that they had increasingly become aloof from popular pressure. These two vignettes, the subject of much criticism and countless jokes, relfected a deep-seated conviction within Spanish political society that the Socialist leaders were behaving like *los de siempre* (the same old people) and that the elements of continuity between franquist and conservative leaders and the Socialists were far greater than elements of change.

A far more serious set of accusations emerged in 1988 regarding a number of instances of influence peddling by many PSOE ex-officials, including ex-minister Miguel Boyer. The accusations did not bear fruit, in part because a number of conservative politicians were implicated at the same time and this obstructed any political consensus to pursue the matter seriously within parliament.

Juan Luis Cebrián, publisher of Spain's most prestigious daily newspaper, argues that many of the PSOE's "vices" come from the franquist tradition; others date from the "consensus mongering" and clientelism of the transition to democracy; and still others result from the youth, inexperience, and pure opportunism of the Socialist elite. He concludes that the PSOE has become little more than "a fabulous electoral machine and a political employment agency."[13] The cost of becoming a party of careerists with little ideological glue uniting the membership may become apparent only when the PSOE loses power and the party no longer serves as a provider of employment. At that point a massive exodus from the PSOE may occur, complicating the party's attempt to develop an opposition strategy. It is worth recalling that the destruction of the UCD in the 1982 elections revealed in part a coalition that had depended solely on the exercise of power and that had revolved around a single charismatic leader.

Defending the Fort: Internal Dissent

The continuation of a regime of strict intraparty discipline has also contributed to the PSOE's image as an intolerant and often antidemocratic party. As usual, the perceived iron man within the PSOE is Vice-

President Alfonso Guerra, whose infamous dictum that *"quien se mueva no sale en la foto"* ("He who moves will not be in the picture") appears to have been made in all seriousness. The ejection from the PSOE of perennial dissenter Pablo Castellano, the leader of the Socialist Left, and the removal of the independent-minded José Rodríguez de la Borbolla as president of the Andalusian PSOE are only two recent examples of Guerra's power within the PSOE and his willingness to use it against a wide spectrum of internal dissent.[14]

Somewhat ironically, the persistence of an atmosphere hostile to ideological diversity and nonconformity, often viewed as a requisite for attracting a broader electorate, will likely hamper the abiliity of the PSOE to integrate more diverse sectors of society into the party organization itself. As is suggested later, the oligarchic internal political structure and the overlapping of party and government are already limiting the party's ability to engage in a serious ideological reassessment as the PSOE attempts to integrate postmaterialist issues and movements into the Socialist Party.

Finally, the dependence on a single leadership team and the absence of any real alternatives in the PSOE run the risk of throwing the Socialist Party into chaos should the current leadership experience a fall from grace, or should the PSOE fall from power.

Party, Government, and the Interests of Democracy

The image of the PSOE as an often antidemocratic party and one willing to tolerate occasional abuses of government power has been bitterly refuted by the top PSOE leadership. Unfortunately, in contesting such an image the leadership has only exacerbated the problem. Guerra increasingly complained that opposition to the government was antidemocratic. For example, when facing parliamentary criticism for his use of the Air Force jet to extract him from traffic, he complained of an "antidemocratic windstorm" aimed at him.[15] According to one observer of the Socialist government,

The identification of government officials with the state, and of democracy with the power of Felipe González's praetorian guard, is not novel. But the use of such arguments continues to worry many. It warns that the government wants to preserve its own power at all costs.[16]

The fact that most PSOE leaders firmly believe that their party has been *forced* to bear the burden of consolidating the process of democratization, given the absence of strong competitors, has cultivated the notion that all opposition to the PSOE must come from antidemocratic sectors. Socialist leaders often express disappointment and resentment that they face criticism for their actions when there are no real political alternatives available. This same logic can be observed at the level of intraparty politics, where the leadership of González has faced no real alternatives and has thus come to view itself as indispensable for the political success of the PSOE and the continuation of democracy in Spain. That the logic is often used to justify authoritarian behavior is one of the many contradictions resulting from the PSOE's uncontested position in government and the leadership's hegemony within the Socialist Party.

BEYOND THE 1980s: THE FUTURE OF SPANISH SOCIALISM

Stuck in Power: Political Burnout without Electoral Consequences

By May 1988, opinion polls showed that the PSOE enjoyed the lowest level of popular support since its election to power in 1982. These data reflected the persistence of high levels of antigovernment social protest (a protracted teachers' strike, continued protests against the industrial reconversion, among others) and widespread concern about the Socialist government's aloofness.

However, the same dynamics that were described in chapter 5 and that allowed the PSOE to win reelection in 1986 continued to operate. The party system still offered no alternative to the PSOE. Although one poll showed the PSOE with only 20 percent of the vote, its competitors were given little to cheer about: the CDS received 10 percent; the AP, 8 percent; and the IU, about 3 percent.[17] Predictably, a large chunk of the electorate was uncommitted. The absence of a credible opposition to the PSOE once again afforded a huge political space within which to maneuver. Indeed, data collected at about the same time by the Centro de Investigaciones Sociológicas indicated that had elections been held in May 1988, the PSOE would have retained its absolute majority.[18]

As has been the case throughout the PSOE years in government, no other political party is seen to be as capable of political compromise, moderation, responsibility, and effective leadership as the Socialists. The popular image of González has clearly tarnished over time, but he remains the most popular and charismatic leader in Spain.

The Socialists continue to stand out as the most coherent and disciplined party in Spain. Given the weakness of opposition parties, the only alternative to a PSOE government appeared to be political fragmentation and instability. The conservative Popular Alliance continues to struggle with personal feuds, a neophyte leader, and a reactionary and anachronistic popular image. The parties of the center remain fragmented and weak, and although Adolfo Suárez has emerged as the chief leader of the political center, there are many obstacles preventing him from mounting a challenge to the PSOE. His poor relationship with the military and financial elite; the distrust he evokes among other centrist groups; the weakness of his political party; the ideological and political competition provided by the PSOE, AP, and regional groups; and his identification with the transition from franquism make him less of an alternative to the PSOE than might be expected given his charisma and leadership skills. The communist left remains fragmented between two rival organizations, although talk of a reunification has begun. Although a political comeback of the PCE is not impossible, it will not likely present a real threat to the PSOE in the near and medium term.

Socialist leaders have responded to many criticisms leveled at them by citing their two consecutive absolute majorities, results that any political party would view with pride. After the 1986 general elections, the PSOE magazine, *El Socialista*, argued that "for four years we have heard about the government's distancing from the people, disenchantment, etc. The elections of this past weekend have put an end to all those doubts."[19] At a May Day rally in 1987, Joaquín Leguina, president of the Madrid Autonomous Community, leader of the powerful Madrid Socialist Federation, and a moderate critic of González, noted with irony that despite the criticisms of the PSOE (especially those leveled at the party by UGT Secretary General Nicolás Redondo), "this is the best government we have."[20]

By 1988, it was still an open question whether the PSOE would suffer any severe hemorrhage of votes in the near or medium future and, more important, whether any other party would be enough of a beneficiary to dislodge the Socialists from power.

If It Works, Don't Fix It: Obstacles to Ideological Development

> It is not clear if it is worse that the programs of ten years ago were not carried out, or that they were not even considered. Upon taking up the responsibility of government, one always has to jettison simplistic, arbitrary and naive aspects that accumulate during time in the opposition, but in dumping these the baby has been discarded with the bath water.
>
> —Ignacio Sotelo[21]

> In only ten years, the Spanish Socialists have gone from republicanism, neutralism, anticapitalism, *autogestión*, to defender of Spain's entry into NATO, and a strong supporter of the efficiency of the market economy.
>
> —Antonio García Satesmases[22]

Things have taken place very quickly and have caught us unpre-

pared.... We need a debate about the social priorities; where should
we go in the future, or rather, where do we want to lead society?
We have to better define the nature of a progressive social project.
                                                                —Joaquín Leguina[23]

   In retrospect the PSOE has surmounted an ominous set of obstacles
since the transition to democracy. It has fully democratized its image in
the public eye and it has buried old conflicts with the Catholic Church,
the monarchy, the military, and the private sector. Moreover, the PSOE
has become the dominant governing party and has provided the only
two majority single-party governments in Spain's entire history. It has
done all this during a generally hard time for European social democracy. Since taking power the PSOE has avoided a political catastrophe
while having had a clearly reformist (if not social democratic) impact on
the economy and political system. Looking to Europe in 1982, Spanish
Socialists saw plenty of social democratic parties out of power, the French
Socialist debacle, but no case of a politically successful socialist party
carrying out progressive social democratic policies.[24] Perhaps for these
reasons the PSOE leadership has put off any debate about ideology,
long-term objectives, or the need to rediscover a "socialist" vision. Spain's
social democratic government has not been forced to justify the implementation of neoliberal political economic policies that directly increase
unemployment and skew the distribution of income and wealth toward
the wealthiest sectors of society. While in power the PSOE has side-
stepped any discussion of whether such neoliberal policies contribute to
the redistributive goals of social democracy.
   Socialist leaders have consistently argued that the creation of a socialist
society may take decades. González has argued that "[it is im]possible to
change a society in four years that has not been able to change for two
centuries.... In Spain we have to measure change by decades if we want
to be serious."[25] The Socialist leaders also hold that economic growth is
a prerequisite for redistribution and that workers must sacrifice in the
short term in order to make long-term progress. Most recently, González
admitted on Spanish television:

It is true, as the unions contend, that workers' salaries have risen more slowly
than the owners' income. That is the way it is all over Europe, and that is the
way it should be at the early stages of recovery. Only this way can profits be
invested in productive sectors of the economy.[26]

These arguments add up to an admission that PSOE leaders view capitalist democracy as the only feasible and desirable political economic
arrangement for Spain. They have thus endeavored to administer Span-

ish capitalism more efficiently and perhaps more equitably than have their conservative and authoritarian predecessors. But Spanish Socialists no longer seek to alter capitalism fundamentally in the name of equality and economic democracy.

The new emphasis on economic modernization, "efficient administration," and the desire to create "Things Well Done" (the PSOE campaign theme for the June 1987 elections) has replaced the old concern for equality and participatory democracy (*autogestión*). The PSOE has adopted a new image based on its technocratic-administrative capability and the charisma of González, and it is rapidly shedding its social democratic skin. The Spanish Socialists have replaced much of the rhetoric of redistribution and social justice with the goal of integrating Spain more completely into Europe and liberalizing and streamlining the Spanish economy so that it can survive this integration.

Some see such a shift as a sign of the maturity of Spanish politics and evidence that the combative class-based politics of industrializing society has given way to an end of ideology of the postindustrial era. The Americanization of Spanish politics, in which parties put their energy into media coverage instead of grass-roots organization, and in which personalities and single issues displace coherent party programs and ideological vision, is often considered a healthy sign that the Spanish polity has matured.

Others have noted a number of potential dangers of the PSOE's lack of social democratic vision. The growth-cum-redistribution consensus worked admirably in northern Europe in the 1950s and 1960s, but attempts to reproduce it in the 1980s, and in Spain, face more serious obstacles. It is unlikely that growth rates similar to those of the European miracle can be replicated during the 1980s and 1990s; and even if such growth were to result, the introduction of labor-saving technology (and the resulting increase of unemployment) will make the redistribution of income more difficult. In addition to the very unequal distribution of income in Spain among both individuals and regions, there is an increasing probability of a more serious division between an employed elite and an unemployed or underemployed mass. Nicolás Redondo, leader of the PSOE-affiliated trade union, the UGT, has charged that "the [government's] version of market economics, presented to us as the only possible policy and as a universal panacea, is only creating more unemployment, more inequality and more misery."[27] In short, if attempts to continue the growth-cum-redistribution model in the wealthier European countries are increasingly questioned by social democrats, the potential flaws and costs of such a strategy in Spain are far more serious.

Though inherently appealing to a society long isolated from Europe, the faith in integration and the desire to discover a Spanish niche in the increasingly integrated European Community also entails risks and potential problems. The creation of "frontier-free" Europe by 1992 may overwhelm entire sectors of the Spanish economy and may add to the ranks of the unemployed. Whether Spain can compete with the rest of Europe is, at the very least, an open question subject to very different interpretations.

To date, the PSOE has made no attempt to find a new political self-definition, one that no longer directly assails capitalism but that might nevertheless give the Socialists a more social democratic image and mission. One PSOE member has complained that the PSOE has "been left with no identity...nothing remains to distinguish it from progressive liberalism."[28] There has been little "greening" of the Spanish Socialists similar to the current developments in the West German SPD, nor have creative solutions such as the Swedish Meidner plan been debated within the PSOE.[29] The Socialists have not placed much stock in appeals to a variety of still inchoate social groups (youth, women, consumers, environmentalists, etc.) that might reinvigorate the party, although the recent decision (at the Thirty-first Congress) to allocate 25 percent of all party posts to women may be a small step in that direction. In the same vein, a decision in mid–1988 to implement an ambitious part-time youth employment program as an attempt to combat the alarmingly high rates of unemployment among eighteen- to twenty-five-year-olds may represent a desire to reach out to this alienated sector of society.

Nevertheless, Socialist leaders are painfully aware that the PSOE has lost its ideological direction. Alfonso Guerra has admitted:

Quite honestly, we cannot deny that we are faced with an attempt to weaken socialist thought and to replace it with a kind of inhumane ultraliberalism. For this very reason it is more important than ever to engage in a serious and rigorous debate that will allow us to clarify where we are headed.[30]

The Spanish Socialists have officially initiated a working group within the PSOE, called Program 2000, to begin such a discussion of a long-term political vision. Under the direction of Alfonso Guerra, the program will solicit written input from all sectors of the party. Already some of the contributions have pointed to serious deficiencies in the behavior of the Socialist government. For example, a report submitted by José Borrell, secretary of state for Finance, concluded that social expenditures under the Socialists grew too slowly. Another report concluded that four million Spaniards were "extremely poor" because of unemployment.[31]

The fact that the group is dominated by the party leadership and has so far completely excluded all members of the PSOE left does not augur well for the enterprise. Program 2000 coordinator Manuel Escudero, a close associate of Guerra, has concluded that the Socialists will continue to promote "growth in order to redistribute," suggesting that the overall emphasis of the PSOE may not change significantly. The absence of the *críticos* from the exercise (they continue to protest the control of the project by Guerra) may limit the contours of the debate. Attempts to engage in such a debate are increasingly constrained by past decisions and are repelled by a centrist momentum within the party. Implementation of a harsh austerity and industrial streamlining plan entailed the marginalization of many party intellectuals and the promotion of technocrats who currently see little need to rediscover a "socialist" vision. A search for new ideas is hardly considered urgent as long as the PSOE is occupied with the tasks of governing. New ideas and shifts in policy would certainly threaten some powerful sectors of the party, and there is little collective desire to rock the boat. Perhaps the most interesting question for the future is whether the stifling of internal debate, the consolidation of a charismatic leadership, and the very political success of the PSOE will prevent Spanish socialism from undertaking a serious reevaluation of the meaning of social democracy in the crisis of advanced capitalism.

If the experience of northern European social democrats is any guide, the real crisis will take place only when the PSOE finds itself in opposition or when it is once again challenged by new parties or social movements (to its left *or* right). Meanwhile, the Spanish Socialists are content to remain in power and to construct a more efficient, though not necessarily more just, capitalist system. How and whether such a task can be reconciled with the traditionally redistributive orientation of social democracy will become more prescient questions as the contradictions of the PSOE's new centrism multiply and as affected social sectors clamor ever more vocally for answers.

Despite their political success, the Spanish Socialists are trapped by the same dilemmas facing all modern social democratic parties.[32] Having rejecting democratic socialism as unfeasible and undesirable, social democrats must now debate whether the same is true for social democracy. The possible outcomes of this debate run the gamut from the continued attraction of neoliberalism, to a renewed faith in Keynesianism, to the development of "postmaterialist" quality-of-life orientations ("greening"), to a creative reaffirmation of the desire to transform capitalism (including *autogestión*, the Swedish Meidner plan, or the labor-sharing socialism articulated by such writers as André Gorz).

Any solutions to these dilemmas will have to take into account some difficult realities. Domestic policies, especially those designed to significantly reform society, must contend with the ever more present international context. The early suspicion with which some European socialists viewed efforts to integrate European economies was not without some foundation. All European social democratic parties have had to strike compromises not only within their own political economic systems but within the larger and more restrictive European and world contexts.

In a period of slower economic growth and more fierce economic competition, social democratic parties will have to adapt their strategies to the new economic realities. If the European left can no longer realistically hope to alter capitalism, the challenge for social democratic parties will nevertheless be to discover ways to distribute costs associated with the contradictions of postindustrial society somewhat more equitably.

NOTES

1. Quoted in Pedro Calvo Hernando, *Todos me dicen Felipe* (Barcelona: Plaza & Janes, 1987), p. 239.

2. Ignacio Sotelo, *Los Socialistas en el poder* (Madrid: Ediciones El País, 1986), p. 18.

3. An excellent example can be found in the PSOE's *Resoluciones, 30 Congresso PSOE* (Madrid: PSOE, 1984), p. 9. The party's attempt to justify its contradictory policies parallels the following discussion of inauspicious environmental factors quite closely.

4. Ludolfo Paramio, "El Septiembre de los conservadores," *El País* (September 1, 1986), p. 3.

5. See, for example, Joaquín Romero-Maura, "The Spanish Political System on the Eve of Spain's Probable Entry into the E.E.C.," (unpublished manuscript, 1979), p. 44.

6. E. Miret Magdalena, "¿Socialismo para qué?" *El País* (April 30, 1987), p. 14.

7. *El País* International Edition (January 25, 1988), p. 12.

8. Quoted in Calvo Hernando, *Todos me dicen Felipe,* p. 60.

9. Quoted in ibid., pp. 95–96.

10. Angel Luís de la Calle, in *El País* International Edition (February 16, 1987), p. 11.

11. Mario Caciagli, *Elecciones y partidos en la transición española* (Madrid: Centro de Investigaciones Sociológicas, 1986), p. 214.

12. Stephen Padgett, "The West German Social Democrats in Opposition 1982–86," *West European Politics* 3 (1987): 334.

13. Juan Luís Cebrián, "Los vicios de la democracia española," *El País* International Edition (February 21, 1987), pp. 9–10.

14. Castellano was expelled for having alleged, in an off-the-record interview with journalists, that PSOE number three man Txiki Benegas had business interests with a top AP leader. Although he was expelled from the PSOE, the Supreme Council of Judicial Power, of which Castellano is a member, found no evidence of wrongdoing and refused to remove him. Castellano was a key founder of the new PSOE in the 1970s and was then viewed as a moderating force vis-à-vis the more revolutionary González leadership.

15. *Tiempo* (May 9, 1988), p. 42.

16. Antxon Sarasqueta, "Las armas de Guerra," *Cambio 16* (April 25, 1988), p. 37.

17. Data published in *Tiempo* (May 9, 1988), p. 42.

18. Ibid.

19. *El Socialista* (June 16, 1986), p. 16.

20. Quoted in *El País* (May 2, 1987), p. 1.

21. Sotelo, *Los Socialistas,* p. 19.

22. Antonio García Santesmases, "Evolución ideológica del socialismo en la España actual," *Sistema* 68–69 (November 1985): 61–78.

23. Quoted in *Tiempo* (May 9, 1988), p. 20. Leguina is secretary general of the Madrid Socialist Federation and is president of the Autonomous Community of Madrid.

24. This point was underscored by a top adviser to González, interviewed by the author in May 1987.

25. Quoted in Calvo Hernando, *Todos me dicen Felipe,* pp. 237–238.

26. Statements made during a television interview, TVE–1, May 28, 1987.

27. Quoted in García Santesmases, "Evolución ideológica, p. 72.

28. Sotelo, *Los Socialistas,* p. 19.

29. On the recent German experience, see William E. Paterson, "The German Social Democratic Party," in William E. Paterson and Alastair H. Thomas, eds., *The Future of Social Democracy: Problems and Prospects of Social Democratic Parties in Western Europe.* (Oxford: Clarendon Press, 1986), pp. 127–152. On Sweden, see Kesselman; also see John D. Stephens, "The Ideological Development of the Swedish Social Democrats," in Bogdan Denitch, ed., *Democratic Socialism: The Mass Left in Advanced Industrial Societies* (Montclair, N.J.: Allanheld, Osmun, 1981), pp. 136–148.

30. Alfonso Guerra, et al., eds., *El futuro del socialismo* (Madrid: Editorial Sistema, 1986), p. 18.

31. *El País* International Edition (April 4, 1988), p. 12.

32. A particularly relative European comparison is treated in Daniel Singer, *Is Socialism Doomed?: The Meaning of Mitterrand* (New York: Oxford University Press, 1988).

Select Bibliography

Alcaide Inchausti, Julio. "Balance económico de cuatro años de gobierno Socialista." *Cuenta y Razón* 25 (December 1986): 61–74.

Alzaga, Oscar. *Lo que el cambio se llevó.* Barcelona: Planeta, 1985.

Armario, Diego. *El triángulo: El PSOE durante la transición.* Valencia: Fernando Torres, 1981.

Asenso, Oscar de Juan. "La constitución española de 1978 y el PSOE." *Sistema* 53 (March 1983): 95–107.

Barciela, Fernando. *La otra historia del PSOE.* Madrid: Emiliano Escolar, 1981.

Barnes, Samuel H., and Antonio López Pina. "Political Mobilization in Old and New Democracies: Spain in Comparative Perspective." Presented at the 1982 Annual Meeting of the American Political Science Association, Denver, September 2–5.

Barnes, Samuel H., Peter McDonough, and Antonio López Pina. "The Development of Partisanship in New Democracies: The Case of Spain." *American Journal of Political Science* 29 (1985): 695–720.

Barnes, Samuel H., Peter McDonough, and Antonio López Pina. "Volatile Parties and Stable Voters in Spain." Presented at the 1985 International Political Science Association World Congress, Paris, France, July 15–20.

Barzelay, Michael. "Andalusian Socialism: Political Ideology and Economic Policy in an Autonomous Community of Spain." Delivered at the Annual Meeting of the American Political Science Association, Washington, D.C., August 30, 1986.

Bell, David, ed. *Democratic Politics in Spain: Spanish Politics after Franco.* London: Frances Pinter, 1983.

Bizcarrondo, Marta. *Arquistaín y la crisis Socialista en la II República (1934–1936).* Madrid: Siglo XXI, 1975.

Bizcarrondo, Marta. "La Segunda República: Ideologías Socialistas," in Santos Juliá, ed., *El Socialismo en Español.* Madrid: Pablo Iglesias, 1986, 255–274.

Blas Guerrero, Andrés de. *El Socialismo radical en la Segunda República*. Madrid: Tucar, 1978.

Blas Guerrero, Andrés de. "UCD, PSOE, PCE, y AP: Las posiciones ideológicas," in R. Morodó, ed., *Los partidos políticos en España*. Barcelona: Labor, 1979.

Blas Guerrero, Andrés de. "Transferencias en la ideología de la izquierda." *Leviatán* 19 (1985): 35–63.

Bonilla Sauras, Manuel. *Los amos del PSOE*. Madrid: Arca de la Alianza Cultural, 1986.

Caciagli, Mario. *Elecciones y partidos en la transición Española*. Madrid: Centro de Investigaciones Sociológicas, 1986.

Calvo Hernando, Pedro. *Todos me dicen Felipe*. Barcelona: Plaza & Janes, 1987.

Cambra, Pilar. *Socialismo no es libertad: El verdadero programa del PSOE*. Madrid: Editorial Dossat, 1979.

Camiller, Patrick. "Spanish Socialism in the Atlantic Order." *New Left Review* 156 (1986): 5–36.

Cantarero del Castillo. *Tragedia del Socialismo español*. Barcelona: DOPESA, 1975.

Carabantes, Andrés. *Balance y futuro del socialismo*. Barcelona: Planeta, 1984.

Carr, Raymond, and Juan Pablo Fusi. *Spain: Dictatorship to Democracy*. 2d ed. London: George Allen and Unwin, 1981.

Carrascal, José María. *La revolución del PSOE*. Barcelona: Plaza & Janes, 1985.

Castillo, Pilar del, and Giacomo Sani. "Las elecciones de 1986: Continuidad sin consolidación," in Juan Linz and José Ramón Montero, eds., *Crísis y cambio: Electores y partidos en la España de los años ochenta*. Madrid: Centro de Estudios Constitucionales, 1986, 625–643.

Centro de Investigaciones Sociológicas. *Economía y sociedad: Evolución y expectativas a corto y medio plazo*. Madrid: Centro de Investigaciones Sociológicas, December 1985.

Chamorro, Eduardo. *Felipe González, un hombre a la espera*. Barcelona: Planeta, 1980.

Chazarra, Antonio, and Jesús García Yruela. "Una reflexión sobre el socialismo español hoy." *Leviatán* 19 (1985): 61–73.

de la Cierva, Ricardo. *Historia del socialismo en España, 1879–1983*. Barcelona: Planeta, 1983.

Claudín, Fernando. "Entrevista con Felipe González." *Zona Abierta* 20 (May–August 1979): 5–21.

Contreras Casado, Manuel. "El Partido Socialista: La trayectoria de un conflicto interno," in Manuel Ramírez, *Estudios Sobre la II República española*. Madrid: Tecnos, 1975, 203–215.

Contreras, Manuel. "Líderes Socialistas de la dictadura a la república." *Sistema* 26 (1978): 59–72.

Contreras, Manuel. *El PSOE en la II República: Organización e ideología*. Madrid: Centro de Investigaciones Sociológicas, 1981.

de la Cuadra, Bonifacio, and Soledad Gallego-Díaz. *Del consenso al desencanto*. Madrid: Editorial Saltés, 1981.

Díaz, Elias. "Sobre los orígines de la fragmentación actual del socialismo español (autocrítica para la unidad)." *Sistema* 15 (1976): 125–137.

Díaz, Elias. "El lado oscuro de la dialéctica: Consideraciones sobre el XXVIII Congreso del PSOE." *Sistema* 32 (1979): 35–50.

Díaz, Elias. "Pensamiento socialista durante el franquismo," in Santos Juliá *El socialismo en España*. Madrid: Editorial Pablo Iglesias, 1986, 367–399.

Diéz Nicolás, Juan. "Análisis y consecuencias de las elecciones generales de 1986." *Cuenta y Razón* 25 (1986): 75–90.

Domenench, Toni, Jordi Guiu, and Félix Ovejero. "13 tesis sobre el futuro de la izquierda." *Mientras Tanto* 26 (May 1986): 35–60.

Documentos de Estrategia. *Comisión Ejecutiva Federal* (October 1983). Madrid: PSOE.

de Esteban, Jorge and Luís López Guerra. *Los partidos políticos en la España actual*. Barcelona: Planeta, 1982.

Federación Socialista Madrileña, Corriente de Izquierda Socialista. "Manifesto a los compañeros socialistas." (Unpublished, November 1980). Madrid.

García Castro, Eladio. "La crísis de la izquierda revolucionária," in Fernando Claudín, ed., *¿Crísis de los partidos políticos?* Madrid: Dédalo, 1980.

García Cotarelo, Ramón. "Los partidos políticos en Europa y en España, opciones y programas. El caso de la izquierda." *Revista de Política Comparada* 2 (1980): 123–167.

García San Miguel, Luís. "Las ideologías políticas en la España actual." *Sistema* 40 (1981): 55–77.

Giner, Salvador. "Southern European Socialism in Transition." *West European Politics* 2 (1984): 41–62.

Gomáriz, Enrique. "La sociología de Felipe González." *Zona Abierta* 20 (May–August 1979): 61–76.

Gómez Llorente, Luís. *Historia del socialismo Español (hasta 1921)*. Madrid: Editorial Cuadernos Para el Diálogo, 1976.

Gómez Llorente, Luís. "En torno a la ideología y la política del PSOE." *Zona Abierta* 20 (1979): 23–36.

Gonzáles Casanova, J. A. "La tarea institucional del PSOE." *Leviatán* 5 (1981): 47–53.

González, Felipe. "La unidad de los Socialistas." *Sistema* 15 (1976): 45–51.

González, Felipe. *España y su futuro*. Madrid: Cuadernos Para el Diálogo, 1978.

Gooch, Anthony. "A Surrealistic Referendum: Spain and NATO." *Government and Opposition* 3 (1986): 300–315.

Guerra, Alfonso. "Los partidos socialistas del sur de Europa y las relaciones socialistas-comunistas." *Sistema* 15 (1976): 53–60.

Guerra, Alfonso. "Situación política tras el golpe de Estado." *Sistema* 42 (1981): 3–15.

Guerra, Alfonso et al., (eds.). *El futuro del Socialismo*. Madrid: Editorial Sistema, 1986.

Guerra, Alfonso. "El Socialismo y la España vertebrada." *Sistema* 68–69 (1986): 5–18.

Guindal, Mariano, and Rodolfo Serrano. *La otra transición: Nicolás Redondo y el sindicalismo español*. Madrid: Unión Editorial, 1986.

Guinea, José Luís. *Los movimientos obreros y sindicales en España de 1933 a 1978*. Madrid: Ibérico Europa de Ediciones, 1978.

Gunther, Richard. "The Spanish Socialist Party: From Clandestine Opposition to Party of Government," in Stanley Payne, ed., *The Politics of Democratic Spain*. Chicago: Chicago Council on Foreign Relations, 1986, 8–49.

Gunther, Richard, Giacomo Sani, and Goldie Shabad. *Spain after Franco: The Making of a Competitive Party System*. Berkeley: University of California Press, 1986.

Heine, Harmut. "Represión y exilio," in Santos Juliá, ed., *El socialismo en España*. Madrid: Pablo Iglesias, 1986, 195–316.

Heywood, Paul. "Spain: 10 June 1987." *Government and Opposition* 4 (1977): 390–401.

Heywood, Paul. "Mirror-Images: The PCE and the PSOE in the Transition to Democracy." *West European Politics* 2 (1987): 193–210.

Izquierda Socialista, Federación Socialista Madrileña. "Manifesto a los compañeros Socialistas" (Unpublished, November 1980). Madrid: PSOE.

Izquierda Socialista, PSOE. *Posiciones de la izquierda Socialista ante el XXX Congreso, PSOE*. Cáceres: PSOE, 1984.

Juliá, Santos. *La izquierda del PSOE, 1935–1936*. Madrid: Siglo XXI, 1977.

Juliá, Santos. *El socialismo en España*. Madrid: Editorial Pablo Iglesias, 1986.

Juliá, Santos. "República, revolución y luchas internas" in Santos Juliá, ed., *El socialismo en España*. Madrid: Pablo Iglesias, 1986, 231–254.

Lancaster, Thomas D. "Economics, Democracy, and Spanish Elections." *Political Behavior* 4 (1984): 353–367.

Lancaster, Thomas D., and Gary Prevost. *Politics and Change in Spain*. New York: Praeger, 1985.

Leviatán. "Las elecciones y el cambio." Special issue, vol. 10 (1982).

Leguina, Joaquín. "Viejas y nuevas ideas de la izquierda." *Leviatán* 19 (1985): 39–51.

Linz, Juan J., and José Ramón Montero. *Electores y partidos en España: Las elecciones de 1982 y su legado*. Madrid: Centro de Estudios Constitucionales, 1986.

López Pintor, Rafael. "The October, 1982 General Election and the Evolution of the Spanish Party System," in Howard Penniman and Eusebio M. Mujal-León, eds., *Spain at the Polls, 1977, 1979, 1982*. Washington, D.C.: American Enterprise Institute/Duke University Press, 1985, 293–313.

Maluquer de Motes, Jordi. *El socialismo en España, 1833–1868*. Barcelona: Grijalbo, 1977.

Maravall, José María. *Dictadura y disentimiento político: Obreros y estudiantes bajo el Franquismo*. Madrid: Alfaguara, 1978.

Maravall, José María. "Eurocomunismo y socialismo en España: La sociología de una competición política," *Sistema* 28 (1979): 3–48.

Maravall, José María. "Del milenio a la practica política: El socialismo como reformismo radical." *Zona Abierta* 20 (1979): 89–97.

Maravall, José María. "La alternativa socialista. La política y el apoyo electoral del PSOE." *Sistema* 35 (March 1980): 3–48.

Maravall, José María. "Transición a la democracia, alienamientos políticos y elecciones en España." *Sistema* 36 (May 1980): 65–105.

Maravall, José María. *La política de la transición, 1975–1980*. Madrid: Taurus, 1981.

Menéndez del Valle, Emilio. "La transición al socialismo en España y las relaciones internacionales." *Sistema* 15 (1976): 115–123.

McDonough, Peter, Antonio López Pina, and Samuel H. Barnes. "The Spanish Public in Political Transition." *British Journal of Political Science* 2 (January 1981): 49–79.

McDonough, Peter, Antonio López Pina, and Samuel H. Barnes. "The Growth of Democratic Legitimacy in Spain." *American Political Science Review* 3 (1983): 736–760.

McDonough, Peter, Samuel H. Barnes, and A. López Pina. "Economic Policy and Public Opinion in Spain." Presented at the 1985 Annual Meeting of Midwest Political Science Association, Chicago, April 17–20.

McDonough, Peter, Antonio López Pina, and Samuel H. Barnes. "The Legitimacy of Democracy in Spain." Presented at the 1985 Annual Meeting of the American Political Science Association, New Orleans, August 29–September 1.

Moral Sandoval, Enrique. "El socialismo y la dictadura de Primo de Rivera," in Santos Juliá, ed., *El socialismo en España*. Madrid: Pablo Iglesias, 1986, 191–212.

Morán, Fernando. *Una política exterior para España*. Barcelona: Planeta, 1980.

Morodó, Raul. "Socialistes et Communistes dans la transition." *Pouvoirs* 8 (1979): 28–43.

Mujal-León, Eusebio M. "The Left and the Catholic Question in Spain." *West European Politics* 2 (April 1982): 32–54.

Mujal-León, Eusebio M. "Foreign Policy of the Socialist Government," in Stanley G. Payne, ed., *The Politics of Democratic Spain*. Chicago: Chicago Council on Foreign Relations, 1986, 197–279.

Munagorri, Iñaki, et al. *Represión, tortura, y gobierno PSOE*. Madrid: Editorial Revolución, 1984.

Nash, Elizabeth. "The Spanish Socialist Party since Franco: From Clandestinity to Government: 1976–1982," in David S. Bell, ed., *Democratic Politics in Spain: Spanish Politics after Franco*. London: St. Martin's Press, 1983, 29–62.

Obiols, Raimón, *Los futuros imperfectos*. Barcelona: Plaza & Janes, 1987.

Ollero Butler, F. "El Congreso Extraordinario del PSOE." *Revista de Derecho Político* 4 (1979): 207 ff.

Oneto, José. *¿A donde va Felipe?* Barcelona: Argos Vergara, 1983.

Oneto, José. *El secuestro del cambio*. Barcelona: Plaza & Janes, 1984.

Padilla, Antonio. *El movimiento Socialista Español*. Barcelona: Planeta, 1977.

Partido Socialista Obrero Español. "50 Preguntas Sobre la OTAN." Madrid: PSOE, 1981.

Partido Socialista Obrero Español. "Documento de estratégia." Comisión Ejecutiva Federal. Madrid: PSOE, 1983.

Partido Socialista Obrero Español. "Conferencia Federal de Organización y Estatutos: Documentos base" Madrid: PSOE March 4–6, 1983.

Partido Socialista Obrero Español. *Estatutos Federales*. Madrid: PSOE, December 14–16, 1984.

Partido Socialista Obrero Español. *Memoria PSOE, 1981–1984: De la oposición al gobierno*. Madrid: Comisión Ejecutiva Federal, PSOE 1984.

Partido Socialista Obrero Español. *Reseña histórica y estructura del PSOE.* Madrid: Comisión Ejecutiva Federal, PSOE, December 1984.

Partido Socialista Obrero Español. *El Gobierno ante la crisis económica: Explicación de la política económica e industrial de los Socialistas.* Madrid: PSOE, April 1984.

Partido Socialista Obrero Español. "Reglamiento Federal de Conflictos." Madrid: PSOE, 1984.

Partido Socialista Obrero Español. *Resoluciones, 30 Congreso PSOE.* Madrid: PSOE, December 13–16, 1984.

Partido Socialista Obrero Español. *31 Congreso PSOE, Resoluciones.* Madrid: PSOE, 1988.

Partido Socialista Obrero Español. *Estatutos Federales.* Madrid: PSOE, 1988.

Peces Barba, G. et al. *La izquierda y la Constitución.* Barcelona: Taula de Canvi, 1978.

Penniman, Howard R., and Eusebio M. Mujal-León, eds. *Spain at the Polls, 1977, 1979, and 1982: A Study of the National Elections.* Washington, D.C.: American Enterprise Institute/Duke University Press, 1985.

Pérez Díaz, Víctor. "Clase obrera y organizaciones obreras en la España de hoy: Política y vida sindical." *Sistema* 32 (September 1979).

Pérez Díaz, Víctor. "Políticas económicas y pautas sociales en la España de la transición: La doble cara del neocorporatismo," in Juan J. Linz, ed. *España: Un presente para el futuro,* Vol. I. Madrid: Instituto de Estudios Económicos, 1984, 23–55.

Pérez Díaz, Víctor. *El retorno de la sociedad civil.* Madrid: Instituto de Estudios Económicos, 1987.

Peydro Caro, Miguel. *Las escisiones del PSOE.* Barcelona: Plaza & Janes, 1980.

Preston, Paul. "The Origins of the Socialist Schism in Spain, 1917–1931." *Journal of Contemporary History* 13 (1977): 101–132.

Preston, Paul. "Decadencia y resurgimiento del PSOE durante el régimen franquista," in Santos Juliá, ed., *El socialismo en España.* Madrid: Pablo Iglesias, 1986, 349–366.

Prevost, Gary. "Change and Continuity in the Spanish Labor Movement." *West European Politics* 7, no. 1 (January 1984).

Prevost, Gary. "The Spanish Labor Movement," in Thomas D. Lancaster and Gary Prevost, eds., *Politics and Change in Spain.* New York: Praeger, 1985, 125–143.

Puhle, Hans-Jürgen. "El PSOE: Un partido dominante y heterogéneo," in Juan J. Linz and José Ramón Montero, eds., *Crisis y cambio: Electores y partidos en la España de los años ochenta.* Madrid: Centro de Estudios Constitucionales, 1986, 319–344.

Ramírez, Miguel. *Estudios sobre la II República Española.* Madrid: Tecnos, 1975.

Santamaría, Julián. "Elecciones generales de 1982 y consolidación de la democracia." *Revista Española de Investigaciones Sociológicas* 28 (1984): 7–17.

Santesmases, Antonio García. "Las dos opciones del PSOE." *Zona Abierta* 20 (May–August 1979): 37–46.

Santesmases, Antonio García. "Evolución ideológica del socialismo en la España actual." *Sistema* 68–69 (November 1985): 61–78.

Santesmases, Antonio García. "El Referendum-OTAN y el futuro de la izquierda." *Mientras Tanto* 25 1/2 (1986): 107–118.

Sarasqueta, Antxon. *Después de Franco, la OTAN.* Barcelona: Plaza & Janes, 1985.

Sarasqueta, Antxon. *El abuso del estado.* Barcelona: Plaza & Janes, 1987.

Seara Vásquez, Modesto. *El socialismo en España.* Mexico City: Universidad Nacional Autónoma de México, 1980.

Serfaty, Meir. "Spain's Socialists: A New Center Party?" *Current History* 492 (1984): 164 ff.

Share, Donald. "Two Transitions: Democratisation and the Evolution of the Spanish Socialist Left." *West European Politics* 1 (1985): 82–103.

Share, Donald. *The Making of Spanish Democracy.* New York: Praeger/Center for the Study of Democratic Institutions, 1986.

Share, Donald. "Spain: Socialists as Neoliberals." *Socialist Review* 1 (1988): 38–67.

Sistema. "Problemas actuales del socialismo Español." Special issue, vol. 15 (1976).

Sistema. "Socialismo y Constitución." Special issue, vols. 17–18 (1977).

Sotelo, Ignacio. *El socialismo democratico.* Madrid: Taurus, 1980.

Sotelo, Ignacio. *Los Socialistas en el poder.* Madrid: Ediciones El País, 1986.

Tezanos, José Félix. "Ante la necesaria apertura de un proceso constituyente en la España actual." *Sistema* 17–18 (1977): 105–121.

Tezanos, José Félix. *Estructura de clases y conflictos de poder en la España post-Franquista.* Madrid: EDICUSA, 1978.

Tezanos, José Félix. "El espacio político y sociológico del socialismo español." *Sistema* 32 (1979): 51–75.

Tezanos, José Félix. "Análisis sociopolítico del voto Socialista en las elecciones de 1979." *Sistema* 31 (1979): 105–121.

Tezanos, José Félix. "Radiografía de dos congresos. Una aportación al estudio sociológico de cuadros del Socialismo español." *Sistema* 35 (1980): 79–99.

Tezanos, José Félix. "La crísis de la conciencia obrera en la España actual." *Sistema* 41 (1981): 105–140.

Tezanos, José Félix. "Identificación de clase y conciencia obrera entre los trabajadores industriales." *Sistema* 43–44 (1981): 82–123.

Tezanos, José Félix. "Estructura y dinámica de la afiliación Socialista en España." *Revista de Estudios Políticos* 23 (September–October 1981): 117–152.

Tezanos, José Félix. *Sociología del Socialismo Español.* Madrid: Tecnos, 1983.

Tezanos, José Félix. "Cambio social y modernización en la España actual." *Revista Española de Investigaciones Sociológicas* 28 (1984): 19–61.

Tezanos, José Félix. "Continuidad y cambio en el Socialismo Español. El PSOE durante la transición democrática," in Julián Santamaría, ed., *Los partidos políticos en España.* Madrid: CIS, forthcoming.

Tezanos, José Félix and José Antonio Gómez Yánez. *Estudio sociológico de participación a los afiliados del PSOE: Informe de los resultados.* Madrid: Grupo Federal de Estudios Sociológicos Secretaria Federal de Organización, 1981.

Tierno Galván, Enrique. *España y el socialismo.* Madrid: Tucar, 1976.

Tuñón de Lara, Manuel. "El Socialismo Español en la Guerra Civil," in Santos Juliá, ed., *El socialismo en España.* Madrid: Pablo Iglesias, 1986, 275–294.

Vilallonga, José Luís de. *Los sables, la corona, y la rosa.* Barcelona: Argos Vergara, 1984.

Vizcaíno Casas, Fernando. *La letra del cambio.* Madrid: Planeta, 1986.

Wert, José Ignacio. "La campaña electoral de Octubre de 1982." *Revista Española de Investigaciones Sociológicas* 28 (1984): 63–84.

Zona Abierta (anonymous). "Análisis de coyuntura: Dos proyectos del gobierno, dos tácticas de la izquierda." Vol. 11 (1977): 5ff.

Index

About the Author

DONALD SHARE is Assistant Professor of Politics and Government at the University of Puget Sound, Washington. His earlier works include *The Making of Spanish Democracy* (Praeger, 1986), and articles published in *Comparative Political Studies*, *The Review of Politics*, and *West European Politics*.